ORGANIZATIONAL
REPORT CARDS

Organizational Report Cards

William T. Gormley, Jr.
David L. Weimer

HARVARD UNIVERSITY PRESS

Cambridge, Massachusetts, London, England   1999

Library of Congress Cataloging-in-Publication Data

Gormley, William T., 1950–
    Organizational report cards / William T. Gormley, Jr., David L. Weimer.
      p. cm.
    Includes bibliographical references and index.
    ISBN 0-674-64350-X (cloth : alk. paper)
     1. Organizational effectiveness—Evaluation.
   I. Weimer, David Leo.
   HD58.9.G67   1999
   658.4—dc21   98-39374

To Duncan MacRae, Jr.,
gentleman and scholar

Preface

Although we had been aware of our shared interests in policy instruments and institutional design for a decade, it was only a few years ago that we thought of collaborating on a research project. We had noticed a proliferation of public reports that compared the performance of organizations such as schools, health maintenance organizations, and hospitals. These "organizational report cards" struck us as particularly intriguing policy instruments. The information that they provide can potentially influence organizations through the choices of their clients, the decisions of their overseers, or the responses of their managers. As policy analysts, we wanted to know when organizational reports cards should be used and how they should be designed to promote important social values. As political scientists, we wanted to understand why they are used in some circumstances rather than others and how they are actually designed. Satisfying our curiosity about organizational report cards offered an excellent opportunity for us to pursue our scholarly interests, learn from each other, and perhaps make a contribution to better public policy.

Our efforts were propelled in a delightful way. The generosity of the Rockefeller Foundation allowed us to spend a month during the summer of 1996 at the Foundation's Study and Conference Center in Bellagio, Italy. In wonderful surroundings, both physical and social, we were able to devote attention to the project free of the unavoidable daily distractions that would have plagued us in our normal routines. Having large blocks of undisturbed time probably made our work together more productive; it certainly made the experience more enjoyable. We benefited from many interesting and helpful conversations with the diverse scholars who shared time with us at Bellagio. We especially thank Manju Jain, Melanie Manion, Zeev Moaz, Zehava Moaz, and Pasquale Pesce for their willingness to engage us in extended discussions about our project.

Our gratitude extends to several other groups of people. First, we wish to thank the many people, too numerous to name individually, who took time to tell us about their efforts to design and implement organizational report cards. Second, we would like to thank colleagues in our departments, and participants in panels at the 1996 Research Conference of the Association for Public Policy Analysis and Management and the 1997 Public Management Conference at the University of Georgia, who offered valuable comments as our work progressed. Third, we would like to thank a number of people who have been especially helpful to us in various ways: Eugene Bardach, Robert Behn, Janet Corrigan, Stanley Engerman, Pamela J. Griffith, Eric Hanushek, Bruce Jacobs, Scott Keeter, Helen Ladd, Jean Mitchell, Mark Moore, Donna Morrison, Dana Mukamel, Nancy Perkins, Beryl Radin, Eric Schneider, Rochelle Sharpe, Edward F. Straw, Carl Van Horn, Aidan Vining, and Joseph Wholey. Fourth, we would like to thank our research assistants, as well as other students, who contributed in various ways to the project: Cristina Boccuti, Lucy Chen, Christian Gross, Liisa Hiatt, Ahmed Kassim, Tamar London, Amy Makinen, Sharon Palmiter, Cynthia Rapp, Hugh Roghmann, Marc Shapiro, and Dan Troy. A special thanks to Chiquita White for preparing the index. Finally, we thank Michael Aronson, Erin Wilson Burns, Andrea Dodge, and Jeff Kehoe for guiding our manuscript to publication.

Contents

Tables and Figures

ORGANIZATIONAL
REPORT CARDS

1

Introduction

Anyone who has ever struggled to master a scholastic subject, or succeeded in doing so, remembers report cards with a mixture of dread and delight. The familiar report card provides teachers with a framework for evaluating the performance of individual students and a medium for disseminating that information to students, their parents or guardians, and academic administrators. This report card is a potentially powerful instrument because of its capacity to draw distinctions across subjects, across time, and across persons; because of its capacity to enlighten and embarrass; and because of its capacity to propel students forward. As a result, it has served as a template for a different kind of report card, which we call the *organizational report card*.

Organizational report cards enable citizens, politicians, clients, and managers to assess the performance of schools, hospitals, day care centers, health maintenance organizations (HMOs), nursing homes, and other organizations that provide services to clients. They encourage accountability to external audiences and they provide valuable feedback to service providers. Organizational report cards are increasingly popular policy instruments because of the growing importance of consumer choice and because of the growing impatience of public policymakers with the low quality and high cost of social service delivery.

The increasing use of organizational report cards is most evident in primary and secondary education. A 1995 survey found that 46 states issue annual educational report cards: 42 of the states publish statistical reports on school districts and 35 states publish reports on individual schools (Council of Chief State School Officers 1995). In over one-half of the states in which reports are made on districts or schools, dissemination to the public or parents is required. For example, since passage of Proposition 98 in 1988, California school boards have been required to prepare School

1

Accountability Reports for each of their elementary and secondary schools and to make them available to parents. Growing experimentation with giving parents greater choice over which schools their children will attend—magnet and charter schools, intra- and inter-district choice, and publicly funded vouchers for use at private schools—suggests that parents will increasingly be a major audience for school report cards.

Health care report cards have also proliferated. At the national level, the National Committee for Quality Assurance (NCQA), a nonprofit organization, serves as a repository of quality-relevant data for HMOs. In addition, the NCQA accredits HMOs and distributes information on plans' current accreditation status. Although the federal government no longer disseminates annual hospital report cards, state governments have taken up the slack. At least 40 states have mandated the collection, analysis, and distribution of health care data (U.S. GAO 1995: 7). In some of these states, the effectiveness of health service delivery organizations, such as hospitals, is systematically assessed (Overman and Cahill 1994: 436).

In addition to preparing or mandating report cards in certain policy domains, the states are themselves the subject of report cards in other policy domains. For example, the Corporation for Enterprise Development, a Washington, D.C., public policy advocacy and research group, publishes an economic development report card for the states every year. *Working Mother* magazine now publishes an annual report card on child care quality, safety, availability, and commitment for all 50 states. And several organizations publish state-by-state summaries of environmental protection efforts.

Local governments are also evaluated. The U.S. Department of Labor publishes data on the performance of local employment and training programs, and popular magazines, such as *Money,* routinely publish rankings of the most livable cities in the United States. The International City and County Management Association shares performance data on fire, police, neighborhood, and business services for large cities and counties, and some civic associations compare their metropolitan area with other comparable metropolitan areas (Osborne and Plastrik 1997: 8).

At first glance, it might appear that organizational report cards would be noncontroversial. After all, they simply divulge information that can later be contested in a public forum. Yet they have aroused controversy in a variety of policy settings. As one might expect, organizations that do poorly on report cards often challenge their fairness. They are often joined by more disinterested critics who recognize the problems inherent in designing valid and reliable performance measures, and who fear the consequences of using poorly constructed ratings or assessments.

What Are Organizational Report Cards?

Recent years have witnessed increased concern about the quality of services provided by organizations in both the private and public sectors. Private firms have sought to serve their customers better through such efforts as Total Quality Management, and public agencies have become more attentive to the quality of services they provide to their clients. A variety of specific mechanisms, or policy instruments, have been used in an effort to enhance accountability. One of these mechanisms is the organizational report card, which we define as a regular effort by an organization to collect data on two or more *other* organizations, transform the data into information relevant to assessing performance, and transmit the information to some audience external to the organizations themselves. Many, though not all, organizational report cards transform data into ratings or rankings of multiple organizations.

As defined, organizational report cards have clear bounds. Our definition's elements allow us to distinguish them from other more familiar performance measures.

Organizational report cards are most similar to performance monitoring systems, which "regularly measure the quality of service delivery and the outcomes (results) achieved in public programs—with monitoring being done at least annually, but, in many cases, quarterly or even more often" (Wholey and Hatry 1992: 605). They differ, however, from performance assessments conducted by the organization itself (see Table 1.1). For example, the Government Performance and Results Act (GPRA, PL103-62) of 1993 requires federal agencies to define strategic goals (clear missions and desired outcomes) and to measure performance to gauge progress toward those goals (U.S. GAO 1996a). Performance information is then to be used as a basis for decisionmaking by the agencies and their congressional overseers. Although organizational report cards are consistent with the spirit of GPRA, they are external assessments, not self-assessments. Thus report cards overlap with the broad category of performance monitoring systems but differ from certain types of such systems.

Report cards share some traits with benchmarking, which compares organizations to the best of their kind or to standards established by knowledgeable professionals (Ammons 1995: 16). However, report cards are

Table 1.1 Organizational Report Cards and Other Performance Measures

	Organizational focus	Regular data collection	External assessment	Data transformation	External audience	Multiple organizations
Organizational report cards	yes	yes	yes	yes	yes	yes
GPRA	yes	yes	no	yes	yes	no
Benchmarking	yes	maybe	maybe	yes	yes	yes
Balanced scorecards	yes	yes	no	yes	maybe	no
Program evaluations	maybe	no	maybe	yes	maybe	maybe
Social indicators	no	yes	yes	yes	yes	no
Disclosure requirements	yes	yes	yes	no	yes	yes

not necessarily limited to comparisons with favorable performers. Also, benchmarking may or may not involve regular data collection and an external assessment.

The concept of a balanced scorecard (Kaplan and Norton 1996) was developed with for-profit firms in mind but is applicable to other organizations as well. A balanced scorecard is somewhat similar to our concept of an organizational report card, but does not compare organizations. Also, balanced scorecards are self-assessment tools developed by managers for managers, not external assessments developed by outsiders for outsiders and managers.

Report cards can be distinguished from the ubiquitous reporting requirements that governments impose on public agencies, and increasingly on private organizations, by recalling the definitional requirement that collected data be *transformed* into information relevant to assessing organizational performance. To qualify as a report card, the data must be put in a form that facilitates interpretation by some external audience. For this reason, common reporting requirements are not report cards.

Program evaluations often attempt to assess the performance of organizations by measuring their impacts. Report cards can be distinguished from program evaluations by the definitional requirement of *regularity*. Program evaluations are typically one-time assessments; report cards are regular and, therefore, anticipated. Also, some program evaluations do not distinguish between organizations when more than one organization is responsible for a given program.

Finally, report cards can be distinguished from social and policy indicators with which they share regularity. Social indicators are "measures of social conditions justifiably included in public statistical systems" and policy indicators are measures "relevant to public policy choices made in view of ethical values" (MacRae 1985: 35). Social indicators, usually aggregate and national in scope, are much broader than report cards. As policy choices are usually relevant to classes of organizations, policy indicators also usually deal with data aggregated across organizations. Consequently, they lack the focus of report cards on *specific organizations*.

The Demand for Report Cards

A number of interests and interest groups have argued in favor of report cards in different policy contexts. Though they have often disagreed on the precise purposes of report cards, the main audience for report cards, the desired scope of report cards, and the ground rules that should govern them, they have agreed that report cards are desirable or at least worth a try.

Individual consumers and consumer advocacy groups have often expressed a wish for more and better information to guide the selection of organizations that deliver services of various kinds. Their hope is that such information will result in better individual choices, better industry performance, or both.

Ordinary citizens, who may or may not consume services directly, also seek more and better information to guide them in political activities, such as voting and lobbying. School performance, for example, has figured prominently in both state and local elections.

Corporate purchasers have been vigorous advocates for report cards. Indeed, corporations have been the prime movers in the quest for certain kinds of report cards, such as those covering health plans. Their expectation is that report cards will give them a valuable competitive edge by enabling them to choose service-delivery organizations that provide better "value for money." The monopsony power in health insurance markets enjoyed by certain large corporations as major purchasers gives them the economic leverage to insist on participation in report card systems as a precondition for employee access.

Governmental purchasers have also pressed for report cards. In health care, for instance, the federal government purchases huge amounts of expensive services through the Medicare and Medicaid programs. Understandably, the federal government wants to know which service providers are performing well. That is especially true in an era of retrenchment and cost-containment.

Government officials, of course, do not simply purchase services; they also set the ground rules for determining how services are purchased or obtained by others. In addition, they monitor performance through investigative hearings and other forms of oversight. For this reason, public policymakers generally want to know how an industry is faring, which industry components are more efficient and effective than others, and which organizations seem to be struggling despite governmental financial support. Report cards can help in these tasks. Furthermore, they may be more palatable politically than more intrusive government regulations.

The mass media have a special interest in report cards. Among the qualities that journalists look for in a story are clarity, contrast, and conflict. Report cards provide all three: they are relatively easy to digest and understand, they bring intra-industry comparisons into bold relief, and they generate controversy by identifying saints and sinners by name. Indeed, newspapers and magazines often produce report cards themselves.

Certain academics, think-tanks, and consulting firms also welcome report cards. In principle, the reports provide large amounts of data that can be accessed with relative ease and they facilitate longitudinal and sometimes cross-sectional comparisons. Report cards provide grist for the mill of policy analysts, industry analysts, and other users of large data bases.

Certain professional groups also find report cards appealing, particularly those who perceive that a competing profession or a competing industry might be undermined by report cards. For example, physicians' groups in some states (such as Maryland, for example) have clamored for HMO report cards, perhaps in the hope that such report cards would discredit the emerging HMO industry. Professional groups may also see report cards as opportunities to promote values of importance to the profession, such as preventive medicine.

The organizations that produce report cards have also fueled demand for such policy instruments. Whether for-profit or nonprofit, such organizations thrive when report cards thrive. They may also be advocates for better report cards, particularly if better report cards require more of the informational services that they offer.

As report cards pose a potential threat to targeted service providers, the relevant industry's position on report cards is often ambivalent and sometimes downright hostile. However, report cards can serve industry purposes rather nicely at times. If they achieve enough attention, they may help to weed out "bad apples" that discredit the industry as a whole. By legitimizing an industry and enhancing consumer confidence, report cards can ensure the industry's long-term economic security. Moreover, report cards may discourage faint-hearted firms from entering the market, thus guaranteeing more customers for those firms that can withstand the scrutiny that report cards generate.

Why Are Report Cards Problematic?

Despite considerable demand for organizational report cards, they do not always fulfill expectations. Obviously, their use requires resources that have opportunity costs. Beyond opportunity costs, however, the design and use of organizational report cards involve a number of generic problems that undercut their value as a policy instrument. Though these problems intertwine, they can be divided into three categories for purposes of discussion: assessment problems, organizational response problems, and consumer reception problems.

Assessment Problems

Report card designers face all the major methodological problems encountered in designing performance monitoring systems and program evaluations, as well as a few additional ones related to the report cards' intended uses. Fundamentally, these problems arise because of limitations in data and theory: not all relevant variables can be measured, and theoretical links between variables that can be measured and those that are conceptually appropriate are often weak.

Organizational production can be conceived of as having four components, beginning with *inputs* (resources) that are subjected to a *process* (the use of the resources in various ways) to produce *outputs* (direct products of the process) that in turn contribute to *outcomes* (valued consequences). Organizational performance, the impact of the organization on outcomes, can be thought of as the relationship between the resources used (inputs) and the values created (outcomes). With respect to schools, for example, inputs include such things as teachers and students, processes include how teachers and students spend their time during the school day, outputs include increased cognitive abilities as measured by tests, and outcomes include the increased capacity of the students to participate effectively in economic, political, and social life.

An organization's performance is its impact on outcomes. Ideally, measures of performance should indicate how effectively organizations convert inputs to outcomes. In practice, however, outcomes, and even important inputs, are often difficult to measure. Output and process variables are usually more easily measured than outcomes, and can often be linked theoretically to them. Consequently, performance measurement often relies on process and output variables as proxies for outcome variables (see Table 1.2). For example, the outputs of increased student scores on standardized tests are typically taken as surrogates for the outcome "education" because of the theoretical relationship between the skills and knowledge being measured by the tests and the ability to function effectively in the economy. With respect to HMOs, customer satisfaction may serve as a proxy measure for the quality of interactions between patients and health care providers. Whether it serves as a proxy for quality of care is more debatable (Anders 1996d).

Table 1.2 The Focus of Report Cards in Selected Policy Domains

Organizations	Focus	Examples
Hospitals	outcomes	deaths from CABG surgery
HMOs	inputs processes outputs	board certified physicians customer satisfaction child immunizations
Public schools	outputs	standardized test scores
Colleges	inputs outputs	SAT scores graduation rates
State governments, economic development	inputs outcomes	development capacity economic performance
Local governments, employment and training	outcomes	job placements
Airlines	outputs	on-time arrivals safety violations
Insurers	processes outcomes	strategic plans loss ratios

The limitations of inputs as proxies for outcomes are even more obvious. Nevertheless, many report cards continue to rely heavily on such techniques. For example, the annual college guide produced by *U.S. News & World Report* gives substantial weight to such input measures as the quality of the student body and faculty resources. Output measures, such as graduation and retention rates, also get considerable emphasis, but outcome measures, such as the alumni giving rate, receive little weight, perhaps because alumni giving is not the most interesting of outcomes. These limitations, though regrettable, are also understandable. Assessing outcomes is extremely difficult, even in the best of circumstances, and available measures of outcomes are seldom impressive.

ASSESSING OUTCOMES   Consider the choice of the particular variables, direct or proxy, for measuring outcomes. We can think of these as the dependent variables in the performance relationship. Several problems arise in choosing these variables.

Distance from Outcomes.   The earlier in the sequence of production, the more the appropriateness of the variables depends on the strength of the theoretical assertions of their links to outcomes. Direct measures of outcomes require no relational theories as they are operationalizations of conceptualized values, though they may raise standard questions of validity and reliability. Output, process, and input variables are one, two, and three steps removed, respectively. Each step relies on a hypothesized relationship that introduces some degree of uncertainty.

Incomplete Measurement of Outcomes.   Problems arise in finding a set of dependent variables that comprehensively measure all the outcomes. Ideally, performance should include all affected values; excluding any dimensions, or margins, leads to an incomplete measure. For example, while mortality rates for surgical units are certainly important and relatively easily measured, post-operative quality-of-life is also certainly important as well even though it may be much more difficult to measure. A surgical unit with a lower mortality rate should not necessarily be ranked more highly than one with a higher rate if the latter produced a much higher quality-of-life for survivors. As we discuss below, failure to measure outcomes comprehensively poses the risk of inducing socially undesirable organizational responses. It also raises the issue of fairness to the organizations whose performances are being assessed, which has both ethical and practical implications: if a report card is unfair, then it may not be viable, and deservedly so. As comprehensive measurement of outcomes is rarely practical, report card designers must inevitably exercise judgment in deciding which outcomes can reasonably be ignored because they are relatively less important or because their exclusion is unlikely to induce undesirable responses.

Uncertain Weights for Combining Outcomes.   In the case of *league tables,* report cards that rank organizations in terms of their performance, the combination of dependent variables into the underlying scale used for the ranking requires designers to select a specific set of weights. In other words, it requires them to make tradeoffs among the various values at stake. When there is no clear consensus about such tradeoffs, comparisons based on the scale are normatively suspect. Even when there might be agreement in the abstract about appropriate tradeoffs, organizations have an incentive to argue for favorable weights once they know their own positions on the dependent variables underlying the scale.

TAKING ACCOUNT OF INPUTS   Once dependent variables to measure outcomes have been selected, designers face the problem of measuring inputs so that the contribution of the organization itself to performance can be assessed. In theory, it only makes sense to compare outcomes across organizations that have comparable mixes of inputs or that have been placed on an equal footing through the use of statistical controls. In practice, variations in inputs are sometimes ignored. Although we are wary of such practices, we recognize that the choice is often between an imperfect report card and no report card at all.

Comprehensive Assessment of Inputs.   Just as the set of variables measuring outcomes should be comprehensive, so too should be the variables measuring inputs. Although it has been common among students of organizational performance to define inputs rather narrowly as the labor and capital resources commanded by the organization (Carter, Klein, and Day 1992: 36), we adopt a broader definition: inputs are all the elements that enter into an organization's production function. They include not only capital and labor directly controlled by the organization, but other factors, such as attributes of the clientele it serves and the environment in which it serves them.

Some inputs, such as budgets, are typically easy to measure. In comparing organizations that deliver services to clients, however, an important and difficult to measure input is the composition of the clientele. Student bodies differ in their distributions of prior academic achievement and parental involvement, factors that affect educational outcomes. HMOs differ in the distribution of the health status of patient populations. Attribution of performance to organizations requires designers to take account of differences in this important input, especially in making explicit comparisons across organizations.

Measuring Inputs.   Measuring the relevant attributes of clientele, and taking account of these attributes in assessing performance, turns out to be quite difficult. Process variables, such as enrollment in subsidized school lunch programs with income eligibility requirements, often must be used as proxies for input variables, such as the socioeconomic status of students' families (itself a proxy for parental contributions to education), that cannot be measured with available data. Complex statistical issues, which reduce the transparency of report cards, arise in attempts to assess organizational performance.

In choosing variables for inclusion in report cards, considerations of cost, validity, accuracy, manipulability, timeliness, and persistence play a role. A brief comparison of two types of data sources for report card variables, administrative records and client surveys, illustrates these considerations and how they are often in conflict.

Organizations routinely collect and organize data for administrative purposes. These administrative records often provide a basis for measuring some inputs, processes, outputs, and outcomes. The cost of using them for report cards is generally low, especially if they are kept in electronic format. Because they are produced regularly, they are often available for use on a timely basis and their collection tends to persist over time. If their accuracy is important for either internal administrative purposes or external oversight relations, then it may be difficult for organizations to manipulate them inappropriately to obtain a better report card.

Often offsetting these advantages, however, are problems of validity and accuracy. Data useful for administrative purposes may not correspond well to the concepts that report card designers seek to operationalize. Even when records have reasonable conceptual validity, they may suffer from incompleteness. For example, patient records may show only medical services provided by the organization itself rather than complete medical histories that would be useful in constructing indexes reflecting the health

status of the patient population. Aside from inaccuracies, administrative records may have important biases. Measures of aggregate student achievement, for instance, usually exclude students who do not take the test as
scheduled or who dropped out of school altogether. Exclusion of these
groups of students from the measure is likely to bias the aggregate score
upward.

Surveys of clientele are an alternative source of data for report cards.
They give report card designers the opportunity to create simple, straightforward measures based on the perceptions of those who actually consume
social services. But perceptions may be rooted more in positive vibrations
(for example, a good bedside manner) than in positive results. Also, surveys are often costly and difficult to implement on a timely basis. If they do
not provide information of immediate value to the organization itself, then
they may not become routinized, thereby reducing the chances that they
will persist as a data source for report cards. Further, reliance on the organization to provide sampling frames or to administer the surveys opens
the door for manipulation. For example, health plans sometimes exclude
disgruntled customers by deleting clients who have been with the plan for
less than six months or a year (Anders 1996d). For these reasons, authentic
outcome measures are usually preferable to customer satisfaction surveys.

Although we have stressed the advantages of measuring outcomes and
of measuring them well, we recognize that yesterday's outcomes are not
always the best predictors of tomorrow's outcomes. For this reason, some
report card designers have supplemented outcome measures with process
or output measures that may help to predict performance in the future.
For example, the Corporation for Enterprise Development (1996), which
rates the economic development performance of state governments, includes a measure of "development capacity." Similarly, A. M. Best (1995),
which rates the riskiness of insurance companies, includes a qualitative
appraisal of insurance companies' strategic plans. Robert Kaplan and David
Norton (1996: 31) would call such measures "performance drivers" because they are expected to drive performance in the future. Such measures,
if vindicated through empirical research, can be useful elements of an
overall appraisal.

Tensions between Persistence and Innovation

Our discussion so far has implicitly assumed that designers seek to create a
report card that will persist over time. There is often a tension between

persistence and innovation, however. Features of report cards that increase their chance of persistence, say regulations requiring that specific data be collected and reported, may make it difficult to improve report cards or fit them to changing circumstances. The less designers care about the appropriateness of their initially selected variables, the usefulness of the report card to intended audiences, and the underlying variability of organizational environments, the more likely it is that the future will reveal ways to improve designs.

Response Problems

Although a key purpose of report cards is to improve organizational performance, there is no guarantee that this will occur. Confronted by unpleasant revelations, an organization may respond by adopting practices aimed at self-improvement, which benefits both the organization and its clients. Alternatively, however, the organization may respond dysfunctionally in an effort to defuse the reputational threat without addressing the root causes of its performance problems. Dysfunctional responses include: nonparticipation, cream skimming, manipulating the numbers, and blaming the messenger.

NONPARTICIPATION   When participation in report card projects is voluntary, many organizations simply decline to participate. This obviously weakens the report card by rendering it less comprehensive. It also has potential adverse consequences for those organizations that do participate. Consider, for example, a 1996 *Newsweek* report card on HMOs. Of 75 health plans contacted, only 43 agreed to participate (Spragins 1996: 56). In fact, the health plans that cooperated were among the best, and those that declined were among the worst. Consequently, a health plan that might have ranked in the middle of all 75 plans could easily rank among the worst of the 43 plans. With information from a skewed sample, a potential client, drawing the wrong inference, might avoid a health plan that in fact is quite respectable. A politician, drawing the wrong inference, might conclude that health plans in a particular state are better or worse than they actually are.

CREAM SKIMMING   It is well known that some clients are harder to handle than others. A welfare recipient who has never held a job for longer than three months is harder to train than a steelworker who worked for the same company for ten years before being laid off. An elderly patient with a heart condition and numerous other ailments is harder to save than a middle-aged patient with a similar heart condition but no comorbidities, such as diabetes or kidney disease. Aware of these distinctions, an organization may be tempted to "skim the cream" or "pick the cherries," choosing the clients who are easiest to serve while leaving more challenging cases to others. A report card that fails to control for relevant client characteristics virtually invites cream skimming. Even well-designed report cards, with elaborate risk-adjustment procedures, can be victimized by cream skimming. For example, critics of New York state's CABG surgery report card have contended that a suspiciously high number of high-risk heart patients from New York appeared in Ohio hospitals following the release of New York's first heart surgery report card (Lagnado 1996). Although the facts in this case have been disputed, the cream-skimming phenomenon has been well documented in various policy areas, such as employment and training (Donahue 1989).

MANIPULATING THE NUMBERS Instead of responding to a negative report card by trying to do better work, an organization may respond by trying to get a better grade without doing a better job. Familiarity with how report card scores are calculated enables organizations to adjust their figures in ways that create a more favorable impression. This phenomenon has been detected, for example, in data submitted by colleges and universities to *U.S. News & World Report* and other publications that rate institutions of higher learning. A key figure of central interest is the admission rate or the percentage of all applicants admitted by the college or university. A low figure suggests high demand and high standards; a high figure suggests low demand and low standards. Without changing their admissions standards, some colleges and universities have boosted their scores through a redefinition of what it means to apply for admission. By defining partial or incomplete applications as authentic applications, colleges and universities have improved their official admissions rates without changing their standards one iota (Knowlton 1995). Whatever one thinks of the ethics of this practice, it illustrates how organizations can focus obsessively on rankings rather than what the rankings are supposed to represent.

BLAMING THE MESSENGER No one likes to be criticized, and organizations are no different than individuals in this respect. When a report card singles out certain organizations for sub-par performance, a common response is to lash out at the report card, its premises, its methodology, and its designers. By blaming the messenger, organizations seek to challenge the legitimacy of the message, which poses a threat to their well-being. This phenomenon has been especially common in the wake of hospital report cards that compare "expected" and "observed" mortality rates at individual hospitals. When the federal government produced such report cards, hospital associations and individual hospitals accused the federal government of sloppy science and eventually persuaded the federal government to discontinue its report cards. Since then, a number of state governments have produced hospital report cards that have also triggered an avalanche of criticism, especially from those hospitals receiving negative evaluations. For example, Florida hospitals sharply criticized the state's first-ever hospital report card on the grounds that its risk adjustment was inadequate because it relied on administrative data (Mitchell 1996). Ironically, Florida's hospitals were largely responsible for the state's use of administrative data, as opposed to clinical data, which would require substantial expenditures by cost-conscious hospitals.

These are not the only negative consequences that may flow from report cards. Report cards, like other policy instruments, sometimes trigger much-needed organizational reforms followed by performance improvements. At other times, however, they trigger various forms of evasion and data manipulation. When their reputations are on the line, organizations may respond in either functional or dysfunctional ways.

Reception Problems

Well-designed report cards that do not encourage dysfunctional behavior by targeted organizations are essential if report cards are to work as intended. But they are not sufficient. The working premise that drives report cards is that report cards work best when they work through clients, citizens, or politicians. Unfortunately, clients, citizens, and politicians may not use report cards at all or they may use them inappropriately for a number of reasons.

WEAK MOTIVATION   Although the American public is far better educated and, presumably, better informed, than a century ago, studies show that the public's storehouse of relevant political information is surprisingly low (Delli Carpini and Keeter 1996). One reason for this is that ordinary citizens have too many other concerns, interests, and responsibilities to be willing to invest in the acquisition of useful political information. There is also some evidence to suggest that participation in the civic life of the community has declined since de Tocqueville characterized us as a "nation of joiners" (Putnam 1996). Despite multiple opportunities for acquiring information about social service organizations, most Americans ultimately have "better," or at least, different things to do with their time.

Politicians have stronger motives to pay attention. Information enables legislators to perform their jobs better, including both policy formulation and legislative oversight. Although political scientists have sometimes characterized legislative oversight as weak, Joel Aberbach (1990) has documented a sharp increase in congressional oversight since the early 1970s. Alan Rosenthal (1996) has observed a similar though more recent trend at the state level. Admittedly, legislative oversight tends to be more reactive than proactive (McCubbins and Schwartz 1984). Nevertheless, many legislators and their staffs are keenly interested in harvesting policy-relevant information.

COGNITIVE LIMITS   There are limits to how much and what kind of information human beings can process. It has long been recognized by psychologists that there are limits to the complexity of information that people can handle (Miller 1956). People appear to deal with uncertainty by relying on heuristics that have systematic biases (Kahneman, Slovic, and Tversky 1982). These cognitive limitations mean that, while most people can make some sense out of relatively crude report cards, most people also have difficulty processing more subtle messages embedded in more complex and sophisticated report cards, especially those that employ statistical models. Thus, as the measurement of performance improves, reception may decline. If so, producers of report cards must decide what balance to strike between good science and user-friendliness.

By virtue of greater interest and better training, politicians and their staffs can process larger quantities of policy-relevant information than ordinary citizens. Their capacity to handle fairly sophisticated reports is undoubtedly greater as well. Nevertheless, studies have shown that legislative personnel also experience cognitive limitations. A recent study of congressional information use found that members of Congress and their staffs sometimes suffer from information overload (Whiteman 1995: 39–40). A study of state legislators' information use found that shorter policy reports were preferred to longer ones (Mooney 1992). The optimal length seemed to be approximately two pages.

INFORMATIONAL INEQUALITIES There will, of course, be some citizens who can and will process fairly complex report cards to good advantage. Many others, however, will be unable to do so. In practice, these differences are likely to coincide with social class differences, thus exacerbating informational inequalities that already exist. High-income and well-educated parents may acquire useful information on the relative merits of different public school districts and choose residential locales accordingly, while lower-income and less well-educated parents keep their children in schools that cannot seem to get the job done. Better-educated consumers may choose a health plan with a report card in hand, while poorly educated consumers settle for what is left. Pressure from well-informed consumers may benefit all consumers by improving the performance of the industry or institution as a whole (Rose-Ackerman 1992: 97–117). But if this does not occur, the game of musical chairs may leave poorly informed consumers standing up.

Informational inequalities among politicians may be less severe because they routinely share information. Strategically situated legislators, such as committee chairs and subcommittee chairs, undoubtedly possess greater information in selected policy domains than their peers. Because information-poor legislators often take cues from information-rich legislators, however, this particular information gap is less worrisome than those that characterize clients and citizens.

Reporting on Report Cards

Organizational report cards have proliferated. Indeed, demands for report cards from a variety of sources are likely to make them an ever more common feature of the environment of social service organizations. Is this trend desirable? What should report cards seek to accomplish and how should they be designed? What role should government play in encouraging, discouraging, or structuring report cards? When should government rely on report cards as a policy instrument for achieving greater accountability of organizations? And when do other policy instruments make more sense?

In the chapters that follow we attempt to answer these questions. In Chapter 2 we develop a theoretical rationale for report cards as techniques for enhancing accountability. We focus on information asymmetries between producers and consumers and coordination problems within organizations. We then discuss the relative merits of report cards and other policy instruments. Finally, we introduce a normative framework for evaluating report cards.

In Chapter 3 we discuss the history and politics of report cards. We find that interest groups, politicians, and bureaucrats have played critical roles in promoting and undermining report cards. The convergence of problems, solutions, and politics has created favorable conditions for report cards in some policy settings. In general, conditions have been more favorable in education policy than in health policy.

In Chapter 4 we analyze the technical (or methodological) challenges that confront report card designers. We discuss the difficulties of measuring outcomes and inputs and establishing connections between the two. We then turn to real-world examples that highlight the difficulties of risk adjustment in complex industries. Despite these problems, and despite the dangers of statistical obfuscation, we argue that risk adjustment is indispensable to credible report cards when client characteristics differ significantly across organizations.

In Chapter 5 we discuss how consumers and policymakers process information, including information contained in report cards. We rely upon communications theory, marketing theory, and research utilization theory to identify promising strategies for packaging information so that it reaches targeted audiences. We then highlight the challenges of producing report cards that are comprehensible and relevant. We argue that the distinction between mass and elite audiences must be taken into account when designing report cards.

In Chapter 6 we examine the actual use of report cards by service delivery organizations. Drawing upon organizational theories, we identify a range of functional and dysfunctional responses that may occur. We focus on organizational incentives, the capacity for change, and tensions between organizational incentives and social goals. Although we cite numerous examples of pathological responses to report cards, we argue that most organizations are capable of reconciling organizational goals with the values animating report cards.

In Chapter 7 we ask whether report cards should be produced by governments or nongovernmental organizations. Our answer is that the production of report cards must be disaggregated into discrete functions or tasks. Once this is accomplished, the comparative advantages of the public and private sectors become much clearer.

Finally, in Chapter 8 we review the evidence and attempt to answer several questions. When are organizational report cards most useful? How useful are they in comparison to traditional policy instruments, such as subsidies and regulations? How useful are they in comparison to report cards that focus on individuals (physicians, teachers, etc.)? And how might organizational report cards be improved so that they meet the needs of consumers and policymakers without treating targeted organizations unfairly?

2

Report Cards As
Policy Instruments

To understand organizational report cards better, it is necessary to specify with greater precision the problems they are supposed to solve. It is also useful to compare report cards with other generic policy instruments. In this chapter, we develop several theoretical justifications for report cards and we distinguish between the report card and its principal competitor, direct government regulation. Then we specify several criteria for report card design that should guide those who have concluded that a report card is an appropriate policy instrument for a particular task.

Accountability and Organizational Report Cards

The concept of accountability has importance in many areas of public policy. It is especially important in thinking about the duties and responsibilities that public agencies owe to elected officials, judges, and citizens. As a polity, we want public agencies to be held accountable for resources they use and the values they create. Markets and private firms are also expected to answer to their customers for the price and quality of the goods and services they produce. Increasingly, the distinction between the public and private sectors has broken down as contracting out has become more common at all levels of government (Kettl 1993). Government agencies often enter into contracts with private firms and with nonprofit organizations to deliver services invested with a public aspect (trash collection, education, child care, and health care, among others). Under such circumstances, citizens have a right to expect that contractors are accountable to them and to their authorized representatives (politicians and political executives), irrespective of whether the contractors are government agencies, for-profit firms, or nonprofit organizations. As Mark Moore (1995: 53) puts it, "whenever public authority is invoked to solve the technical prob-

20

lems in the market, the enterprise takes on public characteristics." Such public characteristics require attentiveness not just to efficiency and effectiveness but to justice and fairness as well.

Along with these trends, government agencies have begun to compete with other government agencies and with private firms for the right to deliver public services to clients. For example, many public schools now compete with other public schools, and in some jurisdictions with private schools, for the right to deliver taxpayer-subsidized educational services to students. Under such circumstances, as public monopolies are gradually transformed into more competitive arrangements, accountability to customers, previously associated with markets, becomes essential if successful performance, as defined by customers, is to be rewarded. In this situation, expectations of justice and fairness (for example, schooling as a right) remain, but expectations of efficiency and effectiveness are heightened.

The case for a particular form or degree of accountability will depend in part on the legal status of the service provider (government versus for-profit versus nonprofit). It will also depend on such factors as the extent of competition in the market, the extent of government funding, and the extent of public concern. Nevertheless, all organizations providing social services should be held accountable to their sovereigns, including public managers, politicians, and citizens. As Stephen Smith and Michael Lipsky (1993: 13) put it, "Democratic governance requires that government adequately hold accountable all agencies that implement public policy, whether they are government bureaus, businesses, or nonprofit contractors." Such agencies should also be held accountable to their clients and to those who make purchasing decisions on their behalf.

Holding persons or organizations accountable requires information about the exercise of their duties. Often, however, those with duties have more information about how well they are carrying them out than do those to whom they are accountable. Such information asymmetries impede accountability. Public policies and private initiatives that reduce these information asymmetries thus facilitate accountability.

Organizational report cards are policy instruments for reducing information asymmetry—and thereby increasing accountability—in the provision of services. From a public policy perspective, report cards are most relevant to services in which there are clear rationales for public accountability. The use of public resources, such as funds and authority, to provide services is one basis for public accountability (Moore 1995: 29). Another is the failure of markets to achieve social values, such as economic efficiency, distributional equity, and public safety. Services produced, purchased, subsidized, or regulated by government clearly call for public accountability. Markets in which information asymmetries interfere with effective consumer choice may also demand better accountability.

Report cards can contribute to accountability in the provision of services in the two general ways indicated in Figure 2.1. First, by better informing consumers, whether the clients of the services themselves or those who purchase services for them, report cards can affect the suppliers they choose, the prices they are willing to pay, and the complaints they are willing to voice. To the extent that these behaviors and propensities are relevant to the interests of suppliers, they facilitate accountability that is "bottom-up" in the sense that it originates from those receiving services. The more informative a report card, and the greater the choices available to consumers, the greater the potential for effective bottom-up accountability. Second, by better informing citizens, politicians, and public managers, report cards can affect their interest in and capacity for oversight. To the extent that oversight in turn affects the resources and discretion of

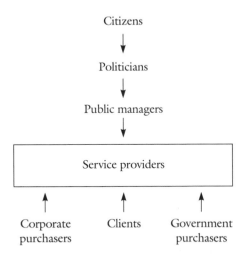

Figure 2.1 Holding service providers accountable

suppliers, it facilitates accountability that is "top-down" in the sense that it originates from those who can potentially employ coercive controls on suppliers.

Note that in Figure 2.1 we distinguish between public managers who have responsibilities in facilitating supply, and therefore have roles as overseers, and managers of the organizations that actually produce the supply. The organizational managers, who bear the greatest responsibility for the quality of the services delivered to clients, are the focal points for both bottom-up and top-down accountability. Although the information provided by report cards may be valuable to the organizational managers in its own right, report cards gain their special force by enhancing bottom-up accountability, top-down accountability, or both.

Information Asymmetries in Markets and Governance

Information asymmetry is a prerequisite for an organizational report card to be an effective policy instrument for enhancing accountability: report cards only make sense if they are in some way informative. The way report cards contribute to greater accountability depends on the nature of the information asymmetries they seek to eliminate. Information asymmetries in service markets offer the possibility for report cards to contribute to greater bottom-up accountability; information asymmetries in governance relations offer the possibility for report cards to contribute to greater top-down accountability. The following sections provide a closer look at the nature of these two types of information asymmetries.

Information Asymmetries in Service Markets

Organizations often have greater knowledge of the various attributes, or margins, of the services they provide than do their clients. When clients or potential clients underestimate service quality, organizations have an incentive to provide them with corrective information, though the organizations may lack ways of doing so credibly. When clients overestimate service quality, however, organizations lack an immediate incentive to provide corrective information. The consequence may be a market failure in the sense that, although corrective information will not be provided by the organizations themselves, aggregate social welfare would be increased if it were.

The seriousness of the market failure depends on the nature of the service, especially whether it is a search, experience, or post-experience good (Vining and Weimer 1988). A service is a *search good* if its quality can be fully determined prior to its consumption. The only problem facing potential consumers is to discover the available combinations of qualities and prices that they would most prefer. Though they may fail to discover the best available combination when searching is costly, they will not make purchases unless they value the service at least as much as its price. Further, the ability of consumers to confirm information provided to them opens up the possibility of credible advertising. Consequently, the market failure is unlikely to be serious.

A service is an *experience good* if its quality can be discovered only through consumption. For example, based on information voluntarily provided by day care centers or schools, it may be difficult for parents to judge the quality of the services provided to their children until after the children have been enrolled for some period of time. Similarly, one may not be able to judge the quality of services provided by HMOs until after one has experienced an episode requiring medical intervention. Experience goods potentially involve a serious market failure.

A service is a *post-experience good* if its quality cannot be fully assessed by an individual consumer even after it is consumed. For example, as surgical outcomes are uncertain, it may not be possible for patients to make accurate assessments of the quality of their operations even well after they have had them. Accurate assessments of quality generally require observation of the long-term outcomes resulting from provision of the service to many clients, making it costly for specialists to develop useful information that they can sell to potential clients. Consequently, the consumption of a post-experience good almost always involves a serious market failure.

Report cards can be thought of as mechanisms for reducing information asymmetries between organizations and those who consume their services. When the services are provided in competitive markets, the information allows consumers to select more appropriate services. Competition for informed customers in turn creates incentives for organizations to improve their performance in providing valued services. Thus, report cards can be seen as facilitating economic efficiency by making competition more effective.

Organizations with limited competition, such as private or public local monopolies, do not face as strong an incentive to respond to consumer demands as do organizations in competitive markets. Weaker competition means that information asymmetries are likely to be relatively large because the organizations need to be less concerned about attracting customers with high quality services. It also means that the information report cards provide to consumers is likely to have less direct impact on organizational performance. In any event, organizations with market power are generally subjected to more stringent governance in the form of various sorts of regulation than are competitive firms. Report cards may play a positive role in the governance relationship as a substitute for or complement to regulation.

Information Asymmetries in Governance Relations

A central insight for understanding organizational behavior is that organizations typically have more information about their performance than do those who oversee them (Niskanen 1971; Bendor, Taylor, and Van Gaalen 1985; Banks and Weingast 1992). Managers of corporations enjoy an informational advantage relative to stockholders and government regulators; bureau heads enjoy an advantage relative to political executives and legislators to whom they are supposed to be accountable. Informational advantages enjoyed by the providers of services relative to governmental sponsors may hinder the achievement of important social values.

Organizational report cards may facilitate oversight by governmental sponsors by making comparative information more readily and routinely available. For example, school report cards may help state regulators identify schools that are performing relatively poorly, perhaps opening the way for some other policy intervention. They may also play a role in helping to mobilize the recipients of important social services to express demands for higher quality. Again, with respect to school report cards, parents of children in schools performing relatively poorly may respond by becoming more active participants in the schooling itself or they may voice their concerns politically in school board elections and bond issues.

Report cards may also play a positive role in stimulating public discussion of values relevant to social services. This stimulation may occur during discussions concerning the content of report cards. But it may also occur as organizations respond to their ratings, perhaps by making assertions about unmeasured values. For example, schools serving relatively disadvantaged populations of students may point to the non-instructional services that they must provide to compensate for deficiencies in material and parental support. Whether in design or response, report cards provide a framework for explicit discussion of values that might otherwise be left out of public discourse.

A number of factors increase the salience of public oversight of services. The service in question may involve externalities that are not fully taken into account by consumers. For example, families may not realize the full gains from educational investments in their children—some gains may spill over to the rest of society in terms of people better able to participate effectively as citizens. Vaccinations and other preventive health measures may reduce risks to the health of others. Low-quality medical care that causes kidney failure inflicts high costs on taxpayers who fund publicly-provided dialysis. Government may be able to increase social welfare by helping to increase the consumption of services with positive externalities and to decrease the consumption of services with negative externalities.

The government may reasonably have a paternalistic concern for consumption of certain services by those who may not be able to act effectively in their own interests. Some persons must rely on agents to make consumption decisions for them. Children rely on parental choices about day care, medical treatments, and schooling. Many parents rely on their children's selection of nursing home care. While people generally act in the best interests of their family members, they sometimes have insufficient information, attention, or integrity to carry out these duties responsibly.

The absence of competition creates opportunities for suppliers to operate inefficiently. For example, the local monopolies school districts enjoy over publicly funded primary and secondary education make it very costly for parents to choose alternative schooling—they must pay tuition at private schools, arrange for home schooling, or change their place of residence to a more desired school district. Poor quality thus will not necessarily result in a loss of clients.

Report Cards and Types of Service Providers

Organizations that supply services almost always enjoy information asymmetries with respect to both their clients and their overseers. Although report cards can aim at closing either or both of these types of information asymmetries, organizations facing competition for customers are more likely to respond to bottom-up accountability than organizations enjoying monopoly positions. Private monopolies by virtue of regulation, and public monopolies by virtue of use of public resources, are likely to be especially responsive to top-down accountability.

Table 2.1 shows these distinctions by indicating the main report card audiences for each of four supply circumstances involving information asymmetries in which report cards are plausible policy instruments. The first row considers competitive suppliers, such as colleges, insurers, and airlines, who sell directly to clients. Here the clients are the obvious targets of the report cards. As they have alternative sources of supply, the information they receive from report cards can potentially affect the market shares of suppliers, which in turn creates incentives for organizational managers to improve their ratings.

As with the first row, the second row focuses on competitive suppliers. Instead of clients primarily funding their own purchases, however, third-party payers play a substantial role. The third-party payers are likely to be the primary audience for report cards. Indeed, employers and the federal government, major third-party payers for health care, have been the driving forces behind the creation of report cards on HMOs. The federal gov-

Table 2.1 Report Cards as Policy Instruments for Dealing with Information Asymmetry

Type of target organization and market setting	Most salient external audiences for report card	Audience-mediated incentives for organizational managers
Suppliers in competitive markets with low levels of third-party payments (e.g. colleges, insurers, airlines)	clients	changes in market share
Suppliers in competitive markets with high levels of third-party payments (e.g. HMOs, hospitals)	payers and clients	changes in market share (including right to participate)
Private monopolies (e.g. local telephone companies)	regulators and clients	changes in rates and discretion
Public monopolies (e.g. public schools, fire departments)	overseers, citizens, and clients	changes in budgets, discretion, and reputation

ernment, as the major purchaser of hospital care for the elderly through Medicare, also provided the initial impetus for report cards on hospitals. Because third-party payers determine the choices available to large groups of clients, suppliers have an even stronger incentive to respond to them than they do to individual clients.

The next two rows consider situations with highly attenuated competition. The third row shows private monopolies such as local telephone companies. Although they do not compete for customers for over-the-wire local services, they are subject to regulation. Regulators, therefore, would be the primary report card targets. Clients are also targets in the sense that they may be motivated to exercise voice either directly to the monopoly or indirectly through participation in the regulatory process (Gormley 1983). The desire for favorable rates, and the fear of loss of discretion, provide incentives to their managers to respond to the information provided by report cards to regulators. Public monopolies (the fourth row), such as school districts, also face little direct competition. Report cards on their services are therefore aimed primarily at overseers and citizens, though, as with private monopolies, clients may be a target because of their potential for exerting influence on their monopoly suppliers through voice—ranging from personalized protest to participation in governance processes—or exit to the jurisdiction of a more favorable local monopoly (Hirschman 1970). Oversight and citizen perceptions motivate the managers of these public monopolies to the extent that they affect the resources they receive and the reputation that they enjoy.

Direct Value of Report Cards to Organizations

Organizations experience both internal and external informational problems. Internally, organizational leaders often face an information asymmetry problem with other members of the organization that raises problems with respect to the exercise of discretion. Externally, organizations may have difficulty learning about, and therefore from, other organizations providing similar services. Report cards may help reduce these informational problems.

An organization can be thought of as a "nexus for a set of contracting relationships" among its members (Jensen and Meckling 1976: 310). Because relationships and tasks within organizations are complex, however, contracts can never be complete in the sense of anticipating all possible contingencies. Members of organizations thus retain considerable discretion. How they exercise this discretion plays an important role in determining the performance of the organization.

For our purposes, the problem of organizational discretion can be thought of in terms of the rational choice theory of institutions (Schotter 1981; Calvert 1995). Organizations provide their members with a framework in which they will engage in repeated interactions. At any particular time, the favorable exercise of discretion from the point of view of the organization may require members to undertake actions that provide them individually with immediate net costs. The expectation that others will undertake such actions in the future, thereby benefitting the entire organization, may present members with the expectation of positive individual net benefits in the future so that the current actions offer a positive present value of net benefits overall. The rational choice theory of institutions models these situations as repeated games in which players can make their decisions conditional on what other players have done in previous rounds of play. Such games have equilibrium strategies in the sense that no player finds it in her self-interest to change her strategy given the strategies of the other players. Among these equilibrium strategies may be some in which the players willingly undertake actions that are not in their myopic self-interest.

There is rarely only one equilibrium strategy in a repeated game, however. This poses a coordination problem for the players. Each could pursue a number of strategies that could result in a relatively desirable equilibrium if matched appropriately with the strategy of the other player. Inappropriate matches, however, could result in reaching a much less desirable equilibrium. In this context, organizational leadership can be thought of as the creation of focal points for coordinating players' strategies (Miller 1992). For example, a leader may make some visible personal sacrifice for the organization, or create exemplars out of others who make exceptional contributions, in order to try to establish such behaviors as new norms. Corporate culture can be thought of as norms and conventions that help organizational members anticipate focal points (Kreps 1990).

Organizations with weak leadership or poor corporate cultures generally perform poorly. Such failures may lead to extinction in competitive markets. Public agencies that do not have to compete for customers, however, can survive without strong leadership or good corporate cultures. They may require focal points from external sources to help their members achieve a better equilibrium (Scholz and Gray 1997). Organizational report cards may be a source of focal points for such organizations.

Organizational leaders often have difficulty assessing the performance of their own organizations. One reason is that information may not be available to help them compare how well their organizations are doing relative to others providing similar services. For example, the head of a surgical unit may not know whether its mortality rate is higher or lower than that of units doing similar procedures at other hospitals. A report card that rated the unit unfavorably might lead its head to compare the unit's procedures with those of better performers. Thus, a report card can potentially facilitate technological improvement among service providers.

Report Cards As Alternatives to Direct Regulation

Information asymmetries and related problems can be solved by what Anne Schneider and Helen Ingram (1990) refer to as "authority tools." The most conspicuous and widely used of these is government regulation. Regulation is a policy instrument that requires or prohibits certain organizational behaviors. Although it is closely associated with so-called regulatory agencies, such as the Environmental Protection Agency, it is in fact widely used by social service agencies as a convenient technique for rectifying information asymmetries and correcting for externalities.

For example, day care centers possess quality-relevant information about staff qualifications, staff turnover, and staff-child ratios that parents lack (Gormley 1995). In an unregulated world, parents would have difficulty protecting their children from unsafe or unhealthy conditions linked to poor staffing. In a regulated world, where all 50 states impose minimum requirements on day care centers, parents at least know that certain basic standards are, or are supposed to be, met. If states take these standards seriously and actually enforce them, then parents can have greater confidence that their children are secure.

Child care regulation illustrates the most common form of government regulation, which is standard-setting. Minimum quality standards, expressed in terms of inputs, processes, or product qualities, seek to eliminate low quality goods or services from the market so that consumers avoid the most serious losses from overestimation of quality. Minimum quality standards are often linked to licensing and inspections to ensure that the standards are met initially and subsequently. Alternatively, some form of certification may take place, with or without inspections.

Because regulation can be highly intrusive, it is often resisted by regulated firms and by other regulated organizations, such as public schools, hospitals, and local governments (Tolchin and Tolchin 1985; Bardach 1989). The business community has been particularly animated in expressing hostility toward government regulation, but other regulated organizations have also decried regulation as overly prescriptive, overly rigid, and overly adversarial. For example, state and local governments have often complained about federal mandates that restrict their discretion or require them to bear the costs of specified actions.

One response to such criticisms has been to shift from "command-and-control" regulation to "incentive-based" regulation, so that regulated organizations can respond more efficiently to the underlying purpose of the regulation rather than to a specific set of rules that may increase costs unduly and unnecessarily. Incentive-based regulation can even be thought of as a form of deregulation in the sense that it gives greater discretion to the objects of regulation.

Deregulation of a number of the social services has been tried. Some states have allowed school districts (or schools) to deviate from state regulatory standards in an effort to experiment with new approaches and strategies. Twenty-five states have established "charter school" programs that allow parents, teachers, or nonprofit corporations to set up their own schools (Judis 1996: 6). Almost 300 schools have already been approved in the six states with the most accommodating laws (Bierlein 1996). Some states have allowed family day care homes to function legally without a regular inspection. The federal government's health care regulatory agency, the Health Care Financing Administration, has relaxed the regulatory requirements that nursing homes must meet. And the Department of Health and Human Services has granted waivers of Medicaid rules to numerous states, allowing considerable experimentation in the delivery of Medicaid services.

Despite these efforts to make regulation more efficient, more effective, and more palatable to regulated organizations, dissatisfaction with regulation as a policy instrument remains widespread. One reason for this is that regulation is a fundamentally coercive process, even if some of its sting is removed. Another reason is that regulation robs regulated organizations of discretion, which can be an indispensable source of creativity and innovation. These concerns have led, in some instances, to total deregulation, with the regulatory agency actually closing its doors (the Civil Aeronautics Board and the Interstate Commerce Commission, for example). They have also encouraged both the public and private sectors to look to information-based policy instruments, such as report cards, as solutions to information asymmetries between service providers and those who care about their performance (consumers, overseers, and managers).

In principle, report cards have two major advantages over regulation. First, report cards are less coercive than direct regulation. Government may have to mandate the collection and reporting of data by organizations to make report cards feasible. These mandates, however, are likely to be less intrusive than regulations that specify the production processes of organizations or set minimum standards of quality for their services. To the extent that reporting burdens are less coercive than regulation, report cards are less likely to foster an adversarial relationship between government and service organizations. Second, report cards aimed at consumers may adequately correct information asymmetries without imposing the standardization that often results from centralized regulatory decisions. Report cards can inform without restricting consumer choice.

These differences between report cards and standards-based regulation are significant. Nevertheless, it should be recognized that report cards, as substitutes for government regulation, also possess certain regulatory characteristics: they require compliant organizations to invest time and money; they pose a potential threat to the organization's reputation and budget; and they have the capacity to induce either functional or dysfunctional organizational responses. For these reasons, the selection of a report card as a policy instrument should be made only after giving consideration to alternatives.

It is also important to acknowledge that regulations and report cards are not the only possible solutions to information asymmetry problems. Another interesting possibility is to rely more heavily on nonprofit organizations for service delivery. Nonprofit organizations are potentially superior to for-profit firms in delivering services involving information asymmetries. Because the personal compensation that nonprofit executives can extract from revenue is limited by law, they have a weaker incentive to exploit the informational deficiencies of their clients. On the one hand, this suggests that nonprofits may be more "trustworthy" than for-profits and thus pose a less serious information asymmetry problem (Hansmann 1987). On the other hand, nonprofits have a weaker incentive than for-profit firms to search for cost-savings that would increase profits.

Nonprofits also offer a potential advantage relative to service delivery by government agencies because they often have greater discretion in the clients they serve and the particular services they provide. For example, shelters for the homeless operated by nonprofits may be able to enforce restrictions on offensive behaviors, like the use of foul language, or require actions, like quiet reflection, that government agencies would find difficult, or even legally impossible, to impose. Nonprofits thus allow greater variety of publicly funded services (Weisbrod 1988). In order to take advantage of such variety, however, potential clients require information about organizational characteristics, including performance. Report cards may play a role in meeting these information needs.

Report cards and public or private accreditation may be close substitutes in many situations. Accreditation involves some external organization certifying that an organization meets some minimum standards in terms of the inputs or processes that it employs to produce goods or services. Private organizations play a major role in accreditation in the United States (Cheit 1990). In some cases, industries organize their own accreditation systems to restrict competition from firms that produce lower quality products. In other cases, government imposes accreditation requirements, but delegates their design and implementation to private organizations. Whereas accreditation can be thought of as a simple signal to consumers that an organization has met some minimum standards, report cards usually provide more detailed information about levels and dimensions of performance. The National Committee for Quality Assurance, for example, makes information on both accreditation status and more detailed quality assessments available, though not yet for most HMOs.

Ripe Conditions for Report Cards

A central premise of the policy instruments literature is that selected instruments should be appropriate to the task at hand (Linder and Peters 1989; Salamon 1989; Weimer 1992). With this in mind, organizational report cards make more sense in some contexts than in others. For example, a report card may be an excellent solution to excessive television violence, because both our political culture and the First Amendment place significant constraints on what government can accomplish through direct regulation in its dealings with either television networks or the film industry. In contrast, a report card may be a poor solution to inadequate prison conditions, because convicted criminals do not enjoy the freedom to select the prison of their choice, based on the amenities provided, and because politicians seldom care deeply about prison quality. Federal district court judges care more, but their concern is with a specific case; thus a report card would probably provide them with more information than they really want.

In thinking about the potential utility of report cards, it is important to distinguish between their roles in bottom-up and top-down accountability. Bottom-up accountability operates through consumers (individual clients and third-party purchasers); top-down accountability operates most immediately through policymakers (legislators and public executives). Because consumers and policymakers have different needs, interests, and capacities, the circumstances that facilitate use by one group may differ considerably from those that favor use by the other.

The Role of Report Cards in Bottom-Up Accountability

Several considerations are relevant to deciding whether report cards have substantial or limited potential to assist consumers in the choices they make. One of them is *interorganizational variation* in services: Do organizations differ sharply in their service delivery strategies or outputs? If they do, then information can, in principle, reveal quality-relevant differences. If they do not—for example, if there is a dime's worth of difference between facilities—then the accumulation and dissemination of large quantities of information may be a pointless exercise. For report cards to be useful to consumers, the values of the variables measuring the outcomes they produce must vary meaningfully.

A second important consideration is the extent of *consumer choice:* Do clients actually have the opportunity to make choices for themselves? If they do, then report cards can be enormously helpful. Often, however, they do not. One limiting factor is *geography.* If there is only one maternity hospital within a 50-mile radius of a given residential neighborhood, then information on the relative performance of various maternity hospitals may not be particularly helpful to consumers. If there is only one elementary school within easy driving distance, then similar considerations apply. In contrast, day care centers and family day care homes are scattered throughout communities, which suggests that the potential for report cards to help parents choose child care facilities is relatively high.

Laws that restrict consumer choice also limit the value of report cards to clients. In many jurisdictions, parents must send their children to the public school designated by the school board and therefore lack the option of choosing from a menu of public schools. As parents gain greater discretion through the introduction of public school choice, charter schools, or vouchers, report cards aimed at them will become more useful and appropriate.

Yet another limiting factor is *corporate cost containment.* As corporations have enlisted HMOs and preferred provider organizations to deliver health care services to their employees, consumer choices have become more constrained. In cases where employees must choose between a single HMO and a single fee-for-service plan, choices are severely constrained and report cards may be of little assistance to individual consumers (though they can be extremely useful to corporate consumers, who often play a useful intermediary role). In cases where employees may choose from a menu of health plans, the potential utility of report cards is higher.

A third consideration is whether a particular industry is heavily dependent on *consumer fees*. If clients are paying a substantial share of the total costs, as in child care, then they may be more attentive to pertinent information (especially price information) than if the government is footing a substantial part of the bill, as it does for nursing homes. On the other hand, as price considerations loom larger, quality considerations may become secondary, thus reducing interest in quality-relevant information.

The Role of Report Cards in Top-Down Accountability

The circumstances that make report cards appealing to consumers are not necessarily those that facilitate use by policymakers. From a policymaker's perspective, a key consideration is the *extent of government funding* for a particular industry or endeavor. This consideration relates to the public-private management distinction but is not identical to it. Although the percentage of nursing homes actually run by government agencies is relatively small, government subsidies to nursing homes are quite substantial (Salamon 1992: 65–66). The latter, we believe, is the more relevant fact. The greater the government's financial commitment to a particular institution, the greater the degree of interest policymakers will show in report cards.

The *salience of the issues addressed* is likely to matter as well. In a study of congressional information use, Whiteman (1985) found that policy reports were more likely to be utilized when they touched on issues of high salience. Although issue salience is not a static phenomenon, some issues tend to occupy a prominent place on particular policy agendas for long periods of time (Kingdon 1984). Elementary and secondary education, for example, has long been highly salient for state policymakers—much more so than child care, which has until recently been regarded as a private concern. This helps to explain why public school report cards have attracted considerable interest and funding at the state level, while child care report cards have received less support and enjoyed less widespread use.

At least some policymakers are likely to be concerned about the overall *performance of the industry* or endeavor. From the vantage point of consumers, variations across organizations are of particular interest. From the vantage point of policymakers, the mean may matter more than the standard deviation. If an industry is doing poorly and organizations differ only at the margins, then report cards cannot really help consumers, unless, of course, there is some roughly comparable industry to which they can turn. In contrast, this is precisely the sort of situation that triggers "fire-alarm oversight" by politicians (McCubbins and Schwartz 1984). Legislative priority-setting is guided in part by the relative performance of different sectors of the economy. A report card that highlights relatively low levels of performance can be extremely instructive to policymakers and is likely to generate considerable interest.

Assessing Report Cards

Before arguing for particular policy remedies, public policy analysts should be explicit about their normative criteria (MacRae 1971; Anderson 1979). This is as important when studying policy instruments as it is when studying policy problems. Unless it is built upon a solid normative foundation, policy analysis runs the risk of being either purely descriptive or prescriptive but ad hoc.

Thus several questions arise: If report cards are to be chosen, then what should they look like? How should they be designed? What principles should guide them? Although we can imagine a wide array of values that might be worth pursuing, we believe that six are particularly important for helping to evaluate answers to these questions:

1. *Validity:* Information provided by a report card should be valid and should meet widely accepted standards of scientific practice. Among other things, it should focus on measures that closely approximate, or are clearly linked to, outcomes and it should adjust for pertinent differences in clients and resources.

2. *Comprehensiveness:* Information presented in a report card should be comprehensive in terms of important dimensions of organizational performance and should include a range of indicators. This is particularly important when the quality of organizational outcomes is multidimen-

sional, as is often the case. The omission of key indicators yields a report card that is incomplete and potentially misleading.

3. *Comprehensibility:* The information presented in a report card should be comprehensible to potential users, including consumers and policymakers. The presentation of data as information, the amount and form of information, and the media through which information is transmitted should all take the cognitive capacities and habits of potential users into account.

4. *Relevance:* The information provided by a report card should be relevant to the needs of potential users. In the case of consumers, it should take into account the dynamics of choice—specifically, how much flexibility consumers have to make particular choices, and when those choices must be made. It should also focus on the right unit of analysis—for example, whether consumers are choosing a physician or a hospital or a health plan; a school or a school district. In the case of policymakers, it should take into account the budget cycle and, more broadly, the ebb and flow of political interest.

5. *Reasonableness:* A report card should be reasonable in the demands it places upon a targeted industry and its organizations. Among other things, this means that sufficient time should be allowed for submitting data and that paperwork requirements should not be unduly burdensome. In other words, the cost of compliance should not be excessive.

6. *Functionality:* A report card should be crafted in such a way that it convinces targeted organizations to engage in appropriate, rather than dysfunctional, behavior. In particular, the report card's theoretical purposes should be compelling—organizations should be persuaded not simply to comply with technical requirements but, more importantly, to embrace the report card's implicit vision as their own.

Conclusion

In succeeding chapters, we rely on the six criteria for assessing report cards to structure our normative inquiry. Validity and comprehensiveness, which involve issues of report card *content,* will be particularly important to Chapter 4. Comprehensibility and relevance, which concern *audience use* of report cards, will be especially pertinent to Chapter 5. Reasonableness and functionality, which relate to *organizational responses* to report cards, will be of critical importance to Chapter 6. More generally, we will use all six criteria to guide and inform our analysis, including when we turn to questions of strategies for designing and implementing report cards.

We recognize, however, that report cards are embedded in a complex political environment encompassing strong-willed interest groups, bureaucratic supporters and opponents, determined policy entrepreneurs, and a general public that can occasionally be galvanized into action. Before applying our normative criteria to actual report cards, we discuss the politics of report cards, especially the politics of education and health report cards in the United States.

3

The Politics of Report Cards

The struggle over values, though central to the debate over report cards, is intimately connected to the clash of competing interests. Representatives of expanding and contracting industries, consumers, professionals, politicians, and journalists have advanced their respective interests in promoting or opposing report cards. The history of report cards is one of interest group politics, bureaucratic politics, and policy analysis, in which the choice of policy instruments has been shaped by economic, political, and technical considerations.

In this chapter, we focus on education and health care report cards, whose precursors first appeared in the nineteenth century. We proceed chronologically, from the origins of report cards to their growth and maturation, to the crises that have threatened to tarnish or destroy them. We then ask whether the politics of report cards is better viewed as an example of information policy or as an offshoot of more specific substantive debates in well-established policy domains, such as education and health care. Our exploration of these issues is informed by several theoretical frameworks of the policymaking process, and sets the stage for our treatment of technical and policy design issues in subsequent chapters.

Origins

While it is difficult to say with precision who invented the organizational report card, it is possible to identify some of the early advocates of report cards for schools and hospitals. In the 1840s Horace Mann, the Massachusetts state legislator and education reformer, recommended systematic comparisons of public schools as a mechanism for inducing improved performance (Tyack and Hansot 1982: 160). In conjunction with allies on the Boston School Board such as Samuel G. Howe, Mann pressed for performance assessments in the hope of highlighting the inadequacies of Boston's schools. In 1845 Mann's dream was partly realized when the Boston School Board administered a uniform written test to students in the top class of each elementary school. The tests revealed numerous errors and sharp variations across schools, just as Mann and Howe had predicted (Tyack 1974: 36–38).

The idea of hospital report cards emerged two decades later in Great Britain, thanks to the vision and perseverance of Florence Nightingale, the legendary nurse and reformer. Horrified by conditions in Army hospitals at home and abroad, Nightingale urged that hospitals develop and publicize statistics on their patients' diseases and mortality rates. With the support of Dr. William Farr, a prominent statistician, she prepared model report cards and persuaded the International Statistical Congress to endorse her approach in 1860. The following year she extracted an agreement from eight London hospitals to publish mortality statistics based loosely on her model forms (Cook 1914: 428–438).

Inventing the organizational report card was relatively easy. Institutionalizing the idea would prove much more difficult. Technical problems, financial problems, industry opposition, public ignorance, and other obstacles prevented report cards from taking root soon after their appearance. Even Florence Nightingale, favored by Queen Victoria, feared by hospital administrators, and thoroughly devoted to her cause, could not persuade Britain's hospitals to prepare reputable report cards on a regular basis. Although several London hospitals agreed to publish annual mortality statistics in 1861, these efforts proved inconsistent and short-lived. As Sir Edward Cook (1914: 434) noted, "The laboriousness, and therefore the costliness, of the work of compilation, the difficulty of securing actual, as well as apparent, uniformity, and a consequent doubt as to the value of conclusions deduced from the figures are presumably among the causes which have defeated Miss Nightingale's scheme."

Despite frustrations and disappointments, the early efforts of Mann, Nightingale, and other organizational report card enthusiasts were extremely important. Although report cards did not spread immediately, and indeed foundered in their own backyards, these initiatives resulted in report card prototypes for future improvement and eventual adoption. They also generated interest in a solution that would eventually prove popular when education and health problems rose on the public agenda and political conditions proved more favorable. In Kingdon's (1995: 116–117) words, they contributed policy solutions to the "policy primeval soup."

Incremental Progress

The nineteenth century proved inhospitable to organizational report cards for a number of reasons. Fledgling institutions, such as schools and hospitals, were sufficiently fragile that they might not have withstood the scrutiny of an impartial and systematic assessment. The science of measurement was quite crude, and it is doubtful that the general public would have understood good measures, bad measures, or the difference between the two. The capacity to produce such measures—whether good or bad—was also quite limited as data collection, storage, tabulation, and analysis were laborious tasks.

The Progressive Era, with its emphasis on professionalism, meritocracy, independent regulatory commissions, a civil service, and technical expertise, seemed more auspicious. And indeed some progress was made, thanks in part to eloquent pleas from Ernest Codman, a respected Boston surgeon, for systematic comparisons based on "end results" (Brennan and Berwick 1996: 96). In 1917 the American College of Surgeons (ACS) prepared a detailed and unflattering report assessing the performance of 692 hospitals. Although the ACS report focused more on hospital practices than on actual outcomes, it created quite a stir when presented at a professional conference at the Waldorf Astoria Hotel in New York City. To conceal the identity of hospitals with poor track records, ACS officials gathered at the hotel furnace around midnight and burned the original reports (Roberts et al. 1987). Clearly, American surgeons believed that hospital report cards were not suitable for a mass audience.

Educational statistics also improved during the Progressive Era and became more widely accepted during World War I, when 1.7 million American servicemen were tested to assess their fitness for particular responsibilities (Tyack 1974: 204). Reassured by the military's satisfaction with wartime testing, newspapers and popular magazines helped to convince parents that there was nothing inappropriate about student testing. By 1932 at least three-fourths of large U.S. cities were using standardized tests in the classroom (Tyack 1974: 208). However, the tests were typically intelligence tests designed to facilitate classroom assignment rather than achievement tests designed to assess the performance of teachers or schools.

The scientific community's capacity to produce a valid organizational report card improved steadily throughout the twentieth century, as did scientific support for such a concept. In the health sciences, Paul Lembcke of Johns Hopkins University developed a medical auditing system aimed at assessing the appropriateness of care in the 1950s and Avedis Donabedian of the University of Michigan developed a theoretical framework for distinguishing among structural, process, and outcome variables in the 1960s (Brennan and Berwick 1996: 105–107). In the 1970s researchers at the RAND Corporation published credible measures of patients' functional status and patient satisfaction (Ware and Snyder 1975; Brennan and Berwick 1996: 114).

Educational testing also grew more sophisticated. Of particular importance, scholars developed the capacity to control for variations in student characteristics and the socioeconomic composition of their schools (and classrooms) through the use of multivariate statistical analysis. Sometimes referred to as "risk adjustment," their common name in health applications, these techniques strengthened the capacity of educational researchers to make fair comparisons across schools. In time, it would help to defuse opposition to report cards from critics who objected to explicit comparisons of inner-city and suburban schools. Similar developments in health care also paved the way for public acceptance (and grudging industry acceptance) of hospital comparisons involving patients who differed sharply in the severity of their illness and their risk of death (Brennan and Berwick 1996: 119).

Converging Streams

According to Kingdon (1995), significant reform may take place when several "streams" converge. The first is the policy stream or a well-developed reform proposal that has emerged from an embryonic idea. The second is the problem stream, or general recognition by people in and around government that a trend or crisis requires some governmental response. The third is the political stream, which encompasses interest group perspectives, public opinion, and election results. When these streams converge, they create a "window of opportunity" for policy entrepreneurs who have the genius to recognize it and the skill to capitalize on it.

For organizational report cards to be institutionalized, three events had to occur. First, suitable templates had to be available to convince skeptics that a technically valid report card could be produced. Second, elites and the attentive public had to be concerned about a problem that report cards could arguably fix. Third, interest groups had to be supportive, or at least not overwhelmingly opposed, and politicians had to perceive electoral advantages to report card legislation. These conditions were met for elementary and secondary education in the 1970s, for hospitals in the 1980s, and for HMOs in the 1990s. Whether change occurred would depend on the insight, energy, and sophistication of policy entrepreneurs.

In elementary and secondary education, the problem stream included growing evidence that our nation's public schools were failing. Although education was the single largest item in state budgets, the results of education spending seemed disappointing. An international study of student performance in 22 countries found that U.S. students ranked in twelfth place (Hechinger and Hechinger 1974). Also, some test scores, such as those for the Scholastic Aptitude Test (SAT), declined during the late 1960s and early 1970s. As critics have pointed out, these problems were often exaggerated (Tyack and Cuban 1995: 30–36). Nevertheless, both cross-sectional and longitudinal studies of public school students yielded disappointing results.

The political stream was also changing in the late 1960s and the early 1970s. Beginning in 1969 annual Gallup surveys revealed growing parental dissatisfaction with school discipline and drug problems, which were thought to interfere with learning (Tyack and Cuban 1995: 32). Disturbed by press reports and by their own negative experiences, parents began to demand greater accountability. Although specific proposals varied considerably (from vouchers to performance contracting), the common impetus was strong parental dissatisfaction with the status quo (Cohen 1978).

Against this backdrop, report cards seemed very appealing. If vouchers were adopted, then report cards would enable parents to choose more wisely. If performance contracting was adopted, then report cards would permit public officials to reward schools that fulfilled the terms of their performance contracts. Even in the absence of such reforms, report cards would enable parents to participate in more meaningful conversations with school teachers and administrators.

As the streams converged, state legislators and school board members acted as policy entrepreneurs. As Cohen and Spillane (1993: 54) explain, "Rising public interest in testing and other political pressures led many states and localities to begin publishing (test) scores in the early 1970s, after decades of secrecy." Later, in the 1980s, these developments would accelerate. At long last, school report cards were being institutionalized.

In contrast to school report cards, hospital report cards were institutionalized at the federal level. This reflected both the federal government's greater financial responsibility for health care costs and the federal government's possession of an unusual data base that lent itself to the production of hospital report cards. It also reflected some of the peculiarities of health care's converging streams.

The problem stream included health care costs that were rising much more rapidly than the rate of inflation. While all health care costs increased sharply in the early 1980s, hospital costs were exceptionally inflationary (Peters 1996: 246), which encouraged tough cost-containment measures. Although the problem was typically defined as rising costs, some analysts characterized the problem as inadequate cost-effectiveness, thus focusing attention simultaneously on cost and quality.

The political stream in health care was changing rapidly, due to several developments. The election of Ronald Reagan as president in 1980 signaled a sharp shift to the right and facilitated efforts to cut federal social programs, including Medicare and Medicaid. The Reagan administration's success in enacting a substantial tax cut in 1981 made it even more difficult to avoid painful spending cuts. Another important trend was the waning influence of the medical profession, which was likely to oppose either federal regulatory requirements or a stronger consumer role (Starr 1982). In Ruggie's (1996: 159) words, "Congress had repeatedly told the AMA and other groups in organized medicine to develop a solution to rising costs, but the profession produced no cost containment strategy whatsoever. As a result, organized medicine lost political clout, its expressed concerns overtaken by the overriding problem of rising health care costs."

Confronted by these developments, Congress and President Reagan approved historic legislation in 1983 that provided for a new system of reimbursing hospitals for services to Medicare and Medicaid patients. Known as the diagnosis-related group approach, this system classified a patient's ailments into one of over 400 specific diagnostic categories (for example, appendicitis), each of which carried a specific price tag. If the hospital spent less than the fixed amount, then it pocketed the difference; if the hospital spent more, then it was responsible for the cost overrun. In 1984 Congress took another historic step by freezing physician payments under Medicare.

With these legislative solutions dominating the headlines, the Health Care Financing Administration (HCFA) opted for a more modest administrative solution designed to assist peer review organizations under contract with the federal government to provide cost and quality oversight.

By combining Medicare claims data with information on deaths, HCFA would alert peer review organizations to hospitals that were less cost-effective than others. This decision, by HCFA's Health Standards and Quality Bureau, seemed innocent enough at the time because the federal government was simply sharing information it already possessed with organizations that desperately needed good information to perform their statutory tasks. Indeed, it is unlikely that HCFA's acting administrator was even consulted on this matter (Krakauer 1997).

HCFA's decision generated controversy, however, when Joel Brinkley of the *New York Times* filed a Freedom of Information Act (FOIA) request demanding access to the hospital mortality data. This was an awkward time for HCFA, whose administrator, Carolyne Davis, had resigned in August 1985. Acting administrator Henry Desmarais found himself on the horns of a dilemma. If HCFA said no to the *New York Times,* then it might well be found guilty of violating FOIA; if it said yes, then it was certain to face a barrage of criticism from the hospital industry. After consulting with HCFA's general counsel, Desmarais released the mortality ratings to the public on March 12, 1986, thus avoiding a legal donnybrook. Although Desmarais soft-pedaled the report by arguing that "right now, the numbers have no intrinsic meaning" (Baldwin 1986: 26), he nevertheless took an historic step. In effect, Desmarais institutionalized the concept of an annual hospital report card available to the general public and to Congress.

Political Mobilizations and Legal Concessions

The origins of school report cards fit Kingdon's model quite snugly. Problem, political, and policy streams converged, creating a window of opportunity. Policy entrepreneurs at the state level, seeking a suitable instrument to promote accountability, advocated school report cards that would facilitate public scrutiny, debate, and, in some instances, choice. Within a short period of time, such report cards became commonplace throughout the United States.

The education case also illustrates what Frank Baumgartner and Bryan Jones (1993) have called a "Downsian mobilization" or a mobilization of enthusiasm. A Downsian mobilization occurs when advocates for a particular solution mobilize to create new institutional arrangements that promise to endure for a considerable period of time. In this instance, reformers convinced a working majority of politicians that better information could improve our nation's public schools. Both top-down and bottom-up reformers were enthusiastic about the idea of an organizational report card—the former because it had potential as a management tool, the latter because it promised to empower parents.

In contrast, the hospital case does not quite fit either framework. Although the streams were shifting, they were not exactly converging. The problem of greatest concern was still cost containment, with quality a decidedly secondary consideration. Thus the match between report cards and the problem *du jour* was not exact. As for the political stream, there was considerable support within the Reagan administration for cost containment and some support for quality monitoring but little enthusiasm for taking on the hospital industry and the medical profession. If a window of opportunity existed, it was neither wide nor firmly open.

Nor was there a Downsian mobilization. HCFA, which made the hospital mortality data public, did so under duress. HCFA's acting administrator was openly skeptical of the data being released. What drove HCFA was not enthusiasm for report cards but a lack of enthusiasm for courtroom disputes. While journalists were understandably enthusiastic about report cards, they did not attempt to mobilize public support for such policy instruments. Instead, they relied on a powerful legal tool to circumvent nervous political executives and force the release of embarrassing information. A legal chess game, not a mobilization of interests, resulted in the public release of the first nationwide hospital report card.

Growth and Maturation

Once established, report cards evolved in different ways. To some extent, this reflected differences in the bureaucracies responsible for producing report cards or in the statutory rules governing such bureaucracies. As Terry Moe (1989) has noted, the implementation of a statute depends significantly on the bargains struck by interest groups at the policy legitimation stage. Those bargains reflect compromises between winners, who seek to limit politicization, and losers, who welcome politicization.

Social and policy trends also determined the fate of report cards. As conditions changed, issues rose and fell on the public's agenda and problems were redefined. In some instances, report cards were actively considered and adopted; in others, they were eclipsed by alternative solutions that enjoyed greater popularity.

Development of Report Card Bureaucracies

For many report cards, an existing government bureaucracy was designated as the "lead agency" responsible for producing the report card. By relying on an established agency, report card advocates were able to lower start-up costs and take advantage of existing expertise. At the same time, however, they inherited competing missions that sometimes posed a threat to report cards. For example, the state departments of education were accustomed to promoting not just educational progress but the interests of teachers and schools as well. When teachers and schools voiced doubts about report cards, this put the state departments of education in an awkward position.

Despite their valuable expertise, existing bureaucracies often found themselves incapable of meeting particular technical challenges posed by report cards. For example, few state departments of education possessed the statistical skills to develop a "risk-adjusted" model of student performance. For such tasks, state departments of education usually turned to outside contractors (Elmore et al. 1996: 95). The same phenomenon was observed in health care at the state level, where health care agencies relied upon contractors to handle econometric modeling tasks.

A notable exception to this general rule was HCFA, which relied on its own personnel to develop and improve econometric models for predicting hospital mortality rates. Statisticians in the Health Standards and Quality Bureau, responsible for the econometric modeling, published articles in professional journals explaining and defending their methodology and reporting findings.

Although government bureaucracies played a significant role in producing report cards, other organizations were also active. In the late 1970s the HMO industry convinced the Carter administration not to assign quality assurance tasks to a government agency. Instead, the HMOs offered to create a private nonprofit organization for that purpose. Named the National Committee for Quality Assurance (NCQA), that organization was not very aggressive during its early years (Anders 1996a: 230). In contrast to the federal Department of Health and Human Services, NCQA could not compel HMOs to produce any information. Like Blanche DuBois, NCQA was forced to rely on the kindness of strangers, most of whom were not particularly kind.

News magazines have also produced a significant number of report cards. *U.S. News & World Report,* for example, now produces annual reports on America's best hospitals, best colleges, and best HMOs. Although these report cards are technically flawed in certain respects, they have become quite popular with the general public. That is especially true of the reports on colleges and hospitals, which have been published for several years in a row.

Interest Group Responses

Reactions of targeted industries to report cards have ranged from outright hostility to grudging acceptance. The hospital industry's reaction to report cards has been particularly negative. Shortly after HCFA released its first list of hospitals with unusually high or low mortality rates in 1986, hospital industry spokespersons lambasted the report (Baldwin 1986). Such criticisms became annual rituals—HCFA would release its report to the press, and the hospital industry would promptly denounce the report.

This was not the hospital industry's first skirmish over performance assessment with an external review body. The Joint Commission on Accreditation of Health Care Organizations (JCAHO), which accredits hospitals and certain other health care organizations, encountered similar difficulties in 1985 when its president, Dennis O'Leary, proposed that hospitals submit a common set of clinical outcome measures so that JCAHO could assess their performance (Bowie 1997). The American Hospital Association teamed up with the American Medical Association (AMA) to torpedo that idea. When revived in 1997, O'Leary's proposal was severely curtailed prior to adoption (Moore 1997). Hospitals will be free to choose from 60 approved vendors of clinical information systems, thus precluding standardization. Also, there are no current plans to make the data public.

The reaction of school teachers and administrators to mandatory school report cards was less negative. Indeed, school teachers and administrators occasionally championed school report cards. For example, the California Teachers Association and the Association of California School Administrators supported a 1988 ballot initiative (Proposition 98) that would require every school district to produce an annual report card (Fetler 1990: 3–6). Admittedly, the requirement was softened by a provision that allowed considerable local discretion in designing report cards. Also, the mandate was linked to a provision that guaranteed a minimum level of funding for public schools and community colleges. Nevertheless, it is difficult to imagine the hospital industry supporting a similar initiative.

Eventually, state hospital associations grew accustomed to state-level hospital report cards. However, that is largely because they were able to shape state report cards to reflect their concerns. For example, California's hospital report card includes letters from individual hospitals that wish to register objections (California OSHPD 1996). Florida's hospital report card takes a different approach—on every other page a statement warns readers about data limitations and urges them to confer with health care professionals to place the data in perspective (Florida Agency for Health Care Administration 1996).

It is important to distinguish these developments from popular social science theories, such as "capture theory," which argues that regulated industries tend to capture their regulators and prevent them from regulating in the public interest (Bernstein 1955; Stigler 1971). If capture theory were correct, then HCFA and its state-level counterparts would never have released hospital mortality figures in the first place. The fact that some concessions were made to the hospital industry suggests not capture but interest group representation in administrative decisionmaking. The close relationship between the JCAHO and the hospital industry does resemble capture, though capture theory refers specifically to government agencies and JCAHO is not a government agency. The relevant point is that in some circumstances private organizations may be even more vulnerable to capture than government agencies.

Social and Economic Trends

Important though they are, bureaucratic politics and interest group politics do not fully explain the evolution of report cards. Changes in society at large and in particular industries also help to explain why the demand for certain types of report cards has grown in intensity.

During the 1970s and the 1980s a number of school systems experimented with various forms of public school choice. Magnet schools proved especially popular, as public schools began to market somewhat different educational products. More generally, school systems developed more flexible approaches to student enrollment, hoping to keep more affluent parents from abandoning urban public school systems altogether. These developments facilitated the growth of school report cards.

One of the more striking changes of recent years has been the growth of enrollment in HMOs. During the 1980s the number of Americans enrolled in HMOs increased from approximately 10 million to approximately 38 million. By the mid-1990s about three out of every four Americans receiving health care through an employer were enrolled in some type of managed care plan. As HMO enrollment has mushroomed, corporate consumers and individual consumers have become much more interested in HMO report cards. Reflecting that interest, the NCQA has grown in size and has managed to accumulate better data.

As Kingdon (1995) would predict, the emergence of a potential market for report cards does not necessarily result in a dramatic surge in the supply of report cards. Sometimes other solutions are coupled to changing problems and political circumstances. Take, for example, the aging of America. Thanks to the miracles of modern medicine, many Americans now live into their seventies or beyond. With this development, the number of Americans living in nursing homes has increased. Yet the production of nursing home report cards has been sporadic at best. One explanation for this is that Congress required all fifty states to establish a long-term care ombudsman to monitor and represent nursing home residents (Gormley 1986). Had that not occurred, reformers might well have insisted on better information to assist a highly vulnerable population.

Another example is the sharp increase in the number of mothers of young children who work outside the home. This trend, which became noticeable in the late 1970s and has continued through the present time, has generated considerable demand for paid child care. One might imagine that this would also create considerable demand for child care report cards. Instead, however, local communities have established resource and referral agencies, which help to connect young children of working mothers with available child care slots. This development appears to have dampened demand for child care report cards, largely because resource and referral agencies have eschewed quality assessments that might imply that some providers are unfit to serve (Gormley 1995: 155–163).

The presence of alternative solutions, however, does not completely eliminate interest in report cards. In the case of nursing homes, some advocacy groups have produced report cards for their metropolitan area or state, and some state governments have developed rudimentary report cards. Some national news magazines have also attempted to assemble national data on nursing home quality. Less progress has been made in child care. However, one national magazine, *Working Mother,* has rated state governments' child care policies, and the state of Colorado has developed an excellent electronic data system on child care facility inspection results that parents can access through their local resource and referral agency.

Crises

New institutions are seldom secure. As Baumgartner and Jones have argued (1993), they are always vulnerable to change as new "images" and new "venues" interact. With report cards, as with other new institutions, several dangers commonly loom overhead. The steady drumbeat of opposition from industry, or particularly affected segments of industry, is always present and sometimes a serious threat. A change of political administrations or a change in party control can be problematic. Any change in venue—for example, from the political branches to the judiciary—can be treacherous. And intergovernmental relations, with its tangled jurisdictions and jurisdictional jealousies, can be as unforgiving as an Amazonian jungle.

Although external threats are more common, internal threats should not be ignored. Without intending to do so, report card backers may trigger a crisis, as when they propose to "push the envelope" by developing, extending, or refining report cards. If their timing is right and they have judged the political winds correctly, then they may succeed. If their timing is wrong and they have miscalculated, then they may jeopardize the future of report cards in a particular policy domain or a particular jurisdiction.

Political Change

When a new administration arrives in Washington, D.C., hearts are aflutter with hope. But seasoned observers are more cautious. As Hugh Heclo (1977) has noted, the executive branch of the federal government often resembles "a government of strangers." Newly appointed political executives, impatient for change, find themselves paired with career bureaucrats, fearful of change. Although tensions between the two camps can be overcome, conflict is highly likely, especially during the transition months.

The arrival of a new HCFA administrator in May 1993 presented the usual mix of opportunities and threats. Bruce Vladeck, a Michigan-trained political scientist, was an acknowledged expert on nursing homes and hospitals. As president of the United Hospital Fund, a research and philanthropic organization, he had studied and supported New York City's nonprofit and municipal hospitals. Thus, it was reasonable to expect him to be troubled by a rating system that routinely found fault with inner-city hospitals.

When Vladeck assumed command, he had three choices: he could keep the report card more or less as is; he could gather new data to improve the report card; or he could end the report card altogether.

Virtually everyone was dissatisfied with the status quo, including the civil servants who might have been supposed to support it. In fact, civil servants responsible for HCFA's econometric modeling were acutely aware of the limitations of their data. Specifically, they recognized that administrative data were inferior to clinical data. With that in mind, they had recommended to Vladeck's predecessor, Gail Wilensky, that Medicare hospitals be mandated to gather clinical data, thus improving the data base dramatically and eliminating a key objection of report card critics. Specifically, they developed a proposal for a Uniform Clinical Data Set, with clinical data gathered by peer review organizations for 10 percent of admissions at all Medicare hospitals (Krakauer 1997). Although Wilensky supported the concept, she did not allocate sufficient resources for successful implementation.

Vladeck, like Wilensky, inherited a flawed data base. Unlike Wilensky, however, he resolved that the time had come to end HCFA's public association with what he called "crummy data." In June 1993, less than one month after taking office, Vladeck announced that the publication of an annual hospital report card would cease. If FOIA requests were filed, then HCFA would comply with the law and release raw data. But HCFA's econometric modeling of hospital mortality rates and the annual report card it yielded would be discontinued indefinitely (Associated Press 1993).

Vladeck's decision was based in part on technical considerations, which we will discuss in Chapter 4. Also, Vladeck, who had championed inner-city hospitals that cared for the poor, was distressed by report cards that routinely lambasted such hospitals for poor performance. However, Vladeck's decision also reflected a barrage of criticism from the hospital industry and the scientific community. In that respect, it illustrates what Baumgartner and Jones (1993) call a "Schattschneider mobilization" or an expansion of the scope of conflict followed by the destruction of a policy subsystem. Over a period of several years, hospital administrators and scientists denounced HCFA's annual hospital report card. In 1993 they succeeded in abolishing it. Shortly after its creation, a small policy subsystem was effectively dismantled.

Legal Skirmishes

In January and February 1995 the Florida Agency for Health Care Administration conducted comprehensive contract compliance reviews of all 29 HMOs in Florida that received Medicaid funding at the time. The reviews were based on surveys or inspections conducted by a team of agency professionals. Encompassing 125 contract-based standards, the reviews served as the basis for an HMO compliance monitoring report, which the state released in March 1995. That report card identified the number and, in broad terms, the nature of deficiencies for each HMO.

The Physicians Corporation of America (PCA), the largest Medicaid contractor in Florida, was not particularly concerned about the state's HMO report card but it was concerned about the broader question of what quality-relevant information might be disclosed by the state. Recently, the PCA had failed in its bid for accreditation by the NCQA. The state, which received a copy of the accreditation report from the NCQA, initially assured the PCA that the document would remain confidential. The state hesitated, however, when it received a request for the NCQA report from the Fort Lauderdale Sun-Sentinel (Schulte 1997). Following an advisory opinion from state attorney general Bob Butterworth, the state reversed itself and announced that the NCQA report, like other quality-relevant information, could be released (Garwood 1997). Shortly thereafter the state began distributing copies of its HMO report card.

Within days after the release of the HMO report card, the PCA filed a motion with the 2nd Judicial Circuit of Leon County requesting an injunction to prohibit the release of any quality-relevant information that identified an HMO by name. In April 1995 Judge F. E. Steinmeyer granted the PCA a partial victory. Steinmeyer agreed with the PCA that a state HMO statute barring the disclosure of "any identifying information" should be construed to encompass not just patients but HMOs as well. This meant that the NCQA report could not be released. However, Steinmeyer also reasoned that the state statute did not apply to information gathered while investigating an HMO as a Medicaid provider. While this seemed to mean that the state's HMO report card could be released, eventually, Steinmeyer granted an injunction barring the release of any quality-relevant information until an appeals court could consider the case.

Little progress was made in resolving the judicial dispute. Pressured by both sides in the controversy, the State Legislature crafted a compromise that Governor Lawton Chiles signed into law in May 1996. Under that compromise, the State Legislature distinguished between information produced before and after July 1, 1996. In the interest of confidentiality, old plan-specific information could not be revealed; in the interest of disclosure, new plan-specific information could be divulged (Berger 1996).

Subject to these ground rules, Florida released a report based on new surveys in September 1996 (Florida Agency for Health Care Administration 1996). In that report the PCA did rather well. Nevertheless, the PCA refused to drop its lawsuit. In September 1996 a state appeals court more emphatically supported the PCA, arguing that the prior statute prohibited the disclosure of quality-relevant information that identified an HMO by name, even if the HMO was being investigated as a Medicaid provider (*State of Florida v. PCA Family Health Plan, Inc.* 1996).

Buoyed by the new state law but deflated by the appeals court ruling, the Agency for Health Care Administration's legal office has advised against divulging the raw data on which the 1996 report was based. The 1996 report, like its ill-fated predecessor, differentiates among health plans but does not specify which quality of care standards each plan failed to meet. Under the legal office's current interpretation, which may or may not be legally correct, the raw survey results that contain more detailed appraisals of each health plan are not to be released.

This episode illustrates the potency of litigation. By challenging the state of Florida in court, a prominent HMO was able to suspend distribution of an HMO report card for a significant period of time. Although the state's politicians ultimately enacted a statute allowing the disclosure of newly-gathered data, the state's lawyers have become extremely risk-averse as a result of this experience. Based on legal counsel, state bureaucrats are now barred from sharing raw data on HMO performance with the general public. In the words of one state official, "We will have filing cabinets of information that can't be released."

Intergovernmental Perils

For decades education policy analysts have recommended the creation of a national testing system to gauge the progress of schoolchildren in different states. In 1988 Congress authorized the states to participate voluntarily in such a system, known as the National Assessment of Educational Progress (NAEP). The hope was that such a system would permit measurement of progress, or lack thereof, in particular subjects in all fifty states.

Although mathematics, science, and reading were targeted for national testing, the group responsible for the mathematics tests made more rapid progress than the others, permitting state-administered mathematics tests in 1990. In 1992 the test was refined and standards-based reporting was adopted. Under this arrangement, each state's performance is compared to a national standard, thus revealing not just how each state does compared with other states but also how each state does compared with the national standard. The same test is to be administered every four years.

NAEP's mathematics test has been a partial success. On the one hand, most states have participated, which is no small accomplishment. On the other hand, NAEP has fallen short of universal participation. In 1992 nine states declined to participate (National Center for Education Statistics 1993: 5). In 1996 seven states declined to participate (National Center for Education Statistics 1997: 6). To make matters worse, some states that participated did not meet the recommended school participation rate for public schools. Thus, some of the state statistics are less reliable than would have been the case if recommended participation rates had been achieved.

States' reasons for not participating appear to be rather diverse. In some states, politicians have expressed philosophical opposition to national tests, which might someday lead to a national curriculum. In other states, politicians and bureaucrats have been reluctant to test their students while they are reforming education practices or administering new tests of their own (Feuer 1997).

Many successful intergovernmental programs are voluntary. However, the more successful programs have almost always offered states compelling financial reasons to participate (Gormley 1989: 173–193; Walker 1995: 227–232). NAEP does not. Without such incentives, NAEP will continue to encounter participation problems, which will limit the utility of interstate comparisons.

The Politics of Information

Do report cards provide information where it is most socially valuable or where it is most politically palatable? Does politics trump policy analysis or vice versa? Is it possible to distinguish between the politics of education report cards and the politics of health report cards or is there no meaningful distinction between the two? These are a few of the questions that we address in the following section.

Optimistic versus Pessimistic Theories

Following Davis Bobrow and John Dryzek (1987), Sam Overman and Anthony Cahill (1994) have distinguished between "optimistic" and "pessimistic" theories of information processing. An optimistic theory views information production as a rational response to market failure and views information use as a sensible adaptive strategy for consumers. A pessimistic theory views discussions about information as politics by other means. According to the pessimistic view, powerful interests seek to avoid the costs of information production and seek to avoid the disclosure of information that could damage their reputations or profit margins.

In a study of health data organizations in two states, Overman and Cahill (1994) found ample evidence to support the pessimistic theory of information processing. For example, the Colorado Hospital Commission dragged its feet in submitting data to the state Health Data Commission. Several Colorado hospitals refused to participate altogether. In Pennsylvania, greater cooperation was achieved. However, even in Pennsylvania, little information reached ordinary consumers.

Like Overman and Cahill, we have found considerable evidence of interest group politics aimed at thwarting organizational report cards. However, some opposition was rooted in legitimate objections to report card methodologies. Also, on balance, we have seen more obstructionism in health care than in education, suggesting that optimistic and pessimistic theories are not equally valid in different policy domains.

Although it is convenient to think of organizational report cards as illustrating a generic "information policy" category, the fact is that organizational report cards are supported and opposed within more traditional policy domains—education, health, employment and training, environmental protection, etc. Thus, in order to understand differential rates of progress for organizational report cards, it is necessary to compare and contrast the policy domains within which they are embedded.

Education Policy versus Health Policy

Education policy and health policy share certain traits in common—most notably, high issue salience and a prominent place on what Roger Cobb and Charles Elder (1983) call the "systemic agenda" or the set of issues that are generally perceived to warrant government attention. They also feature powerful interest groups, including teachers (for example, the National Education Association) and physicians (for example, the AMA). However, education policy and health policy differ in certain respects that could explain the different trajectories of organizational report cards in these two policy domains.

First, health policy is more complex than education policy. The technical skills required of health policy professionals are greater, the characteristic jargon is more forbidding, and the disputes are more arcane. These differences have important implications for report cards. For example, risk adjustment is required in both cases but the risk adjustment is markedly different. In education, it is often sufficient to control for just demographic characteristics; in health, it is also necessary to control for prior medical conditions (or comorbidities), which are less straightforward and less easily measured.

Second, the demand for bottom-up accountability has been stronger and more firmly established in education policy than in health policy. For decades, school boards have been popularly elected and parents have served as members of local parent-teacher associations. For better or for worse, the governance of elementary and secondary education has been notably democratic (Chubb and Moe 1990). In contrast, health care has been marked by greater deference to experts (Starr 1982). Although consumer representation requirements were incorporated into local health care planning processes in the 1970s (Morone and Marmor 1981), health care policymaking is more elitist and less democratic than education policymaking.

Third, quality concerns have been more pronounced in education policy than in health policy. Throughout the 1970s and the 1980s a chorus of critics lambasted our nation's public schools for poor performance. The reforms of these two decades focused almost exclusively on quality improvements. In contrast, health care reformers focused much more sharply on cost containment. For example, state health data organizations were created primarily to curb costs, not to boost quality (Overman and Cahill 1994). With health care spending rising from 5.1 percent in 1960 to almost 14 percent of our Gross Domestic Product today, this emphasis on spending was understandable. In the late 1980s demands for health care quality began to gather momentum (Relman 1988). Even today, however, proponents of health care quality must struggle for economic and political support.

For all these reasons, education report cards have progressed further than health report cards. As we shall see, progress has also varied considerably within each of these broad categories. For example, some elementary and secondary education report cards are clearly more sophisticated than higher education report cards, and some hospital report cards are currently more advanced than nursing home report cards. One reason for sharply different trajectories is politics. Another reason is poor communication among analysts who prepare report cards in different policy domains. It is the latter problem that we hope to ameliorate through this book.

Conclusion

Although technical considerations are important in promoting and improving organizational report cards, they are often tempered by interest group politics, bureaucratic politics, even electoral politics. As William Alonso and Paul Starr (1987: 4) put it, "Statistics cannot be constructed on purely technical grounds alone but require choices that ultimately turn on considerations of purpose and policy." The battle over numbers is not fought by statisticians alone.

For significant policy change to occur, certain conditions are necessary. Although organizational report cards have been championed by prominent reformers since the nineteenth century, it was not until the 1970s and the 1980s that converging problem, policy, and political streams allowed them to proliferate. Breakthroughs were achieved in education policy, then in health policy. Organizational report cards were institutionalized in the public and private sectors, at the federal and state levels.

The historical circumstances under which report cards originated are both interesting and important. It was a FOIA request that catapulted HCFA into the hospital report card business. Reluctant from the very start, HCFA never relished this assignment and never committed the resources needed to silence the objections of its many critics. Moreover, the "quality" constituency that backed report cards could not compete with the "cost containment" constituency that stressed other initiatives. When a new administration and a new HCFA administrator took over in 1993, a fragile policy subsystem was easily dismantled.

The origins of school report cards were more auspicious. The quality of our public schools became a major national issue in the 1970s and it featured prominently in many gubernatorial campaigns. In this instance, quality considerations eclipsed cost considerations in importance, and politicians vied with one another to invent a better mousetrap. When policy analysts argued that it might be nice to count the number of mice being caught, politicians readily agreed. Long familiarity with standardized testing in public schools facilitated this transition. As noted earlier, some states still balk at participating in voluntary national tests. However, stronger financial incentives could result in universal state participation.

The political problems that confront organizational report cards are formidable; other challenges are equally daunting. If report cards are to survive critical scrutiny, then they must be valid and comprehensive. If report cards are to help consumers and policymakers, then they must be relevant and comprehensible. If report cards are to guide service-delivery organizations in constructive ways, then they must be reasonable and functional. These challenges are the subjects of our next three chapters.

4

Assessing Organizational Performance

Americans have a proclivity for ranking things. Newspapers and magazines routinely print, and sometimes even produce, rankings of great variety: cities with the highest quality of life, great films, best beers, and outstanding universities and professional schools, to name just a few. The prevalence of rankings suggests that they appeal to some basic inclination to compare. People seem to find their simplicity and boldness especially attractive. Those ranked poorly usually react strongly, fearing economic repercussions or just plain embarrassment. The capacity of rankings for focusing attention on comparisons makes them potentially a powerful format for communication.

But communication of what? Most things that we wish to compare have multiple dimensions of quality. The designer of a ranking faces the burden of condensing the multiple dimensions into a single scale. Sometimes this is quite reasonable, as when dimensions are highly inter-correlated. Often, however, it requires such arbitrary decisions about the inclusion of dimensions and their relative weights that validity suffers as a result.

These considerations obviously apply to the use of rankings, and ratings, in organizational report cards. Rankings conveyed through league tables and ratings conveyed through classification schemes usually have high salience with organizations and their external audiences. Salience may be heightened even further when rankings and ratings underlie tournaments with monetary or other prizes. Judging the social value of ratings and rankings, however, requires an investigation into the validity of the information that they convey.

If a single dimension exists for appropriately ranking or rating how effectively organizations use their resources to produce desired outcomes, then it is a suitable measure of organizational performance. Constructing a uni-dimensional scale for measuring organizational performance, however, poses many difficult methodological problems, including all those that researchers routinely face in doing program evaluation. In this chapter we consider the most important of these issues conceptually, illustrate them in the context of actual report cards, and offer a general assessment of circumstances in which rankings and ratings based on performance measures should, or should not, be used.

Conceptual Issues in the Design of Performance Measures

The design of scales for assessing organizational performance requires answers to two types of questions: How are outcomes to be measured? And how is the marginal contribution of the organization to the outcomes to be determined? The answer to the first question can be thought of as the choice of a dependent variable for the organization's production function. The answer to the second question can be thought of as the specification of the independent variables in the production function, the identification of those beyond the control of the organization, and the elimination of their effect on the dependent variable to leave the change in the dependent variable that can be attributed to variables under the control of the organization. Borrowing a term used in medical research to describe the process by which the pre-treatment health status of patients is taken into account in the assessment of post-treatment outcomes, we refer to this process as *risk adjustment*.

How Are Outcomes to Be Measured?

The outcomes sought from social services (such as education from schools, health from medical care, cognitive development from day care, and human dignity from long-term nursing care) are usually beyond the practical reach of direct measurement. Designers of performance measures, like program evaluators, often rely on proxies for the desired outcomes (see Figure 4.1). The most common proxies are output measures that have strong theoretical links to outcomes. For example, test scores commonly serve as proxies for education. Obviously, empirical confirmation, relating proxies to more direct measures of outcomes whose use in report cards is infeasible, bolsters confidence in use of the proxies. A growing body of research, for instance, shows that high school test scores measuring cognitive ability do indeed have a positive relationship to subsequent success in the job market (Hanushek 1994: 19–20).

Sometimes process variables may reasonably serve as proxies for outcomes. For example, it may be reasonable in some situations to take shorter hospital stays as a proxy for the more effective restoration of health to people suffering certain acute conditions, though in other situations it may be more a proxy for the stringency of control over the use of medical resources. Even inputs can occasionally serve as reasonable proxies for outcomes, though they usually are unsatisfactory as the basis for performance measurement. For example, strong theory and evidence links staff-to-child ratios in day care settings to cognitive development in children (Abt Associates 1978; Howes and Rubenstein 1985). Treating the staff-to-child

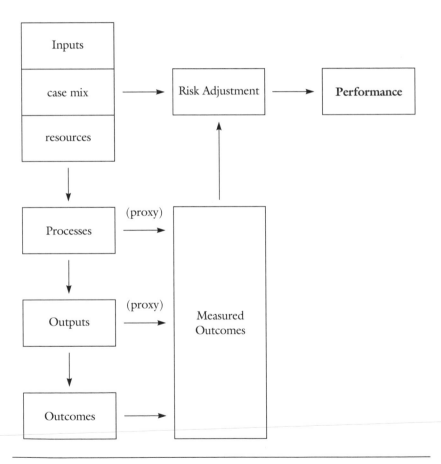

Figure 4.1 Measuring organizational performance

ratio as a measure of performance, however, would not allow an assessment of how well day care centers make use of their staff though it would indicate the extent to which they focus their available resources on a fundamentally important input.

Conceptually, it is desirable to use output rather than process and input variables as proxies for outcomes because outputs are separated by fewer assumed theoretical links. Practically, however, considerations of the availability, accuracy, and integrity of data are important. Consider the choice of a measure of mortality rate either as an outcome itself or as a proxy for the broader outcome, quality of cardiac surgery. Basing it on deaths that occur in some period following surgery, say 30 days, may be a conceptually more valid measure than basing it on deaths that occur while patients are still in the hospital. Using the follow-up period, however, would require that hospital records be supplemented with information from survey or surveillance instruments, which would be costly. Data from the follow-up period might also have less integrity if hospitals are able to produce lower mortality rates by pursuing data for cases that they suspect ended in death with less vigor than they apply to other cases.

The choice of a single variable to serve as the basis of a ranking or rating scale poses difficult issues when either there are several important outcomes, such as mortality and morbidity, or a single outcome is most appropriately represented by a set of variables, such as pain, limited mobility, and other attributes of a particular disease. In the case of multiple outcomes, constructing a scale for ranking or rating requires specification of a function for translating the outcomes into a single dimension. This may be possible if a single value can be applied to all the outcomes. For example, if economic efficiency is taken as the only relevant value, then cost-benefit analysis can be used to measure each outcome in terms of a common money metric based on people's willingness-to-pay to obtain it. Unfortunately for report card designers, not only is efficiency rarely the only value of relevance to social services, but the informational and analytical resources needed to do cost-benefit analysis preclude its routine use in report cards.

The problem of combining multiple outcomes into a single scale that can be used for purposes of ranking organizations is similar to the problem commonly faced by policy analysts in deciding which alternative policy to recommend. The policy analysts' task would be much easier, requiring only prediction, if there were a political consensus about how to map policy impacts on individuals into a single dimension of social welfare.

Unfortunately, political processes rarely address such abstract trade-offs behind a "veil of ignorance." Rather, debate tends to conflate principles with self-interested anticipation so that in practice a consensus about the appropriate social welfare function, the mapping of the welfare of individuals into an overall index of societal well-being, never emerges. Finding a clear political consensus for placing relative social values on each of several organizational outcomes is likely to be similarly elusive.

The challenge of combining multiple measures of a single outcome poses a similar problem. Sometimes the measures themselves have sufficiently similar scales and relationships to the outcome of interest that they can be reasonably added to form a single index. For example, many reading and mathematics tests report scores on standardized scales that theoretically relate to educational outcomes in similar ways. Absent any particular reason to value achievement on one of these tests over achievement on the other, their sum would be a reasonable proxy for the cognitive dimension of education.

Often, however, multiple measures differ in their scales and relationships to outcomes. Imagine, for instance, that "health" is taken as the outcome of a medical service. The outcomes that might be taken as proxies for health include mortality and the absence of limitation on various normal functions. How are they to be combined into a scale? Those designing the scale might impose their own subjective assessments of the relative health value of each outcome, though doing so would almost certainly undercut the validity of the scale. They might instead base their assessments of relative value on surveys of representative populations regarding how they would make hypothetical trade-offs between various morbidities and mortality risks. Such efforts have led to the development of various indexes of quality-adjusted life-years for use in the comparative evaluation of alternative medical treatments. (See, for example, Torrence, Boyle, and Horwood 1982; Hornberger, Redelmeier, and Peterson 1992; Gerard 1992; Drummond, Torrance, and Mason 1993; Culyer and Wagstaff 1993; Gafni, Birch, and Mehrez 1993; Johannesson, Pliskin, and Weinstein 1994; Johannesson and Gerdtham 1996; Dolan, Gudex, Kind and Williams 1996). As such indexes gain more widespread use in medical research, they become more credible as the basis for combining multiple measures of outcomes into a single scale for use in report cards.

Even when the multiple measures appear to be in the same units, care must be taken in aggregating them to obtain valid overall measures. For example, consider the three-step procedure used by the Department of

Transportation (DOT) to construct an overall on-time rating for airlines. First, the average on-time percentage is calculated for each airline at each airport. Second, sets of airport weights are calculated for each airline as the fractions of its flights landing at each airport. Third, the airline's overall score is the weighted average of its scores at all the airports. While the DOT method would seem reasonable to most casual observers, Jonathan Caulkins and colleagues (1993) show how this particular weighting procedure can lead to Simpson's paradox: one airline can have better on-time percentages at each airport than another airline but have a worse overall rating because of the distribution of its flights across airports. Underlying the DOT method is the recognition that on-time arrivals are harder to achieve at more congested or weather sensitive airports; using simple weighted averages, however, does not provide a fully satisfactory way of taking these airport-related differences into account.

Under what, if any, conditions might it be reasonable for a report card designer to choose a single variable as a proxy for a multi-dimensional outcome? First, the variable should tap an important dimension. That is, though it lacks comprehensiveness, it should have validity as a measure of at least one major outcome dimension. The greater the relative substantive importance of the outcome dimension it taps, the more reasonable its exclusive use as the proxy. Second, anticipating organizational responses, the designers should believe that the tapped dimension will command the attention and the respect of targeted organizations. In other words, it should have good functionality.

The use of mortality rates as a proxy for health outcomes of cardiac surgery is an example of a case in which these two conditions probably hold. Mortality is a sufficiently important and, in the context of cardiac surgery, common health outcome that it has reasonable validity as a proxy for health. Further, some distortion of incentives toward reducing mortality at the expense of other health dimensions such as quality of life would probably be considered acceptable by many observers.

How Is Marginal Contribution to Be Measured?

Rankings or ratings based on the selected outcome measure may be useful in some circumstances, irrespective of inputs or effort. Potential clients of organizations may sometimes care only about the gross levels of outcomes they achieve. Students considering MBA study, for example, may find rankings of programs based on reputation in the business world to be an adequate guide for their choices; they may not care that business schools, such as those at Harvard University and Stanford University, derive much of their success from being able to recruit exceptional student bodies rather than from the additions they make to the capabilities of their students. Levels of outcomes may also be of interest to public officials who oversee entire "industries." For example, legislators may wish to identify communities in which children are attaining low levels of educational achievement as a guide for targeting remedial resources to the worst performing groups of students. That the schools serving these communities are performing either especially poorly or especially well may be a secondary concern.

More often, however, report cards appropriately focus on organizational performance. How well is the organization doing relative to other organizations with similar circumstances? What handicap should be applied to allow for "fair" comparisons with other organizations? In other words, what is the organization's value-added?

CATEGORIES OF INPUT VARIABLES Answering these questions requires report card designers to take account of the inputs available to the organization. It is useful to divide organizational inputs into four categories of variables that are potentially relevant to the measurement of performance. These are the variables that one would use to model an organizational production function.

Case-specific characteristics refer to attributes of individual clients that are relevant to the outcome of the service that they receive. With respect to schooling, for instance, cognitive ability, motivation, prior achievement, and parental encouragement help determine how much a student will progress in an academic year. Or, with respect to cardiac surgery, the prevalence of risk factors and comorbidities affects the patient's chances of survival. By taking account of case-specific characteristics, the *gross value-added* to each client can be estimated as the difference between the observed outcome and the counterfactual of what the outcome would have been in the absence of the service provided by the organization. Note that it is gross in the sense that it does not take account of other potentially relevant organizational inputs. If all the other inputs of the organizations being compared were identical, then an appropriate scale for constructing ratings and rankings would be simply the sum of the gross value-added of all an organization's clients.

In some contexts, it is not only the characteristics of the individual client that are relevant, but those of the other clients who are being served at the same time. Such *cohort-specific* characteristics are especially important in measuring the performance of schools. Beginning with the Coleman Report (1966), a consistent finding of educational researchers has been the importance of students' classmates to their achievement. Students whose classmates come from higher socioeconomic backgrounds tend to do better, other things equal, than those from less advantaged backgrounds. We follow Robert Meyer (1996) in referring to estimates of organizational value-added that control for cohort characteristics as *total performance,* a measure of how much the organization contributes to outcomes holding the characteristics of its caseload constant. In other words, it indicates what achievement levels would be obtained if each organization received exactly the same mix of cases. Parents choosing schools for their children, or children choosing nursing homes for their parents, might very well be interested in comparisons based on either gross or total performance, which give direct indications of how much value-added they can expect from specific organizations.

Even if organizations have identical case mixes, however, their performance will differ depending on the resources that they have available for use in delivering services. Determining the performance of an organization requires that account be taken of *resource constraints,* which should be interpreted broadly to include externally imposed rules that restrict or specify how available resources can be used, as well as the resources themselves. For example, in the case of schools, state regulations and district policies may severely restrict the extent to which principals can choose, promote, and fire teachers. In attempting to measure the value-added that can be attributed to specific schools for purposes of state-wide comparisons, designers need not take account of state constraints, because these do not vary across schools. District rules, however, do vary. Not taking account of them would confound school-level and district-level performance. Again following Meyer (1996), we call estimates of value-added that take account of cohort characteristics and resource constraints *intrinsic performance.* Rankings and ratings of how well organizations use their available resources to deal with their caseloads should be based on intrinsic performance.

The remaining category of input variables takes account of *discretionary use of resources.* It includes the choices that organizations make about how they will provide services. There is no conceptual need to identify these variables explicitly in constructing a performance measure, though, as noted below, doing so may be necessary for purposes of statistical estimation. These variables are under the control of the organization, and therefore do not have to be taken into account in handicapping. Simply capturing their combined effects is adequate. Of course, researchers who wished to determine what organizational policies contributed to performance would have to include them explicitly in empirical investigations.

Organizational Production Functions

Organizational performance can be better understood in terms of a model that relates the outcome of interest (dependent variable) to the various organizational inputs (explanatory variables). The most general specification would be based on data for all—or a representative sample—of individual cases handled by the organizations being ranked. For example, a state-wide ranking of schools might be based on test scores of all students, or perhaps only students in several grades. Letting subscripts i and k represent the ith case in the kth organization, the general specification can be written as:

$$O_{ik} = f(case_{ik}, cohort_k, constraints_k, discretionary_k) + error_{ik}$$

where O_{ik} is the outcome measure for case i in organization k, $case_{ik}$ stands for variables measuring the relevant characteristics of case i in organization k, $cohort_k$ stands for variables measuring the composition of the case mix of organization k, $constraints_k$ stands for variables measuring the relevant constraints on organization k, $discretionary_k$ stands for variables measuring the discretionary use of resources by organization k, and $error_{ik}$ represents the random, or unmeasured, component of O_{ik}. The function f could take complicated forms, but is often assumed to be linear in the variables.

Imagine that f were sufficiently simple so that it could be separated into the sum of functions $f_1(case_{ik})$, $f_2(cohort_k)$, $f_3(constraints_k)$, and $f_4(discretionary_k)$. The various measures of value-added for organization k could be found by summing each of the following expressions over its cases:

Gross value-added: $O_{ik} - f_1(case_{ik})$

Total value-added: $O_{ik} - f_1(case_{ik}) - f_2(cohort_k)$

Intrinsic value-added: $O_{ik} - f_1(case_{ik}) - f_2(cohort_k) - f_3(constraints_k)$

Note that these expressions have the term $O_{ik} - f_1(case_{ik})$ in common. If $case_{ik}$ consisted only of the value of the outcome variable prior to the intervention of the organization, then it could simply be subtracted from the outcome measure to form an alternative dependent variable that measured gross value-added directly. For example, if students took exactly the same test at the end of each year, then the production function could be specified by using the difference in test scores as the dependent variable and eliminating prior test scores from the explanatory variables. Unfortunately, using test gains as the dependent variable is usually infeasible because students rarely take sufficiently similar tests in successive years.

Also note that production functions in different substantive areas will use different subsets of the explanatory variables. In the case of elementary and secondary education, for example, a fully specified model would typically include all four categories of inputs. In contrast, cohort-specific characteristics and resource constraints can probably be reasonably excluded from a production function for cardiac surgery that looks only at hospitals within the same state.

A recent study of graduate business schools controlled for three of the four categories of inputs. To determine the contribution of each school to the average starting salary of its graduates, Joseph Tracy and Joel Waldfogel (1997) controlled for student pre-admission test scores and undergraduate grade point averages (case-specific characteristics), the publication rates and salaries of faculty members (resource constraints), and use of the case method (discretionary use of resources), among other variables. They did not control for cohort-specific characteristics because their unit of analysis was the school, not the individual student. The use of such a sophisticated model yielded intriguing results: the top ten business schools included Oklahoma State University, the University of New Mexico, and Wake Forest University—none of which were ranked in the top 20 by popular news magazines (Tracy and Waldfogel 1997: 13). The big difference is that Tracy and Waldfogel measured value-added, while *Business Week* and *U.S. News & World Report* did not.

Estimation of production functions raises a number of difficult econometric issues. These issues have been explored extensively with respect to educational production functions. (See, for example, Dyer, Linn, and Patton 1969; Hanushek 1972; Murnane 1975; Goldstein 1984, 1987, 1991; Raudenbush 1988; Raudenbush and Bryk 1989; Gallagher 1991; Meyer 1991, 1994, 1996). Here we note briefly only two issues of a more general nature.

First, the production function described above is hierarchical in the sense of mixing individual-level and organizational-level variables. If organizational-level variables that affect outcomes are excluded from the model, then the error terms for cases handled by that organization will tend to be correlated. For example, a charismatic principal might motivate teachers so that, after taking account of the measurable school characteristics, students in the school will tend to do better than predicted by the model. If so, their errors will be positively correlated. (In technical terms, the errors are heteroscedastic.) If the model is estimated by ordinary least squares regression, then, although the estimated coefficients on the explanatory variables will be unbiased, their standard errors will be underestimated so that their precision will be overestimated. Fortunately, methods are now available for adjusting standard errors to mitigate the problem of false precision (White 1980).

Second, as reliable data for measuring discretionary use variables may be unavailable, and the discretionary use variables do not appear directly in any of the value-added expressions, they are likely to be excluded from estimated organizational production functions. Their exclusion, however, will bias the estimated coefficients of any included variables with which they are correlated. As the magnitude of the bias will be large only if the magnitudes of both the effects of the discretionary use variables on outcome and their correlations with included variables are large, it is likely that any bias will be small. Nevertheless, some caution is warranted when simplified models are estimated that exclude discretionary use, or any other theoretically important variables.

Organization-Level Outcome Data

Considerations of cost and technical capability often lead evaluators to specify and estimate organizational production functions in terms of organization-level, rather than case-level, data. Assuming that the case-level specification is sufficiently simple, the organization-level specification can be thought of as a simple summation across organizational caseloads that should lead to similar inferences about the importance of the explanatory variables. If the case-level model is complex, say with interactive terms involving case-level explanatory variables, then the organization-level model may not be a simple aggregation of the case-level model so that the two models may yield different inferences. For example, consider a student-level model of achievement in which family wealth is a more important explanatory variable for students with lower levels of prior achievement. (That is, the model has an interaction term involving family wealth and prior achievement.) This relationship could not be fully taken into account in a school-level model based on the average family wealth and the average prior achievement of each school's student body.

Moving from case-level data to organization-level data makes it more difficult to construct models for adequately assessing value-added. One reason is that organization-level data may reflect the characteristics and outcomes of different cases at different times (Meyer 1994). With respect to a school, for instance, the gain in average test score computed as this year's average minus last year's average may not be a good estimate of the average test score gain of students currently in the school: last year's average includes some students who are no longer enrolled and this year's average includes some students who were not enrolled last year. Because the changing composition of caseloads brings into question the validity of measuring value-added in terms of changes in organizational averages, evaluators often retreat to models that do not attempt to take account of case-specific characteristics, but instead assume that they are adequately captured by cohort-specific characteristics. In the context of school comparisons, if the cohort-specific characteristics do not include a measure of prior achievement by the cohort, then the model becomes one of the level of, rather than value-added to, outcome so that the resulting rankings may be poor indicators of the relative performance of schools (Meyer 1991, 1994, 1996).

Expert Assessment

Our discussion so far has assumed that report card designers develop algorithms that specify exactly how quantitative data are to be used to construct measures of organizational performance. Although the algorithms themselves result from numerous decisions of varying degrees of subjectivity, they define procedures that can be applied objectively in routine situations. But this objectivity comes at the price of the exclusion of qualitative information about current and possible future circumstances that cannot be adequately quantified and embedded into algorithms. An alternative approach is to rely on expert knowledge and judgment to incorporate qualitative information into assessments of organizational performance.

BLENDING QUANTITATIVE AND QUALITATIVE INFORMATION INTO RATINGS Expert assessment is a component of what is one of the oldest organizational report cards: A. M.

Best's insurance reports. Since 1899, the privately held New Jersey company, A. M. Best, has rated insurers in terms of their ability to meet obligations to policyholders. The annual Property/Casualty Edition (published since 1900) and Life/Health Edition (since 1906) of *Best's Insurance Reports* cover almost all of the approximately four thousand domestic insurers and the International Edition covers about one thousand foreign insurers. Insurers pay a $500 fee to be listed in the reports (Boroson 1991: B01). A. M. Best also generates revenue from selling advertising to insurers, a variety of weekly, quarterly, and annual publications, and direct information services offered to underwriters and purchasers of insurance. A. M. Best continues to be the dominant, and only comprehensive, producer of insurer report cards, despite losing its monopoly position in recent years to competing services offered by Standard and Poor's, Moody's, Duff and Phelps, and Weiss Research.

A. M. Best bases its rating system on both quantitative and qualitative data (A. M. Best 1995: vii–xi). The major source of quantitative data is insurance company reports filed with state insurance commissioners according to standards set by the National Association of Insurance Commissioners. Other quantitative sources include company reports to policyholders and stockholders, reports of audits conducted by certified public accountants, documents filed with the Securities and Exchange Commission, and A. M. Best's own Supplemental Rating, Background, and Addendum questionnaires administered annually to insurers.

Qualitative information comes from meetings, telephone calls, and correspondence between A. M. Best's analysts and insurance company managers. In addition to seeking information about insurers' operations and current financial circumstances, the analysts discuss insurers' business plans with an eye to future performance. They also allow insurers to respond to assigned ratings before they are published. A. M. Best argues that this quantitative and qualitative information allows it to provide a comprehensive analysis in support of its founding mission: "To perform a constructive and objective role in the insurance industry towards the prevention and detection of insurer insolvency" (A. M. Best 1995: viii).

A. M. Best provides quantitative assessments of insurer profitability, capitalization, and liquidity and qualitative assessments of insurer risk spreading, reinsurance, asset diversification, financial reserves and surpluses, capital structure, management experience and objectives, market presence, and, for health and life insurers, policyholders' confidence. Of greatest salience to most purchasers of insurance, however, are ratings that integrate the quantitative and qualitative information into an index of insurers' ability to meet obligations to policyholders.

The basic ratings are letter grades ranging from A++ to F as follows: A++ and A+ (Superior), A and A− (Excellent), B++ and B+ (Very Good), B and B− (Adequate), C++ and C+ (Fair), C and C− (Marginal), D (Very Vulnerable), E (Under State Supervision), and F(In Liquidation). A number of "modifiers" can be attached to these grades, including "u" to indicate that the insurer's rating is under review because of a recent event and "q" to indicate that a rating is qualified due to possible changes in state insurance regulations. There are also a number of "Not Assigned" categories. Most deal with particular circumstances that make rating inappropriate because of unavailable information. One category, however, includes firms that request that their rating not be published because they disagree with it—only thirteen out of 1,753 rated health and life insurers in 1995 (A. M. Best 1995: xii). All the "Not Assigned" categories are usually interpreted as "bad news" by insurance purchasers (Adams 1986).

The general approach of combining quantitative and qualitative information into letter grades followed by A. M. Best and the other insurer rating services is widely used in the investment world. For example, Moody's Investor Service rates the investment risk of bonds issued by corporations, state and local governments, and public utilities; Standard and Poor's rates the "quality" of common stocks in terms of their earnings and dividend performance.

DISTILLING EXPERT JUDGMENT INTO ALGO-RITHMS   In other applications, rating procedures have been designed to "capture" expert assessment into algorithms based only on objective measures. This approach has been used on occasion to construct priority measures for case handling within organizations. For example, the Bronx District Attorney's Office at one time operated a case rating system based on a regression model that related subjective assessments of relative case priority made by the director of the Major Offense Bureau to objective characteristics of a sample set of cases (Weimer 1980: 147–154). Although this approach does not integrate qualitative information into the assessment process, it does take advantage of expert judgment to create a set of weights that can be used to convert multiple dimensions of quality into a rating.

John G. Lynch and colleagues take the approach a step closer to possible application in report cards by applying it to the development of a service quality index for Florida telephone companies (Lynch, Buzas, and Berg 1994). The Florida Public Service Commission (FPSC) has established 38 quantitative performance standards for telephone companies. It is likely that some of these standards (say, 95 percent of all calls to 911 Service should be answered within 10 seconds) are more important to consumers than others (say, 100 percent of all public coin phones, except those in prisons, schools, and hospitals, must be able to receive incoming calls). Consequently, the percentage of standards met would be a misleading quality index, especially because consumers are likely to care about the magnitudes by which performance was above or below standard.

The approach employed by Lynch and colleagues was to relate hypothetical changes in the quality dimensions to experts' assessments of how these changes would affect quality as perceived by telephone customers. The 39 experts were recruited from among the staffs of the FPSC and local telephone companies. The experts were presented with a series of questions asking them to rate the quality of various combinations of achievement on the performance standards—to avoid overloading the respondents, the ratings were solicited first within clusters of related rules and then across these clusters. These assessments were then analyzed statistically to produce weights for the quality impact of a percentage change in each of the standards.

Although the quality rating developed by Lynch and colleagues is currently not part of a public report card on the quality of services provided by all telephone companies, it is used as part of the FPSC's annual review of selected companies. In 1995, for example, the FPSC initiated over 700,000 test calls to generate scores needed to assess seven local telephone exchange companies (Taylor, Moses, and McDonald 1996). In addition to reporting scores for comparison against performance standards, the FPSC also provided an overall quality score using weights taken from the study by Lynch and colleagues. A company that exactly met all the standards would earn a score of 75 points. Four of the companies were at or above this overall standard. Of the three companies whose scores were below the standard, one had a score of zero because its billing accuracy, which has a large weight, was very low.

INCORPORATING INFORMATION FROM DIRECT OBSERVATION   Expert judgment plays a role in the Public Protection Classification (PPC), which rates over 25,000 public, volunteer, and private fire departments in 48 states. These ratings have relevance to fire insurance rate regulation in 45 states. The PPC has evolved from ratings begun by the National Board of Fire Underwriters at the turn of the century (Granito 1991). It is currently implemented by the Insurance Services Office, an organization created by property and liability insurers in 1971. In order to settle an anti-trust lawsuit, the insurance industry relinquished control of the Insurance Services Office in 1995 and it has since become a for-profit stock company (Covalaski 1995).

The Insurance Services Office updates the PPC every ten to fifteen years, depending on the population of the covered area, when there have been significant changes in public fire protection, or when requested to do so by a local community. The 10 classifications of the PPC are based on application of the Fire Suppression Rating Schedule. Classes 1 to 9 rate fire protection from best to worst; class 10 applies when there is no recognized protection. The ratings are based on the following weights to three categories of performance: 50 percent on the adequacy of the community's fire department, 40 percent on the adequacy of its water supply, and 10 percent on the adequacy of its alarm system (Insurance Services Office 1997).

Data for assessing these categories come from two sources. First, communities submit data using standardized forms. Second, Insurance Services Office personnel conduct field surveys to inspect equipment and water systems, check fire company records to determine the adequacy of maintenance and training, and assess building characteristics relevant to fire suppression. Field surveys can last anywhere from a day to several weeks, depending on the size of the jurisdiction (Straw 1997). In addition to gathering quantitative data that would be difficult to collect accurately through questionnaires, the field agents can make a variety of qualitative assessments and verify the accuracy of data submitted on standardized forms.

It is interesting to note that the Fire Suppression Rating Schedule replaced an earlier system that relied more on input standards. For example, the older system was such that a community could not get full points unless it had traditional water mains, even if it could produce the required water flows for fire suppression (Granito 1992). The Fire Suppression Rating System also evolved to take account of the growing number of buildings that provide their own fire suppression systems, and are rated by the Specific Commercial Property Evaluation System. Because of the special role of the PPC in rate setting, the change in systems was implemented with caps on the rate increases that could occur with first publications of changes in classes.

Report Cards in Practice

Despite the difficulties encountered in the design and implementation of comparisons of organizational performance, they are increasingly being incorporated into report cards. Here we present examples from education and health care to illustrate the various methodological issues discussed above, and to help us address the broader issue of when organizational rankings are likely to be appropriate.

Measuring School Performance

Public concern about the quality of American schools has led to increasing demands from political leaders for greater educational accountability (Cibulka 1991; Manno 1995; Ladd 1996). Researchers have devoted considerable attention to issues surrounding the use of educational indicators as part of accountability systems (Mayston and Jesson 1988; OERI State Accountability Study Group 1988; Pollard 1989; Kaagan and Colby 1989; Odden 1990; Darling-Hammond 1992; Lehnen 1992; Cuttance 1994; Kiesling 1994; Nevo 1994; Council of Chief State School Officers 1995; Willms and Kerckhoff 1995). The majority of report cards comparing educational outcomes, either across or within states, still compare levels of indicators like school test score averages rather than explicit measures of performance. In other words, most school report cards fail to control for inputs in reporting outcomes.

Initial efforts to move toward performance measures attempted to take account of cohort-specific characteristics of schools. For example, the first comparison of California schools attempted to control for the average socioeconomic levels of student bodies by dividing schools into five groups according to an index of parental occupation; comparisons of a variety of indicators were then made within each group (Fetler 1986). More sophisticated efforts to control for socioeconomic levels of student bodies have used statistical models that relate outcome indicators to various proxy variables. In North Carolina, for instance, report cards for the 1991–92 school year presented the performance of each school district in terms of its average test scores compared to those predicted from a model that regressed test scores on measures of family income (percent of students receiving free or reduced price school lunches), parental education, and rates of absenteeism. Interestingly, Charles Clotfelter and Helen Ladd (1994) found that adding racial composition to the equation substantially improved its predictions of average test scores. Including race in the equation produces lower predicted values for schools with high fractions of African-Americans. Racial composition, and indeed all the measures of the socioeconomic levels of student bodies, raise the fear that the effort to create a fair basis of comparison may set lower expectations for schools serving segments of the population that have traditionally had lower levels of achievement. For this reason, the race variable, though its coefficient was statistically significant, was subsequently dropped from North Carolina's school performance model.

Changes in educational accountability reporting in the United Kingdom illustrate the philosophical and methodological controversies involved in making comparisons among schools. Beginning with the Inner London Education Authority, during the early 1980s many local education authorities prepared school rankings based on average test scores adjusted statistically for socioeconomic characteristics of student bodies. The national Department of Education also began using similar methods to construct league tables, or rankings, for the local education authorities themselves. These comparisons were criticized by educational researchers who showed them to be sensitive to the selection of cohort-characteristics, functional forms, and whether ranking is done in terms of residuals (actual test score minus predicted test score) or residuals standardized by their estimated standard errors (Woodhouse and Goldstein 1988). Following the 1988 Education Act, which pushed forward the Thatcher government's efforts to interject greater parental choice into primary and secondary schooling, a decision was made by the Task Group on Assessment and Teaching not to adjust average test scores in school comparisons to avoid complacency among schools serving less affluent student bodies (Cibulka 1991: 193). More recently, the Labour Party, which originally opposed the ranking of schools, called for league tables based on gains in, rather than levels of, student achievement ("School League-Tables" 1994).

In the United States, performance assessment based on student gains has received impetus from growing interest in tying financial incentives to school performance. By 1994, six states and the Dallas Independent School District ran performance-based tournaments (Clotfelter and Ladd 1996). The following sections look at the ranking systems used to support tournaments in South Carolina and Tennessee.

SOUTH CAROLINA SCHOOL INCENTIVE REWARD PROGRAM Since 1977 South Carolina has required its schools and school districts to issue reports that focus on factors identified by the State Board of Education to be "effective in improving schools"

(Gaines 1991: 6). The Education Improvement Act of 1984 greatly expanded the role of report cards as a tool of educational accountability. Each parent annually receives a report card providing a variety of information, including the percentage of students meeting state standards, student and teacher attendance rates, and median years of teacher education (French, Bobbett and Achilles 1994). The Education Improvement Act also introduced the School Incentive Reward Program (SIRP), a tournament among schools based on larger than expected gains in reading and mathematics test scores. Winning schools in the tournament typically receive awards of approximately $15,000 to $20,000 that can be used for a variety of purposes (other than personal compensation for staff), trophy flags for display, and exemption from certain state education regulations (Mandeville 1995; Clotfelter and Ladd 1996: 36). Underlying the tournament is a ranking system that attempts to measure a school's performance in terms of student test score gains, compared to schools with similar inputs.

The SIRP ranking system treats reading and mathematics scores for two tests, the Basic Skills Assessment Program, a South Carolina test administered in grades one, two, three, six, eight, ten, and twelve, and the Comprehensive Tests of Basic Skills, a nationally normed standardized test administered in grades four, five, seven, nine, and eleven, as output measures that serve as proxies for educational outcomes (Richards and Sheu 1992). Each year, the tests are used as the basis for constructing the School Gain Index (SGI), which is the basis for competition within bands.

Comparison bands divide schools according to their predicted test scores. Predictions are based on the following explanatory variables: percentages of students receiving free and subsidized school lunches (a proxy for the socioeconomic status of the student body), the median years of education beyond the bachelor's degree of each school's teachers (a standard input measure), and, for schools with first grades, the percentage of children meeting or exceeding the readiness standard for first grade (a student body composition variable). These variables serve as independent variables in linear regression models with average school test scores as dependent variables. Separate regressions are estimated for both reading and mathematics and for each grade level. To make predictions for the different test and grade levels comparable, the predicted test scores from each regression are transformed to have a mean of zero and a standard deviation of one. These transformed scores are averaged over grades for each school to create an overall index of its predicted performance. Five bands of about 200 schools each are created based on the index.

The banding is intended to take account of input characteristics that are largely beyond the control of the schools. Most importantly, the school lunch variables and the readiness score are proxy measures for family and student inputs into the educational production function. To the extent that these variables fail to capture all important student body characteristics, the banding will not provide a level playing field for the tournament. Moving from a continuous scale to bands also raises the issue of arbitrary boundaries: there may be no clear basis for placing a school either at the bottom of one band or at the top of the adjacent band even though the placement dramatically changes its field of competition.

Competition within each band is in terms of the SGI, which is a measure of relative "value added" of each school. The first step in constructing the SGI involves predicting current-year reading and mathematics scores as functions of previous-year scores for each student. Each of the separate regressions for reading and mathematics by grade level uses previous-year scores for both reading and mathematics in linear, quadratic, and interactive forms as explanatory variables (Clotfelter and Ladd 1996).

The second step involves creating a discrepancy score for each student that measures the excess of the current-year score over that predicted on the basis of the previous-year scores. The discrepancies are just the residuals from the regressions. The residuals from each regression are standardized to have a standard deviation of one.

The third step involves finding an overall standardized gain for each school, which is its SGI. This is done by pooling together the standardized discrepancies for reading and mathematics for students in all grades. The SGI score for the school is the median of the pooled scores. A positive SGI score indicates better than predicted performance; a negative SGI score indicates worse than predicted performance.

In order to receive a financial reward, a school must have a positive SGI. The size of the SGI needed to win differs in each band, with the cutoffs generally lower for the bands with weaker student bodies. Downward adjustments are made to awards if the winning school has not met student and teacher attendance standards. Complaints from schools placed near the bottom of bands led in 1992 to the introduction of a second category of awards based solely on the extent to which predicted SGI was exceeded. Each year awards are given to approximately 25 percent of schools in the state.

Is the SGI a "good" measure of school performance? Putting aside issues related to the choice of specific test scores as proxy measures for educational outcomes, one can identify both strengths and weaknesses in its design. Its use of previous-year test scores as predictors for current-year test scores makes it an explicit measure of "value added." Also, though it is quite complex and requires considerable expertise to implement, its logical structure has contributed to its acceptance and persistence.

Offsetting this strength, however, are two major weaknesses. First, Charles Clotfelter and Helen Ladd (1996: 31) note that the use of school medians as the basis for the SGI makes it insensitive to the outcomes of extreme under- and over-achievers. It is possible that a school could increase the discrepancies of all its under-achievers without increasing its SGI. Schools wishing to increase their SGI can do so by concentrating effort on improving the test scores of those in the middle of the achievement distribution. Basing the SGI on mean discrepancies would give equal weight to gains by all students.

Second, although the tournament takes account of student body composition to some extent through banding, the SGI itself does not. A student's predicted score generally depends not just on the characteristics of the student as measured by previous-year test scores, but also on the capabilities of his or her classmates. Consequently, the predictions do not fully adjust for school inputs. Specifically, Craig Richards and Tian Ming Sheu (1992: 79) interpret the systematically larger average SGI for schools in higher socioeconomic bands as arising from the exclusion of student body characteristics from the prediction equation, leading to under-prediction for the high bands and over-prediction for the low bands. South Carolina has chosen to deal with this bias by setting different standards for winners in each band. Including school-level variables in the prediction equation or estimating separate equations for each band are alternative approaches for improving the predictions through fuller specification of inputs in the educational production function.

TENNESSEE VALUE-ADDED ASSESSMENT SYS-TEM   Report cards for Tennessee school districts and schools followed the state-wide achievement testing mandated by the Comprehensive Education Act of 1984. These report cards presented a variety of outcome measures, including average test scores (Tennessee Basic Skills First Test and Stanford Achievement Test), pass rates on state proficiency tests, and graduation rates. The Department of Education prepared separate reports for each school district, providing information on the three most recent years as well as state averages for comparative purposes. The report cards received considerable attention from local school officials and the mass media. Indeed, some newspapers collected together report cards from individual districts to create front-page comparisons across districts (McLarty and Hudsen 1987).

Although the report cards presented a variety of information on inputs and outputs, they did not meet the growing demand among political leaders in the state for explicit measures of educational performance. There was concern among many legislators that the 1983 tax increase to fund Governor Lamar Alexander's "career ladders" for teachers had not produced significant educational gains. By 1989 it appeared that the state would have to increase expenditures on education further to counter a legal challenge to the overall funding system being brought by small school districts. The governor and legislators wanted greater accountability in return for more spending.

These demands were reflected in the Education Improvement Act, a major reform initiative adopted in 1992, which included a section calling for the creation of the Tennessee Value-Added Assessment System (TVAAS), a statistical model for estimating the contributions of districts, schools, and teachers to student achievement. Performance as measured with the TVAAS is one of several criteria used to identify individual schools that qualify for financial incentive rewards and school districts that are subject to sanctions. In this way, the TVAAS provides ratings to support tournaments as well as to facilitate state-wide comparisons of the performance of school districts and district-wide comparisons of schools and teachers.

Two factors set the stage for the introduction of the TVAAS. First, since 1990, the Department of Education has administered the Tennessee Comprehensive Assessment Program, which includes standardized tests that provide data appropriate for use in measuring educational gains made by students. Specifically, the state adopted norm-referenced tests in five subject areas (reading, language arts, mathematics, science, and social studies) for grades two through eight, and ten. National grade-level distributions for these tests, which are developed by the California Test Bureau/ McGraw-Hill Company, provide a basis for comparing the progress of Tennessee students against national achievement levels. More significantly for purposes of assessing performance, each subject test is presented on a common 1000-point scale for all grade levels so that differences in successive grade-level scores can be interpreted directly as gains in the subject area. For example, a student who scored 650 on the reading test given at the end of grade two and 680 on the reading test given at the end of grade three would be interpreted as gaining 30 points in reading from grade three, which happens to correspond to the change in the national median from grade two to grade three. In order to reduce the risks of direct "teaching to the test," no more than 25 percent of questions on any test have appeared on any previous test (Bock and Wolfe 1996: 81).

Second, during the 1980s William L. Sanders and Robert A. McLean of the University of Tennessee demonstrated a method for estimating the contributions of schools and teachers to student achievement by using multiple years of test scores for individual students. First in Knox County, and later in Blount County and Chattanooga, they showed that their method could detect differences in contributions to achievement across schools and teachers, and that the differences tended to be consistent from year to year. They also showed that there was a high correlation between the effects of teachers as measured within the model and supervisors' subjective evaluations of teachers, and that teacher effects were not school specific. Especially interesting in view of the empirical literature on school effectiveness, they found that school effects were uncorrelated with the racial composition of the student body (Sanders and Horn 1994).

Governor Ned McWherter became an advocate for what was to become the TVAAS after a detailed briefing—originally scheduled for a half-hour but lasting two hours—on value-added assessment from William Sanders in the fall of 1989 (Sanders 1997a). In early 1990, Sanders briefed the oversight committees of the State Legislature and ended up staying on as an advisor for five months. During this time, he drafted much of the language in the Educational Improvement Act dealing with value-added assessment—the act actually cites specific statistical methods and journal articles that would require value-added assessment rather than more proc-ess-oriented assessments advocated by many educational experts. The act enjoyed strong advocacy from Governor McWherter and a broad coalition of supporters: educators were happy to receive more state funds, teachers (and contractors who anticipated building new classrooms) were pleased with mandated reductions in class size, and conservatives looked forward to greater accountability. With passage likely, Sanders went back to the University of Tennessee to begin writing the software that would be re-quired to implement the TVAAS statewide.

The TVAAS employs both fixed-effects models and a "mixed model" that allows estimation of yearly gains in the test scores of individual stu-dents as a function of both nonrandom, or "fixed," variables (indica-tors for schools and school districts) and random variables (indicators for teachers). In contrast to standard regression models that typically treat the random dependent variable as the sum of fixed variables and a random error term, mixed models also include additional random variables as explanatory variables that are assumed to be jointly distributed with the dependent variable. Estimation involves choosing coefficients for the fixed explanatory variables (school and school district effects) and means for the random explanatory variables (teacher effects) that maximize the likelihood of obtaining the values of the random variables (student gains and teacher effects) that were actually observed. If the random variables are assumed to be drawn from multivariate normal distributions, then the estimation procedure will yield best linear unbiased estimators for the fixed effects and best linear unbiased predictors for the random effects. In non-technical terms, the estimated effects can be thought of as draws from distributions centered as tightly as possible around their true values.

Estimation is facilitated by the accumulation of student-level data for the five normed tests for each of the five most recent years. Because many of the input variables that are commonly used in schooling equations can be assumed to be constant for each student over time—clearly the case for race and sex, approximately the case for parental education and family socioeconomic status—students in effect serve as their own controls. It is the use of repeated measures, over both time (up to five years) and tests (five subject areas), that most distinguishes the TVAAS from other methods for assessing school performance, and makes exclusion of most of the input variables commonly employed in educational production functions plausible. It is also unusual in that its structure allows for the appropriate inclusion of data for students who do not have complete test records.

The TVAAS is implemented in three separate models: pure fixed-effect models for school districts and schools within districts, and a mixed model for teachers and schools. The district and school models are relatively simple in functional form. For example, the district model has the form:

$y_{iklmn} = \eta_{iklm} + \epsilon_{iklmn}$ for the ith district, k^{th} year, l^{th} grade, m^{th} subject, and n^{th} student where y_{iklmn} is the observed test score, η_{iklm} is a fixed effect, and ϵ_{iklmn} is the random deviation from the district mean

Measurements over subject areas and years permit estimation of the variance-covariance structure among tests, which adds considerable information to the estimation. The district (and similarly estimated school) effects are presented as percentages of the national median gain for each of the five tests. An overall average of the percentages is also presented. Published reports average these scores over the last three years; presenting these moving averages reduces year-to-year reporting fluctuations.

The contributions of teachers to test scores are estimated using a true mixed model with fixed district effects and random teacher effects around the district mean (Sanders and Horn 1995). As in the district and school effect models, scores for the last five years are used and the estimated variance-covariance matrix among test scores for subjects and grades adds information to the estimation of teacher effects. The model of teacher effects is "layered" in the sense that students' current test scores in a subject are assumed to depend on the contributions of their teachers for the last three years. Thus, teacher effects are assumed to persist beyond the current year, though the contributions of past teachers are netted out when scores from the previous year are subtracted from scores for the current year to calculate net gains.

Several aspects of the estimation of teacher effects, which add greatly to the complexity of the TVAAS, are worth noting briefly. First, the teacher effect is based only on the scores of students who spent a minimum of 75 days per semester with the teacher. Team teachers are assumed to contribute to students in proportion to the fractions of subject instruction that they provide. Linking students to teachers and taking account of actual exposure patterns involves considerable effort to edit data so that matches can be made. Second, estimates of teacher effects take account of different levels of precision that result from varying numbers of students by treating average gains as new information for Bayesian updating of the district-wide distribution of teacher effects. Thus, a teacher with few students would have a mean effect very close to that of the district, while a teacher with many students would have an estimated effect depending largely on the test scores of those students. Third, even though estimation of teacher effects is implemented on a district-by-district basis, considerable computation beyond the capabilities of commercially available software is required. For example, solution of the teacher model for the Memphis school district involves the solution of over 20,000 equations that requires three to five days of computer time (Sanders 1997a).

Teacher effects are not part of a public report card. Each teacher receives a confidential report on his or her performance. The teacher's principal also receives a copy of the report. A third copy is sent to the central office of the teacher's school district where it can be accessed by members of the school board.

Even this brief description of the TVAAS should suggest its computational complexity and massive data requirements. Currently, it can only be implemented with specially designed software developed by the Value-Added Research and Assessment Center at the University of Tennessee at Knoxville, which is directed by Sanders. A 1995 study conducted by the Office of Education Accountability, a unit under the Comptroller of the Treasury, raised a number of concerns about the TVAAS, including whether its statistical elements have been adequately evaluated by qualified experts, whether its documentation is sufficient to allow replication in the event that the computer on which it now operates were to be disabled, whether its complexity undercuts its acceptance by those affected by its results, and whether national norm gains are an appropriate basis for assessing the achievement of Tennessee schools (Baker and Xu 1995).

These concerns led the Office of Educational Accountability to contract with the Ontario Institute for Studies in Education for an independent evaluation of the TVAAS. Although the consultants recommended a number of specific changes in various aspects of the statistical model and the data upon which it is based, they confirmed the basic conceptual validity of the TVAAS, and its use as a valid assessment tool (Bock and Wolfe 1996).

It is not surprising that many educators were initially skeptical of the TVAAS. Controversy is inherent in the relationship between political leaders and educators. The TVAAS was imposed by Governor McWherter and the state legislature rather than being developed in cooperation with the educational community that it holds accountable in very public ways (Fisher 1996: 41). It is also based on standardized tests that many educators view as an inadequate basis for evaluating student achievement. Its very complexity also invites controversy. It attempts to deal with a great variety of methodological issues that might bring the validity of assessment into question. The great complexity, however, limits the extent to which those subject to its assessments can understand how it functions; where methodologically sophisticated researchers see conceptual simplicity and strong validity, some teachers and administrators see a mysterious "black box."

Nevertheless, the TVAAS has moved beyond direct challenge. With familiarity has come general acceptance of its methods and basic results. It enjoys support from editorial writers, parent groups, and a growing number of school administrators who have found TVAAS results useful in their own assessments. Some affluent school districts that show relatively small gains seem to be the main source of opposition. Although a direct attack against the TVAAS is unlikely, opponents could sabotage it by securing legislation that would stop yearly testing in the five subject areas. Indeed, a proposal made by the Education Commissioner in 1997 to cut back on testing would have effectively stopped the TVAAS had it not met with vocal opposition from Tennessee newspapers and legislators committed to educational accountability. Second grade tests were eliminated, but it appears that quite a few schools will administer them voluntarily (Sanders 1997b).

One could also imagine that a successful legal challenge by a newspaper or parents' group to the confidentiality of the teacher effects could radically change the political environment and perhaps result in a direct threat to the TVAAS. At least for now, however, the TVAAS must be judged a very successful tool for measuring the performance of districts, schools, and teachers.

Hospital Mortality Rankings

The increasing cost of health care and the demands it places on the federal budget through the Medicare and Medicaid programs have led to efforts by government to reduce the provision of unnecessary services and the prices at which they are delivered. In 1983, reimbursement of hospitals providing care to the elderly under Medicare was switched from fee-for-service to payments based on both the condition of patients and the type of treatment as specified in diagnosis-related groups (DRGs). The switch to payments based on DRGs raised concerns that hospitals might reduce the quality of care they provide to Medicare patients by inappropriately economizing on services for which they no longer receive reimbursement. At the same time, it resulted in the accumulation of DRG data that opened the possibility for adjusting outcome measures, such as length of stay and mortality, for the seriousness of patients' conditions. As discussed in Chapter 3, the efforts by the federal government to compare hospitals in terms of risk-adjusted mortality rates did not prove ultimately successful and have been discontinued.

Nevertheless, several states now compare hospitals in terms of risk-adjusted mortality rates for specific types of procedures. California uses data routinely collected by the Office of Statewide Health Planning and Development to rate acute care facilities in terms of risk-adjusted in-hospital (within 30 days of admission) death rates for patients admitted with "fresh" heart attacks (California Office of Statewide Planning and Development 1996). Florida also uses administrative data to rate hospitals for a wide range of medical procedures (Florida Agency for Health Care Administration 1996). In contrast, Pennsylvania uses clinical data to rate hospitals in terms of risk-adjusted in-hospital death rates for coronary artery bypass graft (CABG) surgery, and conveys this information along with extensive information on costs in a consumer guide (Pennsylvania Health Care Cost Containment Council 1995). New York's hospital report card for cardiac artery bypass graft surgery also provides risk-adjusted in-hospital mortality rates for acute care facilities. Like Pennsylvania, New York utilizes clinical rather than administrative data. These distinctions are important because studies show that models using clinical data explain a greater percentage of the variance in mortality than models using administrative data (Iezzoni et al. 1992; Hannan et al al. 1992; Hannan, Kilburn, Racz, Shields, and Chassin 1994; Hannan et al. 1997). After looking at the aborted federal hospital rating effort, we turn to the New York State report as an illustration of a more successful use of risk-adjustment.

HCFA HOSPITAL REPORT CARDS   In 1986 the Health Care Financing Administration (HCFA) of the federal Department of Health and Human Services published its first annual report card assessing the performance of the nation's acute-care hospitals. The report card, using data from Medicare records, identified hospitals with higher and lower mortality rates for patients with particular conditions, such as a stroke or congestive heart failure, and for patients receiving particular medical procedures, such as coronary artery bypass surgery. The report card also provided a summary measure that transcended the individual medical categories.

HCFA intended neither patients nor the general public as the audience for its hospital mortality reports. It originally prepared the reports for use by state peer review organizations, which receive contracts from HCFA to review the medical necessity and quality of care for Medicare beneficiaries. The reports were made public only after a journalist from the *New York Times* demanded their release under the Freedom of Information Act. Nevertheless, HCFA invested a substantial amount of staff time in the reports over a period of several years. By 1992, the annual hospital mortality report had become a 55-volume publication.

By 1993, however, HCFA's hospital report cards had also become a political and professional source of embarrassment. Critics from the hospital industry roundly challenged the report cards for making unfair comparisons that did not take each hospital's unique circumstances into account. Indeed, a 1990 survey found that, regardless of mortality rating, hospitals shared highly negative views of the accuracy, usefulness, and interpretability of the reports (Berwick and Wald 1990). Critics from the scholarly community also criticized the report cards in leading medical journals (Rosen and Green 1987; Green et al. 1990; Iezzoni et al. 1992). In June 1993, one month after being sworn in as the head of HCFA, Bruce Vladeck terminated the report card project (Associated Press 1993). Henceforth, he announced, only the raw data (from Medicare records) would be made available to anyone filing a Freedom of Information Act request. After seven stormy years, the federal government's involvement in producing a hospital report card came to a sudden end.

As variables go, death would seem to be unusually straightforward from a measurement point of view. Thus, in one sense, HCFA's basic task was less challenging than that confronting organizations or analysts forced to use more ambiguous dependent variables as measures of outcomes. But measuring death can be problematic. Does one measure deaths that occur while someone is still a patient at the hospital? If so, that might encourage hospitals to discharge their sickest patients prematurely for fear that an in-patient death might damage their reputation. An alternative is to measure deaths that occur within 30 days after admission. But perhaps that is too soon to detect the effects of surgery or other treatments. Instead, one might measure deaths that occur within 180 days after admission. But perhaps that shifts the focus too far to conditions beyond the hospital's control. Initially, HCFA measured deaths that occurred within 30 days after admission. Subsequently, however, HCFA measured deaths that occurred within 30/90/180 days after admission, using separate equations for each time interval. Eventually, the use of a survival model (event history analysis) permitted HCFA to combine the equations into a single model.

The principal methodological challenge that confronted HCFA was how to control for differences in hospital inputs, especially case characteristics. The usual technique used by medical scholars is to study a manageable sample of patients using "clinical" data on patient characteristics, including detailed information on the severity of illness and comorbidities (or other preexisting health conditions that might affect health outcomes). Such risk adjustment enables researchers to control for differences in patient characteristics that are beyond the hospitals' control.

Unfortunately, clinical data on substantial numbers of patients at every hospital in the United States were not available to HCFA (and probably will not be available to HCFA or anyone else for many years to come). Consequently, HCFA had to make do with so-called administrative data available through the files of Medicare patients. Using such data, which it obtained from the Medicare Provider Analysis and Review file derived from Medicare bills submitted by hospitals to HCFA through financial intermediaries (U.S. HCFA 1993: A3), HCFA was able to control for a number of pertinent variables, such as age, gender, hospital admission within the previous six or twelve months (HCFA tried both measures at different times), and reason for admission (U.S. HCFA 1993: Table A-3). HCFA was also able to control for those comorbidities listed in the forms hospitals were required to fill out for each patient. But HCFA could not control adequately for case severity (how advanced the patient's illness was)—a serious flaw, given the close connection between case severity and health outcomes. Also, because government forms limited the number of comorbidities hospitals could list for any individual patient, the comorbidities data, though less problematic than the absence of good case severity data, were incomplete.

To appreciate the dangers of inadequate model specification in this context, it is useful to compare HCFA's model to a more fully specified model, using clinical data for a sample of hospitals. Jesse Green and colleagues (1990), using data from 13 hospitals and more than 34,000 Medicare patients, essentially replicated HCFA's model, then added a case severity variable, which they constructed themselves. Adding case severity to HCFA's model yielded more than an eightfold increase in the percentage of the variation in mortality rates that it explained and altered the authors' appraisal of several hospitals. Some hospitals, which looked worse than average using HCFA's model, looked better than average using the improved model, and vice versa. This study, and others like it, raised significant questions about HCFA's capacity to adjust for risk.

Unlike its use of data, which never really overcame some fundamental problems, HCFA's estimating techniques grew increasingly sophisticated over time. Initially, HCFA used logistic regression analysis, with death (after x days) as the dichotomous dependent variable. Eventually, HCFA used a survival model (or, in sociological terms, event history analysis), which enabled it to use more fine-grained information about outcomes and to combine that information in a single model. Event history analysis is uniquely appropriate to an assessment of hospital mortality rates because it solves what is known as the "censoring" problem. As Allison (1982: 64) has argued, the use of a dichotomous dependent variable (such as dead or alive 30 days after treatment) is both "arbitrary and wasteful of information." It is arbitrary because there is no particular reason to focus on a 30 day interval rather than some other interval. It is wasteful because it ignores the variation on either side of the cutoff point. For example, one might argue that a hospital whose patient died 31 days after treatment deserves a lower quality score than a hospital whose patient died 180 days after treatment. Yet logistic regression would draw no such distinctions within the same equation if the cutoff point were 30 days. In contrast, event history analysis retains all available information about when each patient died and includes that information in the same equation. The impacts of explanatory variables are estimated through maximum likelihood estimation.

As presented to the news media, HCFA's report card listed hospitals that performed significantly better than average and hospitals that performed significantly worse than average, given hospital inputs. Officially, HCFA did not rank hospitals. Rather, it presented only observed and predicted values and standard errors for each hospital. When pressed, however, HCFA administrators occasionally supplied unofficial rankings to eager journalists. Some staff members cautioned against this, but were overruled (Bailey 1996).

NEW YORK STATE CABG SURGERY   In 1989 hospitals in New York State began collecting detailed clinical data on patients about to undergo open heart surgery through the Cardiac Surgery Reporting System (CSRS). The CSRS, which was developed by the Department of Health in consultation with its Cardiac Advisory Committee, a group consisting primarily of practicing cardiac physicians, was intended to provide data that would ultimately be useful to hospitals and the Department of Health in improving the quality of cardiac care, and to consumers in their selection of cardiac surgery services (Hannan, Kilburn, Racz, Shields, and Chassin 1994). The Department of Health began preparing reports on hospitals and individual surgeons beginning with data from 1989, but initially only released the hospital reports out of concern that many surgeons did too few cases in a year to provide reliable estimates of their mortality rates. After losing a lawsuit brought by *Newsday* under the Freedom of Information Act (Zinman 1991), the department began releasing surgeon ratings in 1992. Currently, the department distributes over ten thousand copies each year of its annual report card, which now includes actual, predicted, and risk-adjusted mortality rates for hospitals and for surgeons who have performed more than 200 CABG operations within the prior three years.

The availability of clinical data for patients through the CSRS has facilitated the implementation of a more satisfactory risk-adjustment procedure than the one developed by HCFA based on administrative data. The CSRS includes approximately 40 variables that have been suggested by researchers as possible risk-factors for cardiac patients. Each year a subset of these variables serve as predictors of mortality, defined as in-hospital death following CABG surgery, in a logistic regression model estimated with data from all CABG patients in all hospitals within the state. Predictions of mortality risk for patients serve as the basis for risk-adjusting hospital case loads. As noted above, logistic regression is not as suitable as event history analysis for dealing with "censored" data. Nevertheless, the New York risk-adjusting procedures appear to have been reasonably effective.

Although the particular sets of predictors used in the logistic regressions have varied somewhat from year to year, the model for 1993 can be taken as representative of the general approach. It is based on 16,690 CABG patients, 453 of whom died during surgery or the subsequent hospital stay (New York State Department of Health 1995). A dozen risk factors are independent variables in the logistic regression model. The two demographic variables, age and body surface area, are continuous. The rest of the variables are indicators (dummy variables) for the following conditions: hemodynamic state (unstable, shock); comorbidities (chronic obstructive pulmonary disease, diabetes, renal failure, stroke); extensively calcified aorta; ventricular function (ECG evidence of left ventricular hypertrophy, congestive heart failure in current admission); and previous open heart operations. The large sample size allows for quite precise estimates of the effects of these variables. Among the indicator variables, whose coefficients can be directly compared, shock, previous open heart operations, and renal failure have the largest effects on mortality risk.

The first step in constructing risk-adjusted mortality rates is the calculation of an expected mortality rate for each hospital. A hospital's expected mortality rate is the sum of the predicted mortality probabilities for its patients divided by the number of patients it had. The expected mortality rate can be interpreted as the mortality rate that would be predicted on the basis of the model given the hospital's mix of patients and assuming that the hospital's performance matched that of the state overall.

The second step in constructing the risk-adjusted mortality rate involves taking account of differences in patient mixes across hospitals. This is done by dividing the hospital's observed mortality rate by its predicted mortality rate and then multiplying by the overall observed mortality rate for the state (2.71 percent in 1993). Hospitals for which the observed mortality rate is higher (lower) than the predicted rate will have risk-adjusted mortality rates larger (smaller) than the observed mortality rate for the state as a whole. Although hospitals are listed alphabetically in the report, those whose 95 percent confidence intervals do not cover the statewide rate are noted. Of the 31 hospitals rated in 1993, three were identified as having risk-adjusted mortality rates significantly higher than the statewide rate (two of which were university hospitals), and two were identified as having risk-adjusted mortality rates significantly lower than the statewide rate.

Conclusion: Are Rankings the Holy Grail of Accountability?

Constructing scales appropriate for ranking organizations in terms of their performance poses challenging problems for report card designers. A valid outcome must be specified, relevant inputs determined, appropriate data assembled, and a statistical model specified and applied. The cases presented in this chapter give some indication of the difficulty of doing these tasks well. They also suggest a few generalizations.

First, there is likely to be a trade-off between validity and comprehensibility. The TVAAS, for example, is based on an extensive and highly appropriate data set and employs a very sophisticated and conceptually valid methodology. Although its assessments of districts, schools, and now teachers have become generally understood and accepted within Tennessee, the great complexity of its implementation, and especially its rather extensive data requirements, make it unlikely that it will quickly supplant much less valid systems used in other states. Longitudinal data covering students in multiple subject areas, as used by the TVAAS, provide the best basis for assessing value-added. Unfortunately, states that do not now test students annually would have to accumulate such test scores for three to five years before adopting the TVAAS methodology.

Second, there is likely to be a trade-off between validity and scope of coverage. Larger units are more likely to involve heterogeneity that makes the focus on a single outcome inappropriate. For example, mortality rates may be a reasonable basis for comparing CABG units, but questionable for hospitals. Further, risk adjustment, or value-added assessment, is likely to be more difficult for larger and more heterogenous units because of the larger number of factors that must be taken into account. It also raises the cost and difficulty of moving beyond routinely available administrative data as a basis of assessment.

Third, the risk adjustment that is possible in a small-scale scientific study may not be feasible in a broader, more regular undertaking. Or, to put it a bit differently, there is a trade-off between validity and reasonableness. The one-time costs of supplying data on a sample of patients with a specific ailment for a scientific study may be tolerable to hospitals; in contrast, the recurring costs of supplying data for the entire universe of patients on an annual basis may be unacceptable to them. Hospitals, like schools, are likely to quarrel with any data-gathering regimen that requires a lot of time and money. At the same time, they are likely to object to inadequate risk adjustment, even if their own failure to supply relevant data is the root cause. Such ironies are common in the world of report cards.

Fourth, outcome measures are highly appealing, but the most interesting outcomes are often those that take years to discover. It would be nice to know whether hospitals and health plans improve the ambulatory skills of patients who have had hip surgery, for example. As time passes, however, data become stale. There is, in short, a trade-off between validity and relevance. The problem is compounded by acquisitions and mergers. With HMOs merging at a dizzying rate, what does it mean to say that Plan A, subsequently purchased by Plan B, had a better success rate with patients who had hip surgery five years ago than Plan C, subsequently purchased by Plan D?

In thinking about validity and other values, it is perhaps best to think of validity as the first, but not the only, value to be satisfied. Once some basic threshold of validity has been established, other values must come into play, such as comprehensibility, relevance, reasonableness, and functionality. Thus a measure must be a reasonably good approximation of some desired outcome before it is utilized at all. But further improvements in validity cannot be purchased at any price. Report cards must be timely enough and understandable enough to help consumers and policymakers with today's choices and decisions.

5

Audiences and Their Demands

Good musicians know that a successful performance requires much more than technical sophistication, important though that may be. It also requires sensitivity to the characteristics of one's audience. For relatively unsophisticated audiences, jazz groups often restrict their members to short sporadic solos. For more knowledgeable audiences, soloists have greater discretion to improvise at length without returning quickly to the original melodic statement (Berliner 1994: 459). By taking listener characteristics into account, jazz groups can tailor the same basic repertoire to the capacities and preferences of particular audiences. Similarly, designers of organizational report card must take audience characteristics into account if their report cards are to be understood and appreciated.

Multiple Audiences

There are three principal audiences for report cards: consumers, policymakers, and service providers. Given their enormous importance as the ultimate targets of report cards, we devote an entire chapter (Chapter 6) to service providers, who may work for a government agency, a for-profit firm, or a nonprofit organization. In this chapter, we focus primarily on consumers and policymakers.

Consumers include individuals, such as persons who enroll in a health plan; corporations, such as firms that choose a health plan or a limited menu of health plans for their employees; and government agencies, such as the federal HCFA, which pays for health care received by Medicare and Medicaid clients. Policymakers include elected officials, such as legislators who establish the ground rules for HMOs; appointed officials, including political executives, civil servants, and judges; and citizens, who choose elected officials and sometimes lobby them between elections. Other audiences, such as the mass media and interest groups, also play important roles, though as intermediaries.

Theories of mass communication and marketing help us to understand how to reach citizens and consumers without overburdening them or deceiving them. Unfortunately, most theories of marketing assume that consumers are individuals who are simply making choices for themselves (or perhaps a loved one, such as a child or a parent). In many instances, however, consumers are actually organizations (for example, firms) that make decisions on behalf of large numbers of people (for example, employees). The dynamics of information processing for such groups, whether private or public, may actually have more in common with information use by public policymakers than with information use by individual citizens.

Theories of information utilization (and research utilization) help us to understand how to reach public policymakers with appropriate recognition of both political and time constraints. These same theories also offer some insight into how to reach organizations that make consumption decisions (or, in some instances, pre-decisions) for large numbers of individuals. In contrast to theories of mass communication and marketing, which rely heavily upon psychology and economics, theories of information utilization rely more heavily on the decision sciences, political science, and public administration.

Theories of Mass Communication and Marketing

How do citizens and consumers acquire information that helps them to cope with the challenges of political (or daily) life? For years, students of mass communication and public opinion have reached a relatively bleak conclusion: citizens are not particularly alert or attentive; consequently, they are easily manipulated by the mass media, which set their agenda, prime them to see the world a certain way, and frame the issues that are so vital to public debate. Indictments of the mass media have been especially critical of television, which is thought to entertain without informing, to titillate without educating.

More recently, scholars have adopted a different perspective, which W. Russell Neuman and colleagues (1992) characterize as the "political cognition" perspective. A key premise is that citizens are not inert blobs who simply respond to crude mass media cues. When citizens are interested and alert, they actively seek information from various channels. When citizens

lack time or interest, they take cognitive shortcuts but may learn something nonetheless. In short, people use the mass media differentially to
learn what they think they need to know.

A related theory of mass media effects, known as "uses and gratifica-
tions" theory, asks what the individual hopes to get out of a particular
news story. In Doris Graber's (1989: 159) words, "Individuals ignore
personally irrelevant and unattractively presented messages and pay attention to the kinds of things that they need and that they find gratifying,
provided the expense in time and effort seems reasonable." It is easy to
imagine that organizational report cards might be deemed personally relevant to many consumers. If so, consumers should be more receptive to
stories about report cards than other types of news. Also, the issues that
have triggered report cards—education, health, economic development—
routinely rank in the upper echelon of issues. Here again, organizational
report cards have an edge over other stories. On the other hand, full
utilization of report cards may require consumers to move beyond passive
consumption of daily news to active acquisition of the report card on
which the news story is based. This shift, from the sofa to the telephone or
the computer, is extremely simple in principle but may exceed the interest
threshold of most consumers.

Although news stories about report cards are undoubtedly important,
report cards are also presented directly to consumers—unsolicited in some
instances, upon request in others. Under such circumstances, consumers
may also be expected to behave differently, depending on the personal
relevance of the report card. Like some mass media theories, marketing
theories postulate that information will shape beliefs, attitudes, and behavior, but only under certain conditions. Empirical research supports this
claim. Research on warning labels, for example, highlights the importance
of personal relevance. As Debra Stewart and Ingrid Martin (1994: 5) note,
"Consumers who do not use a product and do not anticipate using a
product have little need for warning information." By analogy, childless
adults and adults whose children have already graduated from school are
less likely to examine school report cards. Similarly, young adults with
healthy parents are less likely to scrutinize nursing home report cards. But
warning labels can influence behavior. For example, sales of diet soft drinks
containing saccharin declined after saccharin warning labels appeared (Orwin et al. 1984).

Of course, warning labels do not appear on organizational report cards.
If report cards contain warnings, then they are rather subtle ones. Nutri-

tional labels, which specify the amounts of fat, cholesterol, sodium, and carbohydrates are directly analogous to report cards, because they invite consumers to make explicit comparisons by using numeric ratings. Experimental studies show that nutritional labels can affect both perceptions and behaviors. Label format and the inclusion of reference values (information on recommended daily amounts for both positive and negative nutrients) can also influence both perceptions and behavior (Burton et al. 1994). However, excessive information, or information overload, can be counterproductive. For example, Wesley Magat and W. Kip Viscusi (1992: 102–104) found that additional information on an insect spray label reduced consumer recall of the most important information on the label. Susan Hadden (1986: 233–238) argues that consistent summary symbols, like those used on consumer products in Canada since 1970, are desirable to draw attention to important messages that might otherwise be lost when large quantities of information are provided.

Admittedly, experiments are artificial situations. They thrust information in the faces of consumers who might otherwise ignore the information altogether. But nonexperimental studies also suggest that nutritional labels can make a difference. For example, consumption of high-fiber cereals increased after nutritional labels appeared on cereal boxes (Ippolito and Mathios 1991). The case of cereals is particularly interesting, because it almost certainly involved an interaction effect between nutritional labels (analogous to report cards) and mass media messages on dietary fiber's health effects (analogous to mass media coverage of report cards). News stories and advertisements citing report cards may trigger consumer interest in report cards themselves; once acclimated to reading report cards, consumers may use them regularly and to good advantage.

Additional insights into the design of effective report cards are suggested by the public information campaign, a policy instrument that explicitly uses mass marketing techniques to achieve some policy result. Drawing on a large technical literature and 100 reports of public information campaigns, Janet A. Weiss and Mary Tschirhart (1994: 85–92) identify three tasks that the campaigns must accomplish to be effective. First, the campaign must capture the attention of the right audience. This requires the identification of the target audience, the selection of the channels of communication that will be used to reach it, and methods for drawing attention to the messages provided on the various channels. Second, the campaign must deliver a credible message that the audience understands. This requires a credible source, a clear message that fits with prior knowledge, and a sufficient duration of exposure for the messages to be understood. Third, the campaign must deliver a message that influences the audience. It must provide useful information that directs attention to the issue at hand, triggers relevant norms, changes values or preferences, or creates social contexts favorable to the desired outcomes.

A marketing perspective may well be more applicable to some types of report cards than to others. Report cards that rate or rank organizations according to some explicit criteria have a strong normative message; their intent is not just to inform but to persuade. They are positive advertisements for some organizations, negative advertisements for others. In contrast, report cards that present large amounts of data without interpreting the data tend to be less action-oriented. Report cards that stress breadth rather than depth may be especially valuable to citizens, who need information about an industry as a whole; report cards that provide considerable detail on particular organizations may be more helpful to consumers, who must decide which organization to patronize.

Theories of Research and Information Utilization

Some theories of research utilization have treated research as being roughly equivalent to other less formidable parcels of information. From this perspective, research that meets the immediate needs of policymakers will be integrated into the decisionmaking process; research that fails to do so will be ignored. Timing is so crucial to policymakers that pressure often mounts to release findings from research in progress before the research is actually complete. This happened, for example, with the famous New Jersey Income-Maintenance Experiment, which was interrupted in order to inform congressional debates on welfare reform (Kershaw and Fair 1977).

Although the direct, immediate use of policy-relevant research undoubtedly occurs, other theories, that take a more long-term view of research utilization, are more compelling. Carol Weiss (1977), for example, has developed what she calls an "enlightenment model" of research utilization. According to this model, policy research has a greater impact in the long run than in the short run. Over time, research findings enlighten policymakers, provide them with useful conceptual tools and insights, and sometimes even change their beliefs. But these changes are seldom perceptible in the short run.

Other theorists and researchers have reached similar conclusions. Martha Feldman (1989), for instance, used organizational theory to develop a long-term organizational learning perspective, which she successfully applied to policy research at the Department of Energy (DOE). At DOE, research reports often sat around gathering dust. At the right moment, however, policymakers reached for the dusty research file, learned from it, and incorporated the lessons into new administrative rules. Thus the role of policy research was to develop a "storehouse" of research reports whose immediate relevance was often limited but whose eventual relevance was often high.

Patricia Thomas (1987) observes that policy findings and ideas often seem to be completely ignored when they are first produced, yet spring up, like water that has percolated through limestone, into debate over public policy issues some time in the future. Just as with studies stockpiled in agency files, circumstances may bring attention to research that otherwise seems to have been forgotten.

Social science research can also gain value as individual studies accumulate. Findings gain credibility as they are reported from different studies using different data and methods. Thinking of the bird droppings on some islands that accumulate into soil worth mining for fertilizer, Aidan Vining refers to this process as the "guano theory" of social science utilization. For example, the large body of economic research showing the inefficiency of regulation of fares and routes in the airline industry that accumulated over several decades was a valuable resource for proponents of deregulation (Derthick and Quirk 1985).

Of course, report cards differ from policy research projects, though considerable effort is invested in producing both. The primary purpose of many report cards is not to provide macro-level policy guidance but rather to facilitate micro-level choice. Whereas policy research is usually episodic, report cards are, by definition, regular. Also, policy research may or may not be comparative. In contrast, report cards, by definition, always involve some basis of comparison. Policy research is also typically more ambiguous than report cards, although this need not be the case. For all these reasons, report cards may have a somewhat greater potential than policy research to influence policymakers in the short run. This is especially true if the report card is designed to be comprehensible and relevant.

Report Cards in Practice

Designers of report cards vary significantly in their sensitivity to the "audience problem" and indeed in the audiences they are trying to reach. Many public school report cards seem to have been prepared with an elite audience in mind, judging from both their content and their distributional arrangements. In contrast, many higher education report cards seem to have been prepared with a mass audience in mind, as in the case of the one published annually by *U.S. News & World Report*. Health care report cards also differ in the audiences they are likely to reach. Some reflect good strategic thinking about audience characteristics; others suggest muddled thinking that could easily jeopardize utilization.

Pittsburgh HMOs

Health Pages, a New York–based magazine, publishes irregularly in a select group of metropolitan areas. It prepares a tailor-made magazine, focusing on HMOs, when local business leaders agree to purchase large quantities of magazines for their employees (at least 20,000 copies), thus making the venture financially viable. *Health Pages* has published magazines in seven metropolitan areas, sometimes more than once. In Pittsburgh, Pennsylvania the magazine published three editions before its partner, the Pittsburgh Business Group on Health, chose to proceed on its own.

The Fall/Winter 1995 edition of *Health Pages-Pittsburgh* includes scorecards for three of six managed plans in the Pittsburgh metropolitan area (three declined to participate). The data used to calculate the scores were audited by the National Committee for Quality Assurance (NCQA), a nonprofit organization based in Washington, D.C., thus authenticating the numbers furnished by the health plans. The Fall/Winter 1995 edition includes brief articles on hysterectomy and its alternatives, home health services, and other subjects. It also includes detailed tables on Pittsburgh allergists and gynecologists, with information on their educational background, hospital affiliations, health plan affiliations, board certification, and fees for selected surgical procedures.

Health Pages-Pittsburgh is unusually comprehensible and very user-friendly. It features a readable summary of the scorecard's content and methodology and a helpful glossary. Bar graphs make it easy to compare plans on a particular dimension, such as cholesterol screening or diabetic retinal screening. And each bar graph is accompanied by a brief narrative that explains the medical procedure or activity and places it in perspective.

Especially commendable is *Health Pages'* emphasis on educating consumers to interpret bar graphs properly. In presenting figures on coronary bypass operations and Cesarean sections, the magazine notes that some experts believe these procedures have been used too often (Smith 1995:

21, 23). More generally, the magazine cautions that "a very low value may indicate the plan isn't doing enough of these procedures and a very high value may raise concerns about inefficiencies in monitoring the use of unnecessary procedures" (Smith 1995: 17).

Health Pages also places the Pittsburgh findings in national perspective whenever possible. For example, in addition to comparing the three health plans for cholesterol screening, breast cancer screening, pap smears, and other activities, the magazine notes the Department of Health and Human Services' goal for each activity by the year 2000 (Smith 1995: 21–23). In addition to noting the percentage of Pittsburgh gynecologists who are board certified, the magazine notes that Pittsburgh gynecologists are more likely to be board certified than gynecologists elsewhere (Smith 1995: 34). Such comparisons serve to reduce or heighten concern, as appropriate.

Although *Health Pages* has produced a highly comprehensible and relevant report card, there is still room for improvement. While there are valuable cross-sectional comparisons, there are no longitudinal comparisons. Individuals who can only choose between one of the health plans and a fee-for-service plan cannot know whether their company's health plan has gotten better or worse. Also, only three of the metropolitan area's six health plans participated in the report card venture, thus reducing the utility of the report. One of the six declined to participate for a good reason (it was being restructured). Nevertheless, the absence of full participation is regrettable.

Health Plans

A growing body of research considers the general factors that facilitate and impede the communication of information to consumers about the quality of health care. While some studies are based on consumer behavior, most make use of focus groups or surveys to investigate how well consumers understand various types of informational content and format.

One general finding of this research is that consumers' knowledge of the health care context affects their understanding of the routinely used health care indicators. Because a 1995 national survey found that a majority of respondents did not think that they had a good understanding of health plan elements (Isaacs 1996: 32), this line of research has direct relevance to report card design. Using survey analysis, an experiment, and focus groups, Judith Hibbard, Shoshanna Sofaer, and Jacquelyn Jewett (1996) found that while consumers saw condition-specific performance measures (such as mammography and five-year survival rates for breast cancer) as salient, their knowledge of the health care context played an important role in how well they understood these measures. Another study based on a large number of focus groups found that quality indicators are typically not well understood and often misinterpreted (Jewett and Hibbard 1996). More generally, personal characteristics as well as situational factors seem to influence how consumers respond to quality indicators (McGee and Knutson 1994: 6). A review of report cards prepared by six large purchasers of group health insurance pointed to the importance of supporting the report cards with education on health care systems and measures, especially for retirees (Hoy, Wicks, and Forland 1996: 27).

Another general finding is that consumers appear not to process quantitative information as easily as report card designers might expect. A study based on focus groups conducted by the Pacific Business Group on Health, which represents more than 30 major West Coast employers, found that consumers preferred letter grades like "A," "B," and "C" to categories like "above average," "average," and "below average" to actual rates for various performance measures (Schauffler, Halpin and Rodriguez 1996: 81–82). Participants in the focus groups also reported that numbers often took too much time to interpret, and "that they had difficulty reading charts with bars and graphs, interpreting information about confidence intervals, and understanding population targets" (Schauffler, Halpin and Rodriguez 1996: 82). In their content analysis study of focus group discussions, Judith Hibbard and Jacquelyn Jewett (1996:85–86) found that 43 percent of statements indicating low-comprehension of quality indicators reflected problems with basic concepts such as rates and quantitative comparisons across plans.

A third finding is that consumers' information needs are highly diverse and idiosyncratic. In focus groups with Oregon consumers, Pamela Hanes and Merwyn Greenlick (1996: 25–26) discovered that "consumers want to be able to 'mine down' into topics they consider to be personally relevant, while skimming the more generic information." A computer kiosk can be used to achieve this objective. Indeed, Oregon consumers found the idea of a computer kiosk appealing because it would enable them to customize the level of detail provided. A well-designed web site can accomplish the same goal.

Finally, it appears that report cards that limit their focus to the choices actually available to consumers are more likely to communicate effectively than more comprehensive report cards that include many nonavailable choices. David Knutson and colleagues (1996) surveyed members of the State of Minnesota Employee Group Insurance Program before and after they made their 1995 enrollment decisions. State employees received an employer-specific report card comparing their six choices while university employees did not. Both groups were subsequently exposed to a community-wide report card covering 46 plans that was developed by an independent organization and distributed through local newspapers. It should not be surprising that the employee-specific report card was much more likely to be seen than the community-wide report card; but it was also more intensely read (Knutson et al. 1996: 121). Report cards that focus on available choices probably enjoy advantages both in terms of salience and simplicity. Even something as seemingly trivial as having a sufficiently small number of comparisons that they fit on the same page may encourage use.

Nursing Homes

Although *Consumer Reports* is best known for its excellent product comparisons, the magazine has occasionally focused on the delivery of services within a particular industry. In the fall of 1995 the magazine ran a three-part series on nursing homes and their alternatives (for example, home health care). It included an explicit rating of 43 for-profit chains and religious groups with multiple nursing homes ("When a Loved One Needs Care" 1995). To compute ratings, the magazine focused on 69 quality standards and counted the number of citations (or code violations) in the last four inspection reports for each nursing home examined (it is not clear how many nursing homes per group were investigated). The umbrella group then received an overall score, based on the mean number of citations. In addition, the magazine reported the percentage of individual homes within each umbrella group that were much better and much worse than average. Thus a group with one truly awful facility might receive a poor overall score but look better in the other two categories.

Consumer Reports' nursing home report is unusually comprehensible. The quantitative analysis presents the data in three different ways, taking both the mean and the standard deviation into account. Yet these terms do not appear in the table or text, in case they might confuse the reader. Also, the quantitative analysis is preceded by a highly readable article that summarizes steps consumers should take in trying to find "the right nursing home" for their needs. Based on anonymous personal visits to 53 nursing homes and conversations with industry experts, the article includes lots of helpful hints and tips. For example, *Consumer Reports* warns against such natural inclinations as judging a facility by its decor ("When a Loved One Needs Care" 1995: 523). The magazine also suggests that consumers confer with their state or county ombudsman, who may not reveal which nursing homes are bad but who may reveal which ones are good ("When a Loved One Needs Care" 1995: 520).

Though impressive, *Consumer Reports'* nursing home report card does suffer from some weaknesses. Although the magazine discusses a wide variety of quality dimensions, such as food, dignity, smells, and grooming, it does not offer separate quantitative scores (or, for that matter, qualitative comparisons) for each dimension. In this sense, *Consumer Reports'* report card differs sharply from *Health Pages'* report card. A consumer who cares a great deal about bed sores and safety hazards but not as much about planned activities cannot determine from the chart or article whether a particular group is better or worse along these dimensions. This reduces the relevance of the report card to the questions that particular consumers ask.

Perhaps the most serious weakness of the report is in its treatment of nursing home auspices. At one point, *Consumer Reports* states that for-profit and religious groups are about equally represented in the top third of the sample ("When a Loved One Needs Care" 1995: 519). Yet careful econometric research has demonstrated that religious nursing homes do a better job than for-profit nursing homes, at least in certain areas, such as the use of sedatives (Weisbrod 1988: 149–151). Satisfaction with resources provided by religious nursing homes (and by nonprofits generally) is also higher (Weisbrod 1988: 151–154). By treating quality as a unidimensional concept and by failing to control for variations in facility size and other characteristics, the magazine may have placed too much emphasis on comprehensibility and not enough on validity.

Even though the statistical information presented by *Consumer Reports* is relatively straightforward, it nevertheless raises an interesting methodological issue concerning whether or not state differences should be netted from the ratings based on code violations. On the one hand, states vary in how vigorously they enforce codes, suggesting that state-level effects can be interpreted as differences in enforcement effort that affect the probability that code violations will be detected. On the other hand, there may be real differences among the states, perhaps resulting from different levels of enforcement or variation in other relevant state characteristics.

Indiana School Districts

Indiana, like many other states, requires its school districts to prepare and disseminate report cards for the public schools within their respective jurisdictions. The report cards cover a wide range of topics, including both performance indicators (for example, test score results, student attendance rates, and graduation rates) and financial indicators (for example, receipts and expenditures, salary schedules, and assessed valuation for the prior and current year). Each school district must arrange to have its report card published in a local newspaper once a year.

At first glance, Indiana would seem to have placed considerable emphasis on comprehensiveness. Certainly, its report cards cover a wide range of variables, as indicated above. However, the inclusion of detailed information on financial variables already published elsewhere limits opportunities to provide more useful contextual information and may overload consumers, thus undermining comprehensibility.

The absence of detailed information on the socioeconomic characteristics of the student body is a conspicuous weakness. Without such information, parents cannot assess the "value added" by their school, even if they were capable of performing a rough multiple regression analysis on their own. Moreover, very few parents have the capacity or the inclination to perform a multiple regression analysis. Thus the absence of controls for key inputs makes it extremely difficult for consumers to make fair comparisons.

Report card format is also a serious problem. Despite a state requirement for reporting and a checklist of information that must be provided, there is no standard format for all school districts within the state (Lehnen et al. 1995: 5.2). Thus parents who wish to compare the school district in which they currently reside with one they are considering cannot make easy comparisons because the information is packaged differently by different school districts. This severely reduces the relevance of the report cards to parents who are often particularly interested in comparing one school district to another.

Many of these problems are remediable, as Lehnen et al. (1995) have argued. School districts could be required to submit their information using a common standardized format. They could be required to include explanatory labels, text, graphics, and tables. They could be required to publish the information in their local newspaper every year at the same time and hold a community meeting 60 days later so that interested parents could discuss the report card with school officials.

More broadly, Indiana could follow South Carolina's example and make an effort to put school performance in proper perspective. Without controls for school inputs, Indiana's report cards run the risk of portraying particular schools as failures simply because they are attempting to educate disadvantaged children. Without such controls, the reports are likely to be discounted by parents, school professionals, and policymakers. A survey of 30 randomly selected Indiana school districts supports this assertion. Although nearly two-thirds of the school districts said that the report cards were somewhat useful, only 7 percent said that the report cards were very useful and 31 percent said that the report cards were of little or no use (Lehnen et al. 1995: 4.1). Focus groups in three different parts of the state suggested that other education stakeholders, including parents, also have reservations about report card content, format, and distribution (Lehnen et al. 1995).

In 1996, Indiana amended its education code in an effort to make school report cards more effective. In addition to requiring the provision of specific types of information, the amendments direct the state superintendent of education to determine additional information that school corporations must compile on a district or school level, and to specify a common format for publication, including tables, graphics, and explanatory text. The law authorizes, but does not mandate, that school boards hold public hearings within 60 days of publication of their report cards.

Greensboro and Sacramento Public Schools

Although it is useful to know what parents think about school report cards currently in use, it is also instructive to ask them what they think about alternative report card prototypes. A team from the University of North Carolina at Greensboro did precisely that, through telephone interviews with one hundred parents of students enrolled in the Greensboro, North Carolina public schools and sixty-six parents of children enrolled in the Sacramento, California public schools. In addition, the team asked twelve Greensboro parents to examine four report card prototypes and discuss them. Ten Greensboro area school board members and six Sacramento school board members also participated in the project.

Parents generally regarded a list of ten potential topics for school report cards as either "somewhat important" or "very important." If there were no need to forgo some information in order to obtain additional information, then parents preferred to have it all, at least in theory. If forced to choose, however, then parents preferred information on school success (graduation rate, promotion rates, number of "A" grades, number of AP placements, number of units of credits earned, satisfaction of requirements for university entry, special honors and awards, and athletic accomplishments) and school environment (school safety and involvement of parents) to information on standardized test scores and student engagement (Jaeger et al. 1993: 10). They also preferred all of these items to information on school facilities, services available, staffing and teachers, and programs offered. Interestingly, these were not the choices that journalists or school superintendents would have predicted. In particular, members of these groups overestimated parental interest in standardized test scores (Jaeger et al. 1994: 20).

These findings are particularly interesting, because school board members differed from parents in their information priorities. For school board members, standardized test scores were far more important than other factors, including school environment and school success, which parents ranked so high (Jaeger et al. 1994: 26). Thus a report card aimed simultaneously at parents and school board members would need to recognize that the interests of these two audiences are not identical. A report card that includes diverse indicators can address this problem of divergent interests. But perhaps there are problems with report cards that run too long.

When asked to choose the format of a school report card, parents preferred somewhat longer report cards (four pages) to somewhat shorter report cards (two pages) by a wide margin (Jaeger et al. 1994: 28). They also preferred a tabular format to a narrative format but by a small margin (Jaeger et al. 1994: 28). School board members also preferred the longer tabular format to other formats (Jaeger et al. 1994: 39). Thus, in this particular instance, different audiences responded similarly to different formats, at least in the abstract.

There is, however, an important and somewhat surprising distinction between parental format preferences and the format that actually helps parents the most. After reading different types of report cards, the 12 Greensboro parents were asked to classify the represented schools in terms of quality (good, mediocre, poor). Using report cards that followed their preferred format (longer, tabular), parents accurately classified individual schools 75 percent of the time. Using report cards that followed a less preferred format (longer, narrative), parents responded accurately 91 percent of the time (Jaeger et al. 1994: 41). Clearly, more research with larger samples is needed on this subject. However, this research suggests that report card designers may have to choose between a format that parents say they like best and a format that actually informs parents more effectively.

Insurance Ratings: Evidence of Market Impact

The near century-long existence of A. M. Best indicates that the marketplace values the information that it provides about the solvency of insurers. The entry of other firms into the field in recent years further attests to the demand for such information. Yet one might wonder about the extent to which the marketplace is valuing the solvency ratings of insurers rather than more descriptive information, such as which insurers are active in which markets. States set minimum reserve requirements for insurers and require them to participate in guaranty funds that insure to varying degrees against the adverse impacts of their insolvency on their clients. Do the ratings actually have an impact on consumer choices?

A very direct impact operates through contract provisions that restrict the selection of insurers. Mortgage and other contracts often specify minimum ratings for acceptable insurers (Adams 1986). These restrictions in turn create strong incentives for insurers, especially those specializing in the property and liability lines covered in contracts, to obtain higher ratings.

Do ratings affect the prices that insurers can charge for their products? Although no one has looked directly at this question, David Sommer (1996) found that portfolio risk and capital-asset ratios affected prices in ways consistent with the hypothesis that the market is willing to pay more for insurance provided by firms with lower levels of insolvency risk. Specifically, he finds a statistically significant negative relationship between insolvency risk and price. In other words, the market penalizes insurers with high default risk through lower prices. As the ratings made by A. M. Best and its competitors are the major sources of information about insurer solvency available to consumers, and there is some statistical evidence that the ratings actually predict insolvency as well as do financial variables (Ambrose and Seward 1988), it seems reasonable to attribute the price effect to the ratings.

Rating changes might also affect the stock prices of insurers to the extent that they provide new information to investors. The fact that the major business publications, such as the *Wall Street Journal,* routinely run stories about rating changes for major insurers is consistent with such an effect. Nevertheless, a systematic investigation failed to find any effect of A. M. Best rating changes on stock prices, indicating that the ratings did not provide new information to investors (Singh and Power 1994). These results contrast with findings on the market impacts of other financial rating systems: Moody's and Standard and Poor's downgrading of corporate bond ratings reduce stock prices (Holthausen and Leftwich 1986) and changes in their ratings of municipal bonds affect bond prices (Ingram, Brooks, and Copeland 1983).

Reaching a Mass Audience

Although some report cards reach consumers directly, most report cards are first "filtered" by other individuals and organizations (see Figure 5.1). News organizations and advocacy groups are the most familiar intermediaries. Employers sometimes serve as conduits for report cards, as when they select a menu of health plans for their employees' consideration and furnish some information on each. Increasingly, report cards are accessed through the Internet, which means, in effect, that some consumers learn a great deal while others learn little or nothing.

The challenge of reaching a mass audience with information that is valid

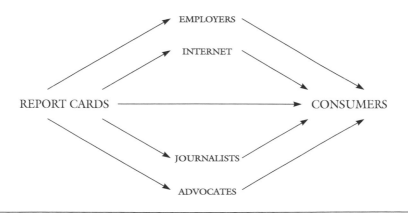

Figure 5.1 Reaching a mass audience

and comprehensive but also comprehensible and relevant is a formidable one. Inadequate education, time, knowledge, and interest serve as barriers at the receiving end. Inadequate funding, time, data, and insight into audience characteristics serve as barriers at the sending end. To overcome these barriers, some imagination is required.

Customer Satisfaction Surveys

A popular technique for communicating with individual consumers is the customer satisfaction survey. Such surveys, which have become more common in business in recent years, have become staples of HMO report cards. The standard approach is to use some sort of Likert scale to find out what customers think. For example, the NCQA uses eight measures to assess HMO enrollees' satisfaction with access and quality.

The customer satisfaction survey flows logically from the Total Quality Management movement's emphasis on customer service and customer feedback (Deming 1982). It also aptly reflects the sentiment expressed in a popular tune from the musical *Ain't Misbehavin'*: "Find out what they like / And how they like it / And let 'em have it just that way!"

A customer satisfaction survey is almost always comprehensible. It has the advantage of being easy to digest, a natural extension of the consumer's heavy reliance upon word of mouth as an information source but a significant step beyond that. Although it requires the collection of new data and demands considerable care in the selection of appropriate samples, it is not particularly expensive. And it is relatively easy to administer, whether in-house or by contracting with a survey research firm.

There are, however, some significant drawbacks to customer satisfaction surveys. One is that satisfaction levels are often extremely high, with very small standard deviations. A survey that reveals no statistically significant differences across firms within a particular industry (or across schools within a particular school district) may be comforting to the industry (or school district) but may not be very helpful to consumers, especially if it fails to capture dissatisfaction with important dimensions of organizational performance. This tendency toward convergence is exacerbated by decisions to merge positive response categories, such as excellent / very good / good. For example, ratings of Pittsburgh HMOs, discussed earlier, have merged the top three satisfaction categories, yielding virtually indistinguishable satisfaction levels that range from 88 percent to 91 percent (Smith 1995).

A second problem is that customers' perceptions may be wrong. The old adage that the customer is always right is more a tribute to market power than to the wisdom or perspicacity of consumers. Most parents say that they are very satisfied with the quality of child care their child receives (Hofferth et al. 1991), but studies show that parents have good reason to be concerned about child care quality (Kisker et al. 1991; Galinsky et al. 1995; Helburn et al. 1995). In fact, customer satisfaction may be a coping mechanism. Through cognitive dissonance reduction, customers narrow the gap between hopes and perceptions and learn to accept conditions that are quite difficult to change. Yet the premise behind report cards is that many of these conditions can in fact be changed. Thus a report card that relies heavily on easily inflated customer satisfaction measures of quality may be limiting its potential to induce significant organizational change.

A third problem is that many consumers have reservations about customer satisfaction data. On the one hand, consumers seem to prefer customer satisfaction data to complex indicators of undesirable events, such as hospital deaths after a heart attack (Hibbard and Jewett 1996). On the other hand, consumers seem to prefer advice from family members and friends to customer satisfaction data. That, at any rate, is true of senior citizens (Edgman-Levitan and Cleary 1996: 47–50). Whatever consumers may say in focus groups or in response to survey questions, the evidence to date indicates no discernible impacts of customer satisfaction surveys on HMO disenrollments (Newcomer et al. 1996). Perhaps that is because so many customer satisfaction surveys paint a rosy image of all evaluated organizations.

Are there alternatives to standard customer satisfaction surveys that might capture consumer sentiment and experience without conveying the false impression that all is sweetness and light? One such alternative is to report the number of customer complaints against particular firms within an industry. For example, before its demise the Interstate Commerce Commission (ICC) regularly reported the number of complaints against interstate moving companies (U.S. ICC 1995). This information, when combined with the number of shipments per firm, can be useful in assessing the performance of interstate carriers. Unfortunately, the ICC did not compute complaint/shipment ratios, thus requiring consumers to make their own calculations with a pocket calculator or by hand. Also, there are fundamental problems with raw complaint data. A "smear" campaign aimed at a particular firm could be misleading and unfair.

A superior approach is to report the number of substantiated complaints along with some measure of business volume. The New York State Insurance Department (1995) uses this approach in ranking automobile insurance companies. Its rankings are based on the number of "upheld" complaints per million dollars of premiums earned in the state—an overall average of about one upheld complaint per five million dollars of premiums in 1995. In addition to a comprehensive listing of complaint ratios and rankings of all insurers, the report provides three effective summary tables showing performance during the last three years: the twenty-five auto insurers with the lowest complaint ratios; the ten with the highest complaint ratios; and the ten with the largest premium volumes. A convenient list of commonly asked questions and answers at the beginning of the report greatly increases its comprehensibility.

Greater use of upheld complaints could be especially promising in child care, where complaints are promptly investigated by state licensing officials, who keep up-to-date files chronicling the complaints and their resolution (Gormley 1995). Unfortunately, such information is not routinely shared with consumers, although state licensing agencies sometimes make it available to consumers who make the pilgrimage to the child care licensing office in the state capital. Ideally, that information should be pooled and shared with consumers, using resource and referral agencies, libraries, and public schools as intermediaries.

Electronic Communication

In many respects, the electronic media have displaced the print media as preferred vehicles for mass communication. Americans rely more heavily on television than on newspapers for news. A 1989 survey that allowed respondents to name one or more media as their major source of news found that 66 percent named television, 36 percent named newspapers, and 14 percent named radio—somewhat surprisingly, they also regarded television as a more credible news source than newspapers (Bogart 1989: 243). Americans spend more time watching television than reading books. Movies are still enormously popular, as are their spinoffs, videotapes. And growing numbers of Americans surf the Internet for news, ideas, and gossip. All of these developments open up new opportunities for effective mass communication. In particular, they suggest that report card designers should consider alternatives and supplements to the printed word as they seek to engage, educate, and inform a diverse cross-section of citizens.

Communicating with people from all walks of life, varied backgrounds, and limited attention spans is a challenge, but it can be done. It is easy to imagine a light-hearted video in which consumers learn to cope with the challenges of health care choice in a competitive era. A family might hastily choose a horrible health plan with doctors reminiscent of the Three Stooges. Misery ensues, as a minor stomach ailment escalates into a journey into medical hell. Then a report card, in a cameo appearance, helps the family to undo the damage and select a plan with physicians who actually seem to know the difference between the large and small intestines. The danger of such a film is that it might be construed as casting aspersions on the honor of the medical profession. But the considerable advantage is that it would serve as an inducement to take report cards seriously and persuade viewers of the high stakes of health plan choices. In this instance, a video might be combined with a printed report card, available upon request.

Alternatively, report cards might be made available through the Internet. Already, the NCQA furnishes information on the accreditation status of HMOs via a World Wide Web site (www.ncqa.org/accred/asr/asrlist.htm). The next logical step would be to supply detailed quality-relevant information on each HMO through the same mechanism. Specifically, consumers could call up each HMO's HEDIS (Health Plan and Employer Data and Information Set) file on the Internet and extract as much information as desired.

HMO report cards lend themselves to World Wide Web dissemination because enormous amounts of quality-relevant data are available through a single national organization, namely, the NCQA. Child care report cards, to the extent that they exist at all, are developed through a much more decentralized process and might best be distributed through libraries and public schools within individual states. Alternatively, child care report cards might be distributed through the Internet by the National Association of Child Care Resource and Referral Agencies, which could insist on some standardized format and some minimum information to ensure comparability.

These are exciting possibilities, but they do have one major drawback, which is that they may exacerbate the gap between the rich and the poor, the well educated and the poorly educated, the connected and the unconnected. That is true of any new information system, but it is especially true of the Internet and other communications media that are currently accessible to a relatively small number of citizens. If the Internet is to displace printed documents as the principal vehicle for disseminating report cards, then it should be accessible, both financially and technically, to most citizens. Internet access through public libraries, which appears to be increasingly common, may eventually make the Internet an appropriate vehicle for dissemination of report cards to the general public.

Another drawback of the Internet is that it may not be the right vehicle for the current generation of senior citizens, many of whom define a web site as a place where spiders hang out. For them, the solution may be printed information (in large type, and not too much of it) plus personal counseling to help resolve questions that arise. The availability of personal counseling is also important for disadvantaged citizens, including those with low levels of literacy (Hanes and Greenlick, 1996: 26). Indeed, as counseling can assist a wide variety of consumers, report card designers should consider ways to facilitate interaction between consumers and people able to help interpret report cards. For many groups of consumers, telephone numbers and addresses of counselors may be among the most important information provided by a report card.

Reaching an Elite Audience

In one respect, it is much easier for report card designers to reach an elite audience than it is for them to reach a mass audience. Elites are accustomed to processing large amounts of paper, including, in many instances, tables, charts, and technical reports. Thus traditional formats, relying heavily or exclusively on the printed word and on paper, may be perfectly satisfactory for policymakers and other elites.

On the other hand, policymakers are notoriously impatient with boring, pedantic, long-winded reports that do not cut to the chase quickly enough. Also, policymakers usually want reports that are clearly policy-relevant. Thus, when attempting to reach policymakers, report card designers may be tempted to interpret the data and offer recommendations. If such interpretation is perceived as over-interpretation, however, then the report card, though relevant, may lose credibility.

Enhanced Report Cards

Because policymakers are action-oriented, an enhanced report card, with an executive summary and policy recommendations, has a certain appeal. The executive summary highlights core ideas, frames issues and tells the policymaker whether the report card is interesting, plausible, and potentially useful (see Figure 5.2). The recommendations tell the policymaker whether the report card's designers are kindred spirits or ideological foes. Such a report card could facilitate what David Whiteman (1985) has called "strategic" utilization by policymakers.

On the other hand, one wonders whether report card designers have any business taking these additional steps. One of the virtues of a good report card is that it allows people to make up their own minds. An argumentative report card with a clear point of view might well be confused with a political tract. This could easily backfire, undermining rather than promoting utilization by policymakers. It could also sharply reduce cooperation by targeted organizations. An organization that anticipates a low rating or ranking may be nervous enough; an organization that fears outright criticism may, if it can, decline to participate in the project altogether.

Another type of enhanced report card is one that emphasizes econometric sophistication. While a mass audience usually lacks the capacity to understand model specification, estimating techniques, and statistical significance levels, an elite audience may welcome detailed explanations of such subjects. If the stakes are high (whether to fund a new program or approach, whether to devolve power to lower levels of government, whether to regulate or deregulate), then the need for such background information is particularly strong. The more explicit the methodological premises and techniques, the easier it will be for critics to analyze the report card, which is precisely as it should be. A report card based on faulty premises deserves to be skewered and discredited; a report card whose methods are beyond reproach deserves attention and respect.

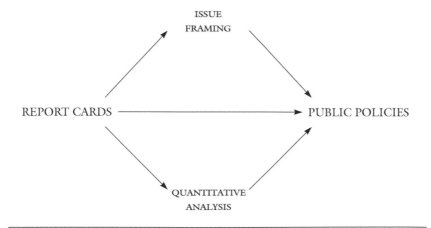

Figure 5.2 Reaching an elite audience

In recommending econometric sophistication for report cards aimed at elites, we are not also recommending density, redundancy, or opaqueness. Technical information can be presented clearly and crisply, and we have seen many examples of such presentations. Detailed information on estimating techniques can usually be relegated to an appendix. The operationalization of particular variables can be discussed briefly in the text, at greater length in footnotes or an appendix. Above all, tables and charts should tell a clear story and should not require a Ph.D. to interpret.

A tougher question to resolve is whether report cards aimed at elites should include an explicit ranking of organizations based on a single dimension. Such a ranking, as exemplified by public school report cards in South Carolina and Dallas, Texas (Clotfelter and Ladd 1996), can be extremely helpful to policymakers. It facilitates the use of tournaments, in which organizations whose performance exceeds expectations receive financial awards for the organization itself or its personnel. It also condenses information in a way that facilitates utilization.

On the other hand, a ranking may be unfair to organizations that do poorly in one or two areas but excel in one or two others. It may also serve policymakers poorly if it substitutes for multidimensional analysis rather than complements it. Policymakers, like consumers, need to know not just which organizations perform better than others but also in which areas they excel and in which areas they struggle.

Some organizations do not shrink from explicit rankings but make it clear that different organizations are bellwethers in different domains. For example, the Corporation for Enterprise Development (CFED), a nonprofit research group, assigns letter grades to state governments based on their economic development performance (CFED 1996). However, the CFED gives each state a different letter grade for economic performance, business vitality, development capacity, and subcategories within each broad category. This approach facilitates use because letter grades capture people's interest and attention (Clones 1997). At the same time, it reminds users (such as businesses thinking of relocating or expanding) that the best state for one aspect of economic development may not be the best state for another.

Report Cards as Agenda-Setters and Agenda-Sustainers

The content of report cards is undeniably important, for both elite and mass audiences. A report card whose validity is suspect will not command respect. A report card with an overly narrow focus will be off-target for many potential users. A report card laced with jargon and unexplained procedures will leave people bewildered and confused.

Nevertheless, it is also important to recognize that, especially for elite audiences, the fact that a report card has been issued is a significant event, regardless of the content of the report card. That is because a report card, as a regularized mechanism for appraising the state of an industry or a policy sector, has the capacity to rivet elite attention on a public problem, if only for a brief period of time. Whether this actually happens depends in large measure on the degree of mass media attention it attracts. Press coverage of an issue can influence elite agendas by shaping the public's agenda (McCombs and Shaw 1972; Cobb and Elder 1983; Kingdon 1984) or by sustaining the illusion that the public's agenda has been influenced (Protess et al. 1987). In either case, the very issuance of a report card places an issue on a particular institutional agenda or sustains interest in an issue that has already secured agenda status.

Are there some techniques that can help to magnify the agenda-setting or agenda-sustaining power of report cards? Certainly, one technique would be to release the report card at an opportune moment in the budget cycle. At the federal level, this might be during the late winter or early spring, when House Appropriations subcommittee hearings are in full bloom. Another technique would be to release the report card on almost any weekend, when journalists are scrambling to find newsworthy stories. A third technique would be to link the report card to an annual conference, thus guaranteeing an attentive audience of potential users. For example, a school report card could be released at an annual conference of teachers or principals; a hospital report card could be released at an annual conference of physicians or hospital administrators.

The bottom line is that the timing of a report card's release can make a big difference. As John Kingdon (1984) has argued, the confluence of a problem stream, a solution stream, and a political stream creates precious opportunities for policy entrepreneurship. A report card released at just the right time can influence public policy; a report card released at a time when political elites are preoccupied with other matters is unlikely to have much policy impact.

Value Trade-offs

In stressing audience characteristics, we have underscored the importance of relevance and comprehensibility. It is important to recall, however, that relevance and comprehensibility are not the only criteria for evaluating report cards. Validity and comprehensiveness are also of critical importance. In practice, trade-offs must be made between key values, such as validity, on the one hand, and comprehensibility, on the other. The former may call for more data and more technical sophistication, while the latter may call for less data and greater simplicity. The relative weight to be assigned to a given value when designing a report card will depend a great deal on the context. Although a precise recipe cannot be formulated in advance, two aspects of context are especially useful in identifying appropriate report card types for different occasions.

One important aspect of context is the complexity of creating valid and comprehensive measures for assessing organizational performance. This complexity has several sources. First, validly attributing measured outcomes to organizational performance poses difficult inferential problems when organizations serve client populations with very different characteristics—plausibly establishing the counterfactual of what would have happened to the clients without the services of the organization often requires complex statistical procedures. Second, providing a comprehensive measure of organizational performance is obviously more complex the greater the number of relevant attributes, or quality margins, of the services being provided. Producing an overall assessment requires either assigning weights to the various attributes to produce a summary scale of performance, or presenting scales for specific qualities with an evaluative framework for assessing them qualitatively. Third, selecting and interpreting proxies used for outcomes, or even outputs, when appropriate data are unavailable to measure them directly adds to complexity. Proxies must be related theoretically to outcomes, and their limitations taken into account.

Another important aspect of context is the interpretational ability of the audience through which the report card is intended to enhance accountability. Comprehensibility and relevance depend on the capacity of an audience for understanding and interpreting the information provided in report cards. One important factor in the interpretational capacity of the audience is the degree of interest that its members have in gaining the information. The stronger their interests, the more time and energy they will be willing to invest in interpretation. A second factor is the knowledge and skills that members of the audience have available to help them interpret information. The more intellectual resources they command, the greater the interpretational burden they will be able to bear.

Table 5.1 shows how these two important aspects of context combine to make different types of report card designs appropriate. If both the complexity of performance assessment and the interpretational capacity of the audience are low, then *popular report cards* that employ relatively simple measures, direct comparisons, and straightforward presentation are likely to be appropriate. If both the complexity of performance assessment and the interpretational capacity of the audience are high, then *technical report cards* that embody sophisticated performance assessments are likely to be appropriate. If the complexity of performance assessment is high, but the interpretational capacity of the audience is low, then *translated hybrid report cards* that combine some methodological simplification with careful translation of technical issues into terms more interesting and understandable to the audience are likely to be appropriate. If the complexity of performance assessment is low and the interpretational capacity of the audience is high, then *nuanced hybrid report cards* that provide nuanced presentational treatment of issues related to validity and comprehensiveness are likely to be appropriate.

To return to our earlier analogy, a sophisticated jazz audience may be able to appreciate a performance by the Art Ensemble of Chicago, despite its cryptic melody lines and discordant harmonies. In contrast, newcomers to jazz are likely to find the same music harsh and atonal. Music also differs in its technical demands on performers. The chord changes for "Giant Steps," for example, are more daunting than those for "Blue Moon." Booking agents and group leaders must take these considerations into account. At times, some translation may be required, as when Wynton Marsalis explains a difficult piece to a young audience. At other times, a sophisticated audience may benefit from a soulful rendition of a simple tune. With music, as with report cards, both the audience and the task have implications for content and presentation.

Table 5.1 Appropriate Report Card Types

Complexity of performance assessment	Interpretational capacity of audience	
	Low	High
Low	Popular	Hybrid: Nuanced
High	Hybrid: Translated	Technical

Strengthening the Evidence on Audience Impact

Research on the reception of report cards has, for the most part, relied upon self-assessments to determine impact. Focus group researchers ask respondents what type of information they would most like to know about health plans. Survey researchers ask respondents whether they used last year's survey results and, if so, how. While these research efforts are useful, they rely too heavily on a single research technique, and they focus almost exclusively on a mass audience. More research is needed that looks at actual behavior, that examines elite audiences, and that makes comparisons across audiences, across report cards, and over time.

A critical, but inconclusively answered, question in health care research is whether report cards (on hospitals, HMOs, or nursing homes) have any impact on market shares. In principle, health care organizations with good grades should see their market shares increase; those with bad grades should see their market shares decline. General research looking at the effect of quality on hospital choice (Luft et al. 1990) and market concentration on nursing home quality (Zinn 1994) has shown mixed results. An intriguing case study at American Express showed a sharp improvement in market share for a high-scoring HMO, a sharp decline for a low-scoring HMO, following the company's release of a report card (Strategic Consulting Services 1994: 3). A single case study might be anomalous, but more recent research suggests the potential for report cards to have an impact on market shares. For example, Dana Mukamel and Alvin Mushlin (1998) find that hospitals and surgeons with better reported outcomes in the New York State cardiac surgery report card have experienced growth in market shares, and Michael Chernew and Dennis Scanlon (1998) report that an index of the quality of medical care provided by health plans offered to employees of a large company had a statistically significant effect on their enrollment choices, though four other quality measures seemed to have no, or only a small, effect. A statistical analysis of the effect of the HCFA hospital report cards on hospital choice by Stephen Mennemeyer and his colleagues (1997) found a very small negative relationship between reported mortality rates and patient discharges (a caseload measure) that was swamped in magnitude by the effects of newspaper stories about single unexpected deaths.

The only direct assessment of the impact of outcome measures provided by report cards on patients' choices of physicians or hospitals suggests that inadequate dissemination has kept the report cards from reaching all patients who would potentially use them. In 1996 Eric C. Schneider and Arnold Epstein (1998) conducted surveys with 474 patients who had undergone CABG surgery in four Pennsylvania hospitals. They found that only 20 percent of respondents knew of the *Consumer Guide to Coronary Artery Bypass Graft (CABG) Surgery* and only 12 percent knew of it before surgery. Of those who knew of it before surgery, about 20 percent attributed to it a moderate or major impact on their choice of either hospital or physician. However, when the guide was described to respondents who had not heard of it, 56 percent said that they were either very or somewhat interested in seeing a copy. Further, 58 percent said that they would probably or definitely change surgeons if they found that their surgeon had a higher than expected mortality rate in the previous year (Schneider and Epstein 1998: 1638).

A related question is whether advertising that alludes to report cards has any impact on market shares. A recent television and radio marketing campaign by Kaiser Permanente in the Washington, D.C. area suggests that such effects are likely to be small. Of persons who recalled seeing or hearing Kaiser Permanente advertising late in 1996, only 3 percent remembered a reference to NCQA accreditation or a favorable rating by *U.S. News & World Report* (Market Research 1997: 9). On the other hand, 27 percent of all respondents did recall the advertising and Kaiser Permanente's overall market share did improve (Woods 1997). Clearly, additional research into this question is needed.

Although it is tempting to focus on the choices made by the ultimate consumers of health care or education services, it may be more prudent to focus initially on the choices made by those who will determine the menu of choices available to consumers. In the case of HMOs, that means shifting the unit of analysis from the employee to the employer. Every year employers decide whether particular health plans will be added to or deleted from their menu of employee options. According to the U.S. GAO (1996b: 5), sixty percent of large corporations consider accreditation status by the NCQA when deciding to purchase health insurance from an HMO. But what exactly does this mean? How do changes in accreditation status compare, for example, to changes in cost? Do employers distinguish between full accreditation and temporary accreditation or only between accreditation and no accreditation? And do large corporations pay greater attention to quality than small firms? An in-depth analysis of decisions made by companies within a large metropolitan area, served by a wide variety of health plans, could reveal whether a change in accreditation status has any impact on the health plan decisions that employers make, either instantly or a year or two later. If market shares are to change, then employers' health plan menu decisions must change first. Thus research that focuses on employers' choices could anticipate consumer changes yet to come.

Clearly, much research remains to be done. Despite the proliferation of report cards, we do not know whether consumers learn more from news accounts based on report cards, from advertisements that allude to report cards, or from report cards themselves. We do not know the optimal content or format of a report card aimed at consumers, as opposed to a report card aimed at public policymakers. We do not know the relative impact of quality-relevant information, as opposed to information that focuses on costs. And we do not know whether public policymakers learn more from report cards or from public policy analysis. Like report cards themselves, research on report cards is still in its embryonic stages.

Conclusion

Designing organizational report cards so that they effectively communicate useful information to their audiences poses difficult challenges. Effective communication with either consumers or policymakers requires designers to package report cards so that they will gain attention, understanding, and credibility, and thus have at least the potential for providing information that is relevant to decisions. Most report cards now appear as printed documents with targeted dissemination or reports in the print media. Their dissemination will almost certainly follow general trends toward greater use of electronic media, raising important issues of access. The extent to which report cards successfully reach their intended audiences of consumers and policymakers largely determines the influence that they will have with a third audience, the organizations themselves. It is to this topic that we turn next.

6

Organizational Responses

Although organizational report cards by intention and design aim most immediately at influencing those who consume, procure, or oversee the services produced by organizations, their ultimate targets are the organizations themselves. To the extent that report cards affect the choices of consumers, the decisions of budgetary sponsors, or the deference granted by political overseers, they inevitably affect the financial, reputational, and discretionary resources available to organizations. With varying degrees of foresight, organizational leaders will anticipate these effects. Also, with varying degrees of effectiveness, these leaders will attempt to respond in ways that advance the interests of their organizations. The nature of these responses largely determines report cards' long-run impacts, both those that are socially desirable and those that are socially undesirable.

Conceptual Basis for Anticipating Organizational Response

Informed decisions about the use of report cards thus require their designers to predict the organizational responses that they will elicit. The great variety of organizational forms and environments means that prediction must of necessity be contextual. Nevertheless, consideration of three general factors offers a useful starting point. First, what incentives do report cards create and how strong are they? Second, how flexible is the organization that is subject to the incentives? And third, how well do the incentives align with socially desirable goals?

Incentives Created by Report Cards: Leaders and Their External Environment

The leaders of organizations almost always care about the resources that are available to their organizations. The personal fortunes of managers of private firms generally depend on the profit that they reap for the firms' owners. The managers of nonprofit organizations must generate revenue to maintain or expand their operations, and success in doing so creates opportunities for career advancement. Although the effects of organizational resources on the personal interests of the heads of government bureaus funded through budget allocations can be quite complex (Downs 1967; Niskanen 1973, 1975; Dunleavy 1991), the weight of empirical evidence is consistent with the assumption that bureau chiefs generally prefer larger to smaller budgets (Blais and Dion 1991: 355–361). Consequently, the extent to which report cards can affect the flow of resources to organizations is likely to determine the strength of the incentives that they present to organizational leaders.

Reputation may affect the flow of resources to organizations by influencing consumer decisions or public funding. But leaders also care about the reputations of their organizations beyond these financial impacts. Aside from the intrinsic value most people place on being perceived as effective, organizational leaders stand to gain prestige and career mobility when their organizations are well regarded. Avoiding embarrassment is an important way to preserve reputation. Indeed, based on his study of federal bureau heads, Herbert Kaufman (1981: 26) argues that fear of being caught in embarrassing situations is one of the major motivations for intelligence gathering by organizational leaders.

Leaders care about the reputations of their organizations for managerial reasons as well as personal reasons. Organizational members typically have motivations similar to those of leaders. They may enjoy psychic, if not career, benefits from belonging to well-regarded organizations. Consequently, recruiting, retaining, and motivating members is likely to be easier for organizations that enjoy favorable reputations.

A favorable reputation among an organization's external audiences generally translates into greater discretion in the use of resources as well as reductions in the costs of its governance relationships. The managers of for-profit firms are likely to enjoy more discretion from owners when their firms' reputations are more favorable. Favorable reputations and avoidance of embarrassing situations reduce the chances of scrutiny by private and public consumer advocates, takeover bids by hostile management groups, and increased government regulation—activities that can place heavy demands on managerial attention and require the expenditure of substantial organizational resources. The managers of nonprofit organizations have similar concerns with respect to their boards of directors, donors, and regulators. Indeed, Steven Smith and Michael Lipsky (1993) argue that nonprofit organizations have become too attentive to the concerns of government officials in particular. The heads of government bureaus typically face oversight from legislative committees and central budget agencies. A favorable reputation may earn the bureau leeway in hiring, the use of its budget, and policy initiatives (Sapolsky 1972). An unfavorable reputation, especially one arising from sensational events that trigger "fire alarms" (McCubbins and Schwartz 1984), invites scrutiny that almost always demands costly responses and may sometimes result in substantial losses of discretion over organizational inputs and processes (Weimer 1983).

In summary, organizational report cards can potentially influence leaders by affecting two things that they value. First, report cards can have a direct impact on the flow of resources to organizations by informing consumer choice. Second, they can influence organizations' governance relations (the interactions between organizations and those external groups, such as owners, regulators, or budgetary sponsors, to whom organizational leaders are legally accountable), by contributing to organizational reputations. The governance relations may affect both the flow of resources and discretion over their use. The salience of these avenues of influence for any particular organization depends on the competition the organization faces in its product market and the particular nature of its governance relations (Vining and Weimer 1990).

Other things being equal, the more organizations rely on the competitive sale of products or services as sources of revenue, the greater the potential for report cards to affect organizations through the informing of consumer choice. At one extreme, consider organizations that must compete for customers. Information that makes them relatively more attractive can attract customers; information that makes them relatively less attractive can drive them away. Because these changes affect the accrual of revenue, organizational leaders are likely to be very sensitive to report cards. Sensitivity is likely to be heightened when buyers of the products or services have monopsony power—losing a few individual subscribers may be irritating to an HMO; losing all the employees of a major employer may be devastating.

At the other extreme are organizations that enjoy monopoly positions in their markets: information about their products or services will have little potential for changing the number of customers or their revenue flows. For example, local police departments face no competition for their supply of publicly provided law enforcement. A similar, but less extreme, case is publicly funded primary and secondary education, which is currently supplied in most locales by school districts that have local monopolies. Public school districts do face competition from other districts in their metropolitan areas, but the costs of residential relocation mute it. Parents willing to forgo public funding can switch to the private sector market. Although there is some evidence that private school competition favorably affects public school performance (Hoxby 1994; Gormley 1995: 135–140), it is currently limited by the monopoly position of public school districts. The facilitation of greater competition in the supply of publicly funded schooling through educational vouchers or charter schools, however, would greatly increase the potential impact of school report cards by tying consumer preferences more closely to organizational resources.

More tentative generalizations based on the nature of organizational governance relations, which are typically multiple and complex, suggest themselves. For example, managers of private firms serve at the pleasure of owners, but they also often conduct business subject to restrictions imposed by regulatory agencies. The heads of school districts typically serve at the pleasure of elected school boards, but their actions are regulated by state agencies. Bureau heads are embedded in governance relations with other executive agencies, legislative committees, and, increasingly, individual legislators (Gormley 1989). Nevertheless, the relevance of the governance relationship to organizational resources offers a basis for prediction.

The greater the dependence of organizational resources on the governance relation, the greater the potential strength of report cards for motivating organizational leaders. The strongest incentives probably arise in situations in which organizations must maintain certification to either participate in particular markets or receive payments from the government or other third parties. For example, hospital administrators are likely to be very attentive to any threats to limit their delivery of financially lucrative services or receive payments from Medicaid, Medicare, or private health insurers. Reliance on government for direct grants is also likely to create strong incentives if the threat of either their elimination or reduction is credible. For example, state aid to school districts does not generally depend on the governance relations between individual school districts and the state—formula budgeting usually prevails. Tournaments tied to report cards, such as the one among South Carolina schools, can be interpreted as efforts to introduce a clearer link between performance and funding in the governance of schools. Of course, the willingness of school boards to allocate budget increases and voters to approve bond issues is likely to be influenced by information provided in report cards.

Organizational Flexibility: Leaders and Their Internal Tasks

Whatever the strength of the incentives to organizational leaders induced by report cards, their ultimate effects will depend largely on the capabilities of the leaders to change organizational behaviors. Both the formal structure and the beliefs, norms, and habits that comprise organizational culture are relevant to predicting the ways that the incentives given to organizational leaders will translate into changes in behavior. So too will the presence of various professionals who form organizational sub-cultures whose norms may lead them to respond directly to the information conveyed in report cards as well as indirectly through their responses to the initiatives of organizational leaders.

The effective application of rewards and punishments within organizations requires effective monitoring. Organizations vary in the ease with which leaders can monitor the behavior of organizational members. The delivery of social services, for example, generally places considerable discretion in the hands of lower-level organizational members, or operatives, who deal directly with "clients," and the patterns of their individual decisions largely determine organizational performance (Lipsky 1980). Some aspects of performance may be more easily monitored than others because of asymmetries in hierarchical decision-making processes. For instance, overly lenient plea bargain offers made by assistant prosecutors are likely to be accepted by defendants and therefore not subject to further routine review by other prosecutors, whereas overly harsh plea bargain offers are likely to be rejected and therefore reconsidered as cases move to subsequent stages in the disposition process (Weimer 1980).

The cost of monitoring is likely to increase as levels of hierarchy increase (Light 1995). For example, it will generally be more difficult for the administrator of a hospital to monitor the practices of cardiac surgeons, along with all the other units in the hospital, than it will be for the head of the cardiac surgery unit. Report cards targeted at lower-level managers in deep hierarchies have greater potential for eliciting behavioral changes than report cards targeted at their superiors because the managers are likely to be better able to monitor operatives than superiors who are farther removed from day-to-day operations. More generally, the closer the target of the report card is to operatives organizationally, the more likely that monitoring will support the effective use of formal rewards and punishments.

The cost of monitoring also depends on the difficulty of assessing individual contributions to outputs. Some actions of operators cannot be directly observed and therefore their measurement requires the expenditure of resources. Outputs may be the result of various actions taken by multiple operators and therefore difficult to link to the actions of individuals. These are the problems of hidden action and team production that are central questions addressed in principal-agent models of hierarchy. (For overviews, see Holmstrom and Tirole 1989; Sappington 1991; and Banks 1995.) These problems make impractical the creation of formal rewards and penalties (contracts in the principal-agent literature) to induce operators (agents) to act as if they were single-mindedly pursuing the interests of their managers (principals).

The discretion that organizational leaders have over formal rewards and punishments also varies greatly, but it is generally much greater for the managers of private firms than the heads of government bureaus. Bureaus tend to produce outputs that are more difficult to measure and value than private firms—bureaus often produce public goods that are not traded in markets or deliver services at administratively set prices. Whereas the owners of firms can usually value managerial performance by looking at their profitability compared to the profitability of other firms in the industry, the overseers of bureaus rarely have such direct measures. The greater ease of evaluating performance allows the owners of firms to rely on mechanisms of ex post control, such as profit-sharing arrangements, rather than mechanisms of ex ante control, such as specifications of particular inputs and processes (Thompson and Jones 1986). In contrast, the overseers of bureaus typically place constraints on bureaucrats through ex ante controls such as line-item budgeting, personnel ceilings, and procedural rules to limit discretion and facilitate detection of the deviations from overseers' preferences that do occur (Johnson and Libecap 1989). Consequently, private managers generally have greater opportunity to use formal incentives to coax a response to report cards than do their public sector counterparts.

Whether or not organizational leaders face sufficiently low monitoring costs and enjoy adequate discretion to use formal rewards and punishments to motivate behavior in response to report cards, they are likely to find that the norms and habits that comprise organizational culture play an important role in determining the overall organizational response. Organizational culture comprises the common beliefs, norms, and habits of organizational members. The importance of organizational culture goes back at least to Chester Bernard, who wrote about the "moral element" in his 1938 book, *The Functions of the Executive*. Subsequent writers on bureaucracy have repeatedly noted the importance of mission, "a culture that is widely shared and warmly endorsed by operators and managers alike" (Wilson 1989: 95), to understanding organizational performance (Rainey 1996). In recent years, the importance of achieving an effective corporate culture has become a standard message in the popular literature on business management.

Psychological theories of cognition and motivation provide one conceptual basis for understanding the role of mission in organizations (Weiss 1996). Missions serve as "knowledge structures" that "shape the ways people perceive, understand, and remember raw data; they permit people to construct meaning out of information" (Weiss 1996: 123). They provide a basis for individuals to interpret incentives as rewards and punishments, influence the extent to which individuals place value on rewards to other members of the collectives to which they belong, and help determine the nature of intrinsic motivations (Weiss 1996: 127–133). Eliciting changes in routines and behaviors that go against the prevailing mission of an organization poses great difficulties for leaders.

At the same time, however, externally imposed requirements for the collection of data may themselves be a resource for changing organizational missions (Weiss and Gruber 1984; Innes 1988; Levitt and March 1988). For example, Janet Weiss and Judith Gruber (1984) found that the annual survey of school districts conducted by the federal Office of Civil Rights to gather information on discrimination issues had several apparent effects on the districts beyond their perceived threat as a basis for legal action. The survey, especially in its early years, apparently affected the ways personnel in school districts framed their thinking about issues of race and sex, which in turn helped alter school missions and the way teachers and administrators viewed their jobs. Further, because the reports of survey results are public documents, they aided external groups that wished to alter school district policy.

Another conceptual basis for the notion of mission is the rational choice theory of institutions, which seeks to understand norms, conventions, and habits in terms of the self-interested behavior of individuals engaged in repeated social interactions (Kreps 1990; Miller 1992; Calvert 1995). Some social situations can be characterized abstractly as games in which the equilibrium strategies of the players, if the game is to be played only once, yield outcomes that are Pareto inferior to other possible outcomes that are not equilibria. If the game is repeated indefinitely, however, then there are likely to be equilibria involving strategies based on players' actions in previous rounds that yield outcomes that are Pareto superior to the equilibrium outcomes in single-play. For example, not cooperating is the equilibrium strategy in single play of the well-known Prisoners' Dilemma. When the game is repeated with an indefinite stopping time, however, then strategies like "tit-for-tat," which require one to cooperate in the first round and then cooperate only if the other player cooperated in the previous round, can result in continued cooperation as the outcome (Axelrod 1984). Repeated games, however, generally have many possible equilibrium strategies (Fudenberg and Maskin 1986). This raises a problem of coordination: How will the players know which strategies to choose so as to achieve one of the more desirable equilibria? Organizational culture, or indeed leadership, can be thought of within this framework as providing focal points that help organizational members coordinate their strategies in particular ways.

Report cards could very well be a resource for leaders in their efforts to provide focal points for coordinating strategies. The leaders, however, must be able to link the information in the report cards to specific equilibria that would be preferable to the status quo, identify the strategies that the members must follow to achieve one of the desired equilibria, and find a way to induce them to adopt the strategies. For example, the reputation of an organization for customer service requires employees routinely to make extra efforts to solve problems that arise. As the extra effort is costly to the individual, however, few will be willing to make it if they think that others will not, and overall customer service will be poor. On the other hand, if members routinely contribute, then individuals will be reluctant to withhold extra effort out of fear of being viewed, and treated, as shirkers, and consequently good customer service will be an organizational norm. Persuading organizational members to move from the "never extra effort" equilibrium to the "always extra effort" equilibrium might be aided by a report card demonstrating that competitors have achieved higher levels of customer satisfaction.

Different organizational forms may be conducive to different types of missions. Consider especially nonprofit organizations, whose legal restrictions on the distribution of financial residuals to managers may make them more "trustworthy" than for-profit firms in situations in which consumers are uninformed, and whose capacity for targeting services may allow them to serve heterogeneous demands better than government bureaus that must offer equality of access (Weisbrod 1988). The nondistribution restriction of not-for-profits may attract managers and employees with somewhat different motivations than those who select for-profit firms. To the extent that this is the case, nonprofits may be better able to create and maintain missions that support the quality of organizational outputs. For example, with respect to day care, analysis of national data suggests that nonprofit centers have better educated staff, greater staff to child ratios, and lower teacher turnover rates (all proxies for the quality of care) than do for-profit centers; explicit comparisons of detected problems and substantiated complaints in Vermont also give nonprofits a quality edge (Gormley 1995: 68–75). To the extent that nonprofits are indeed more likely to have missions that promote direct concern about quality of service than for-profits, their members are more likely to be responsive to efforts by leaders to improve service quality in response to report cards.

The overall mission of an organization may be affected by the presence of members, such as doctors, lawyers, and engineers, who bring with them professional norms and allegiances (Kaufman 1960; Katzmann 1980; Wilson 1980). Their responses to the initiatives of leaders, or to the signals given by the report cards themselves, are likely to depend on how consistent these organizational pressures are with their professional cultures. Indeed, one strategy for advancing self-regulation within organizations is to impose decision processes that empower members of particular professions whose norms are likely to lead them to make more socially desirable decisions than other members of the organizations (Bardach and Kagan 1982: 226–232). For example, an industrial hygienist may be more willing to stop a production process that poses a potential risk to workers than would a production manager.

Professional norms may mute or reinforce responses to financial incentives provided through tournaments that involve competition among groups of organizations. For example, in response to jail overcrowding in the mid-1980s, the New York City Office of Management and Budget created a tournament among the district attorney's offices in four boroughs that rewarded the offices in proportion to their reductions in the number of old pending felony cases and the number of long-term pre-trial detainees. Analysts' fears that assistant district attorneys might sacrifice other objectives relevant to quality prosecution to increase their offices' share of the tournament prizes were not realized, most likely because of the high level of professionalism within these offices (Church and Heumann 1989). One could easily imagine this same professionalism reinforcing incentives tied to conviction rates or some other dimension of performance valued intrinsically by lawyers.

Professionals may be especially sensitive to report cards that affect their reputations among their peers. Professors at research universities, for instance, seem to pay close attention to the rankings of graduate programs prepared by the National Research Council—political scientists even publish articles in their professional newsletter that statistically adjust the National Research Council rankings to take account of faculty size, the university's general reputation, and other factors that change relative rankings (Katz and Eagles 1996; Lowery and Silver 1996; Miller, Tien, and Peebler 1996). Such reactions might result even if the rankings have no noticeable impact on the resources flowing to the organization or even in the absence of intervention by organizational leaders.

Finally, professional norms may limit the extent to which organizations manipulate data to improve the appearance of performance. It is only natural that organizations attempt to put the best face on their performance. Members of professions that value the integrity of data may refuse to participate in deceitful manipulations, perhaps blowing the whistle on gross distortions. The existence of such norms may be a resource for report card designers in their efforts to create systems for the reporting of reliable data.

Alignment of Incentives with Social Goals

The incentives of leaders and their capacity to change behaviors within their organizations speak to the likely magnitude of the effects of report cards. The desirability of these effects, however, depends on the extent to which the incentives induced by report cards push organizations toward the achievement of social goals. What is reported and how it is received by the organization's relevant audiences determine the direction of the incentives perceived by the organizational leader.

Ideally, a report card validly measures every relevant dimension of organizational performance and the audiences of the report card effectively use these measures to inform their decisions. Practically, however, report cards are likely to fall short of the ideal in two ways.

First, report cards rarely measure all the relevant dimensions of organizational outcomes, and the dimensions that are covered rarely have perfect validity. Services such as day care, schooling, and hospital care have many margins of quality that cannot easily be captured in quantitative measures. Inevitably, even when report cards provide multiple indicators of quality, some of these margins are neglected. Validity problems arise when inputs, processes, or outputs serve as proxies for outcomes.

Sociologists have long been concerned with the organizationally dysfunctional behavior that arises when attention to imperfect proxies displaces attention to unmeasured organizational outcomes. Robert Merton (1957: 199) called this problem "goal displacement." A particularly interesting illustration of goal displacement is the use of clearance rates, the fraction of crimes for which the police have identified a suspect, to measure the effectiveness of police investigators. In one police department studied by Jerome Skolnick (1966: 174–179), police officers would often exchange "reduction of counts, concealment of actual criminality, and freedom from further investigation of prior offenses" (175) in return for admissions of offenses that would clear cases and improve the officers' clearance rates. A reversal of the "hierarchy of punishment" inconsistent with organizational goals often resulted: suspects who had committed more crimes received lighter sentences. Peter Blau (1972: 56) describes how evaluations of employment office personnel based on counts of interviews accelerated their pace of work but also led them to dismiss many clients without finding them jobs; additional dimensions of evaluation were eventually added to reduce the strength of the incentive for this dysfunctional behavior.

Of course, central planners who attempt to use simple formulas to reward output face goal displacement problems on a routine basis. Stories told by former Soviet factory managers illustrate responses to imperfect reward structures. For example, at one time men's small shoes were rewarded more highly than boys' large shoes even though they require the same quantities of various inputs; not surprisingly, an overabundance of the former and a shortage of the latter resulted (Berliner 1957: 121).

More recently and closer to home, U.S. Senate committee hearings revealed dysfunctional behavior by Internal Revenue Service (IRS) officials in regional offices, who authorized a reign of terror against innocent taxpayers. Instead of focusing on desired outcomes, such as the fair treatment of both law-abiding and cheating taxpayers, many IRS officials focused on easily measured outputs, such as liens, levies, and seizures (Hirsh 1997). They did so because they were rewarded for sanctions imposed, without regard to whether the sanctions were justified. A classic example of goal displacement, these practices, once revealed, led to apologies and reforms (Crenshaw 1997).

Second, report card audiences pay varying degrees of attention to the measures that are provided. Some indicators will be more salient to audiences than others. To the extent that salience reflects informed preferences, this variability helps send appropriate signals to organizations. To the extent that salience reflects perceptual differences, however, it may confuse the signals sent to organizations. For example, even amidst multiple indicators, summary rankings and ratings, which necessarily reduce multiple dimensions into a unidimensional scale, are likely to attract relatively more attention than measures that require more active comparisons by report card users.

Functional and Dysfunctional Responses

Our overview of organizational incentives, both external and internal, provides a very general framework for thinking about responses to report cards. A catalog of possible generic responses to report cards provides a complementary framework that can perhaps be helpful at a more practical level (see Figure 6.1). In particular, it focuses attention on the types of functional and dysfunctional responses that may occur.

In this context, we consider organizational responses functional if they increase the social value of organizational outcomes; they are dysfunctional if they decrease the social value of organizational outcomes. Functional responses typically increase the quantities of valued outputs, emphasize dimensions of valued outputs that were previously neglected, or reduce the levels of inputs required to produce levels of outputs. Dysfunctional responses may promote some of these responses while undermining others so that the net overall effect is negative. They may also involve the diversion of resources to activities that improve report card measures without improving the outcomes that they are supposed to promote.

Functional Responses

Four generic categories of responses are likely to be functional: improvement in organizational processes, reallocation of inputs to more valuable uses, focusing managerial attention on key issues, and enhancement of organizational mission.

PROCESS IMPROVEMENT Organizations use a variety of processes to convert inputs to outputs. The desire to improve performance on some report card measure may induce organizations to evaluate, and perhaps change, the processes that they are using. One possible source of such innovation is the observation and adoption of the processes used in similar, but apparently more successful, organizations. For example, surgeons may closely observe the procedures used in units at other hospitals that appear to have substantially lower mortality rates. Another source of innovation is the reassessment of currently used processes that may have become inappropriate because of changing inputs (such as clientele charac-

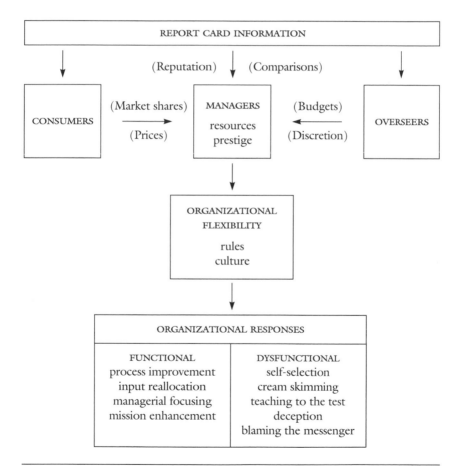

Figure 6.1 Organizational responses to report cards

teristics) or obsolete because of changing technology (such as improvements in computer hardware and software). The reassessments prompted by report cards may be largely internal, or they may involve consultants, vendors, or various sorts of advisory committees.

INPUT REALLOCATION   Organizations allocate inputs across a range of processes to produce some mix of outputs. If the clients or overseers of an organization respond to a report card in a way that suggests that they place a higher marginal value on one output than another, then the organization may shift inputs so as to produce relatively more of the former and less of the latter. For example, public attention to student attendance rates might lead a school to shift administrative resources from some other activity to calling parents whose children are absent to ascertain the reasons for absence. As long as the social value of the forgone activities is less than the social value of the resulting increase in attendance rates, the input change increases the overall social value of schooling.

MANAGERIAL FOCUSING   The time, energy, and attention of organizational leaders are scarce resources. Report cards may provide information that helps them to focus on areas where their involvement can improve organizational performance. Especially in large organizations, problems of coordination among units may prevent them from effectively using available resources. Sometimes focusing the attention of the managers of relevant units on the problems may enable them to work out more effective arrangements for coordination; at other times authoritative decisions may be necessary to resolve impasses. In any event, by simply showing special interest in some aspect of organizational activity, the leader may encourage others to think about it and perhaps find ways of making better use of available resources.

MISSION ENHANCEMENT   Whether one views either psychological theories of cognition and motivation or the rational choice perspectives as the conceptual basis for understanding organizational mission, report cards are a potential resource for leaders seeking to influence the norms, beliefs, and habits of organizational members. Unfavorable comparisons with other organizations in some dimension of organizational performance, for example, may give leaders a focal point for bringing about changes in behavior, such as showing greater courtesy to customers, that might be difficult to achieve through formal systems of rewards and punishments. A signal from outside the organization that a problem exists may be useful in changing beliefs; the leader's attention to the signal may help convince members that their individual efforts will be matched by others so that a change in organizational performance will actually occur. Teachers who believe that efforts they make to improve classroom discipline will be reinforced by the similar efforts of their colleagues and supervisors, for instance, are more likely to be willing to make the efforts.

Dysfunctional Responses

Five generic categories of responses are likely to be dysfunctional: self-selection, cream skimming, teaching to the test, deception, and blaming the messenger.

SELF-SELECTION   Participation in report card projects is sometimes voluntary. Under such circumstances, some organizations will decline to participate. In particular, organizations that expect to do badly in the report card will seek to avoid participation that may sully their reputation. In contrast, organizations that expect to do well are more likely to participate. This phenomenon, a sort of "self-selection," has two consequences: first, the sample of participating organizations is skewed in a positive direction, thus sending false signals about the performance of the industry as a whole; and second, the sample of participating organizations is smaller than it might otherwise be, thus limiting its utility to consumers.

CREAM SKIMMING   Every organization recognizes that the selection of cases or clients (inputs) will affect the organization's success rate (outcomes). For this reason, report cards have the potential to encourage or reward "cream skimming" or "cherry picking," the selection of clients who are already more successful or who are more capable than other clients of rapid improvement. Under such circumstances, organizations can boost their success rate artificially by abandoning "hard" cases and by welcoming "easy" cases. For example, hospitals can admit patients who are not extremely sick, and job training programs can enroll persons who have already been gainfully employed. This is profoundly disturbing in connection with the delivery of social services, because society generally expects publicly supported social service organizations to tackle the hardest cases.

TEACHING TO THE TEST If a savvy organization recognizes the connection between inputs and the perception of success, then it also appreciates the even closer connection between outputs and its report card rating. It may pay so much attention to elements of the report card rating that it loses sight of the broader goals the report card is supposed to promote. This phenomenon, the most direct form of goal displacement, is sometimes called "teaching to the test" because it has been observed in public schools where teachers often drill their students on narrow segments of the curriculum covered by standardized tests in order to improve their scores. Teaching to the test may result in students with higher reading scores who lack creativity, students with higher mathematics scores who can answer the kinds of algebra questions that appear on tests but who are baffled by other kinds of questions, or students with good grammar who have nothing substantive to say. If so, we would say that report cards have "succeeded" with a vengeance. A school or a hospital whose quality appears to have improved but whose actual quality has declined has won a pyrrhic victory. And consumers have not won at all.

DECEPTION A fourth response problem that raises serious questions about report cards is deception. Organizations that face budget cutbacks, lower enrollments of clients, or lower profits if they score poorly on report cards will be tempted to break the rules of appropriate behavior in order to stave off such consequences. Deception may occur, ranging from practices of questionable propriety to practices that are clearly unethical. This phenomenon has been detected in higher education report cards, such as those published by *U.S. News & World Report*. Although the magazine's indicators are fairly straightforward, they allow universities some "wiggle room" in calculating scholastic achievement scores for the student body. Through various artful devices, some universities have managed to reduce the impact of students who are poor test-takers, such as foreign students. For example, Boston University has included in its SAT averages the math scores but not the verbal scores of foreign students, who usually do well in math but poorly in English (Stecklow 1995: B1). This practice results in report cards that are misleading because some universities are being evaluated based on their entire student body while other universities are not. A similar problem exists in elementary and secondary education, where anxious teachers and principals have sometimes encouraged children with learning disabilities to stay at home on days when standardized tests are administered (Kantrowitz and Springen 1997).

BLAMING THE MESSENGER When Lyndon Johnson was president, aides would quaver at the prospect of delivering bad news, because they knew that this would unleash a presidential tirade with repercussions ranging from abuse to dismissal (Reedy 1970). This phenomenon, known as "blaming the messenger," was not unique to President Johnson. Many people, including all too often organizational leaders, lash out at the most proximate source of their distress, whether that source is responsible or not (Tompkins 1993: 163). Blaming the messenger is dysfunctional to the extent that it diverts managerial attention and organizational resources away from solving the basic problems underlying aggravating messages. The cost of the diversion may extend beyond the organization itself if it stops or substantially undercuts the validity of a generally desirable report card. As politicians often defer to experts on technical issues, lack of consensus among experts may be sufficient to delay or stop a policy (Jenkins-Smith and Weimer 1985). In the case of report cards with sophisticated risk-adjustment procedures, methodological challenges by poorly performing organizations may sufficiently undercut political support for the report card and thereby delay its implementation by forcing its redesign.

Report Cards in Practice

Because report cards are in their infancy in most fields, sophisticated studies of their organizational impacts are limited in number. Nevertheless, there is now some scattered evidence on organizational responses to report cards. In the cases considered below, we examine evidence ranging from impact evaluations to interviews with informed observers.

Hospitals and Physicians

New York is one of a handful of states with a well-developed hospital outcome and physician report card. As discussed in Chapter 4, the New York State Cardiac Surgery Reporting System focuses on coronary artery bypass graft (CABG) surgery. Apparent declines in the mortality rate since the report card was introduced suggest that it has had the intended effect of improving the performance of CABG surgeons. Those skeptical of this interpretation, however, point to a variety of behaviors that could either produce an apparent decline when none in fact has occurred or lead to undesirable consequences.

Evidence of the success of the report card comes from the first four years of its use. The initial report card, which compared hospitals only and was released in 1990, covered the first half of 1989. Following a successful suit initiated by *Newsday* under the Freedom of Information Act, the New York State Department of Health began making surgeon-specific mortality rates available to the public in 1991 covering the years 1989 and 1990. An assessment of the impact of the report card takes 1989, the year prior to the first public report, as providing the pre-report card mortality rate and subsequent years as providing post-report card mortality rates. Changes in the mortality rate after 1989 are interpreted as effects of the report card.

This approach has been followed by Edward L. Hannan and colleagues (Hannan, Kilburn, Racz, Shields, and Chassin 1994). They report steady declines in actual mortality rates: 3.52 percent, 3.14 percent, 3.08 percent, and 2.78 percent, for 1989, 1990, 1991, and 1992, respectively. Using a consistent risk adjustment procedure for the four-year period, they found that risk-adjusted mortality rates declined even more dramatically: 4.17 percent, 3.28 percent, 3.03 percent, and 2.45 percent, for 1989, 1990, 1991, and 1992, respectively. Thus, over the four-year period actual mortality rates declined by 21 percent and risk-adjusted mortality rates declined by 41 percent.

Subsequent analysis of data for this period suggests that the declines represent more than either a shift in caseloads from higher-risk/low-volume surgeons to lower-risk/high-volume surgeons or a weeding out of the highest risk surgeons. Though the percentage of patients whose surgeons performed fewer than 50 operations per year declined by 25 percent from 7.6 percent in 1989 to 5.7 percent in 1992, actual and risk-adjusted declines occurred across volume categories (Hannan, Siu, Kumar, Kilburn, and Chassin 1995). Reductions also occurred across groups classified as having high, low, and medium risk-adjusted mortality rates in 1989 (Hannan, Kumar, Racz, Siu, and Chassin 1994).

Some of the initial declines in the risk-adjusted mortality rate probably resulted from more comprehensive collection of data on risk factors. Once surgeons became aware of the risk adjustment procedures, they had an incentive to claim inappropriately factors that contribute to higher risk. Although data for the report card are audited by the Department of Health, there may still remain opportunities for manipulating the risk data. Indeed, fairly large increases in the prevalence of several important risk factors occurred between 1989 and 1990 that could have been due to the release of the first report card. The reported prevalence of congestive heart failure increased from 1.7 percent to 2.9 percent; chronic obstructive pulmonary disease from 6.9 percent to 12.4 percent; unstable angina from 14.9 percent to 21.1 percent; and low ejection fraction from 18.9 percent to 23.1 percent (Green and Wintfeld 1995: 1231). Though these increases were almost certainly induced by the report card, it is not clear how much of the change simply represented more comprehensive reporting. Coupled with definitional changes in renal failure in 1991 that resulted in its prevalence increasing from 0.5 percent in 1990 to 2.8 percent in 1991, the report card induced increases in reported risk factors increased the expected mortality rate for the state from 2.7 percent to 3.7 percent from 1989 to 1991 (Green and Wintfeld 1995: 1231). Consequently, some of the reported reductions in risk-adjusted mortality rates may be due to changes in reporting behavior rather than real reductions in mortality risk.

Critics of the New York State CABG surgery report card have challenged claims of its impact on mortality rates because, without comparable data for states that did not institute report cards, one cannot rule out the possibility that the New York data simply reflect a national trend. Indeed, there is some evidence of declines in the late 1980s in both actual and risk-adjusted mortality rates for elderly CABG surgery patients (Green and Wintfeld 1995: 1231), and a recent study of risk-adjusted mortality rates in Massachusetts, which does not have a CABG report card, reports declines comparable to those for New York between 1990 and 1994 (Ghali, Ash, Hall, and Moskowitz 1997).

Eric Peterson and colleagues (1997) provide the most direct test and the clearest evidence concerning the impact of the CABG surgery report card on mortality rates. They used national Medicare data to investigate the observed and risk-adjusted mortality rates for patients 65 years or older for the period 1987 through 1992. Over this period, which spans the introduction of the report card, the observed mortality rate for New York declined by 33 percent as compared to 19 percent for the rest of the United States. Over the period from 1989 to 1992, the first four years in which hospitals collected clinical data for the report card, the observed mortality rate for New York declined by 22 percent as compared to 9 percent for the rest of the United States. Risk adjusting for age, race, sex, acute myocardial infarction (AMI) at admission, and a comorbidity index, the authors estimated that over the period 1987 through 1992, the average yearly risk-adjusted mortality rate fell 10.5 percent per year for New York as compared to 5.8 percent per year in the rest of the country, with the declines over the 1989 through 1992 period the steepest in New

York. In all of these comparisons, declines in mortality rates were statistically significantly larger in New York than in the rest of the country. Only Northern New England (Maine, New Hampshire, and Vermont), where hospitals began receiving comparative mortality data and assistance through the Northern New England Cardiovascular Study Group in 1990 (O'Connor et al. 1996), showed larger average annual declines over the study period. It is interesting to note that Pennsylvania, which like New York introduced a public cardiac surgery report card during this period, also showed statistically significant improvements relative to the rest of the country. Massachusetts showed declines, but they were statistically significantly smaller than those for New York.

Peterson and colleagues also addressed claims that New York mortality reductions were due in part to cream skimming, with very sick patients being denied surgery or sent out of state. The likelihood that the riskiest elderly New York patients, those admitted with AMI, would receive CABG surgery increased over the study period. Further, over the study period there was a statistically significant decline in the fraction of New York residents receiving their surgery in other states. These findings suggest that cream skimming has not been a major contributor to mortality declines in New York.

The findings of Peterson and colleagues are fully consistent with the New York State CABG surgery report card having contributed to declines in mortality. The major caution against viewing these findings as conclusive proof of efficacy is the possibility that both the introduction of the report card and declining mortality are simultaneously caused by some other factor. The faster rate of decline after the introduction of the report card is somewhat reassuring, but, as is often the case in evaluating system-wide policy interventions, it does not completely rule out the possibility of other explanations.

How might the report card be contributing to mortality declines? The cases of Strong Memorial Hospital in Rochester and St. Peter's Hospital in Albany suggest that they induce hospitals to take a fresh look at their procedures.

Report cards from 1991 through 1996 showed Strong Memorial Hospital to have an above-average risk-adjusted mortality rate. In commenting on the below average rate reported in 1997, the chief of cardiac surgery said, "This is the culmination of three years of hard work involving everyone at this institution who deals with cardiac patients" (Smith 1997: A1). The changes included the hiring of new cardiac surgeons and a complete reorganization of the heart surgery program advised by a visiting team of nationally prominent heart surgeons.

After their initial rage at being ranked third-worst among the 31 hospitals in New York state that perform CABG surgery, the cardiac surgeons at St. Peter's began a systematic investigation of their procedures (Montague 1996). They found that they did comparatively well with low-risk patients, but that they had a very poor comparative record with respect to high-risk emergency cases. Reviewing their procedures for these high-risk cases, they discovered that they used intra-aortic balloons to stabilize weak hearts only 20 percent of the time. Increasing the rate of use to 85 percent, the approximate rate of use for such cases in the state overall, and altering protocols for intravenous drug use and heart numbing procedures, led to a dramatic decline in mortality for their high-risk patients. In 1993, they had no mortalities for their 36 high-risk grafts as compared to a 30 percent mortality rate for the 42 high-risk grafts they performed in 1991 and 1992 (Montague 1996: 35).

The response of St. Peter's cardiac surgeons illustrates the sort of behavior that organizational report cards are intended to induce. An organization ranked poorly on some important performance dimension: (1) identifies the source of its poor ranking, (2) reviews its own procedures, (3) compares them to those of better performing organizations, (4) identifies apparently more effective procedures, and (5) adopts and implements them. To the extent that the reductions in mortality rates are due to such procedural improvements, the report card must be considered effective.

St. Peter's Hospital is not the only hospital that seems to have learned some valuable lessons as a result of negative publicity from report cards. Following the release of a report card on California hospitals in 1993 by the state Office of Statewide Health Planning and Development (OSHPD), a large hospital system, encompassing 15 hospitals, decided to investigate further. The system's first response was that the data must be flawed—a common reaction among hospitals. Upon further investigation, however, administrators discovered that not all of their physicians were using widely accepted World Health Organization criteria for determining whether an AMI or heart attack had taken place. As a result, some patients with gastro-intestinal problems were incorrectly being classified as having cardiovascular problems. This discovery led to improvements in record keeping and diagnostic practices. Without the report card, it is doubtful that this hospital system would have moved so quickly to rectify its problems (Zach 1996).

Other California hospitals have also taken the OSHPD report card seriously, though quality of care has not necessarily improved as a result. For example, the Placentia Linda Hospital, which received a negative rating in 1996, noticed significant discrepancies between its measures of good patient care and OSHPD's measures of the same phenomenon. To heighten their sensitivity to OSHPD's variables, and improve their subsequent report card rating, the Placentia Linda Hospital highlighted and prioritized OSHPD's variables (Rivers 1996). This is a classic example of "teaching to the test." Although it is easy to criticize such a practice, it is important to distinguish, as Robert Behn (1996: 12) does, between "honest cheating" and "dishonest cheating." This is clearly an example of honest cheating, in which an organization knows how its performance will be measured and responds accordingly. Whether that is good or bad depends on whether the measure is a good surrogate for quality.

These examples suggest that organizations do indeed care about their reputations, especially in a competitive market. However, the degree of responsiveness is likely to depend on the organizations' managers—their professional orientation, their attitude toward organizational threats, and their willingness to change. David Nash (1996) found evidence of this in a study of Philadelphia-area hospitals. When Pennsylvania's CABG report card appeared, some Philadelphia-area hospitals looked good while others looked bad. At hospitals that had both poor report cards and disinterested chief executive officers, nothing much happened. At a hospital that had both a poor report card and a concerned chief executive officer, significant reforms ensued. The moral of the story is that leadership matters (Behn 1991; Schneider and Teske 1995). If report cards are perceived as good measures of quality, and if quality is valued by organization leaders, then report card impacts can be considerable.

HMOs

From our perspective, HMOs are particularly interesting, because they are being prodded these days by two sets of report cards. The first are hospital (and physician) report cards, which interest them in their role as consumers of hospital (and physician) services. The second are HMO report cards, which directly evaluate their performance and implicitly seek to change their behavior. Hospital report cards are now prepared and distributed by many state governments; HMO report cards are now available, for many

HMOs, from the National Committee for Quality Assurance (NCQA), from private consulting firms, and from HMOs themselves.

In general, HMOs regard both hospitals and hospital report cards with suspicion. Because HMOs were created explicitly to contain costs, whereas hospitals were established to provide medical care, HMOs have a cost-cutting culture rooted in a cost-cutting organizational mission. As Wilson (1989: 95–96) has observed, a sense of mission is easier to establish when an organization is first created. To newly-established HMOs, cost-cutting comes more naturally than to older, well-established hospitals.

Cost-cutting considerations may lead HMOs to ignore hospital report card results if hospitals with good report card grades charge more for major surgery. There is some evidence to suggest that this is in fact taking place. For example, Good Samaritan Hospital in Los Angeles recorded a 10.4 percent mortality rate for CABG surgery during the 1991–1993 period; during the same period, UCLA (with a relatively similar patient mix) recorded a 7.9 percent mortality rate. Nevertheless, Good Samaritan continued to win contracts from such for-profit HMOs as PacifiCare and FHP International (Anders 1996a: 99–102). A key reason is that UCLA's fee rates exceeded that of Good Samaritan. Such facts may be especially relevant to for-profit health plans.

The same phenomenon can be found in other states. In Philadelphia, for example, Hahnemann University Hospital had a 1993 bypass surgery death rate twice as high as that of nearby Temple University Hospital. In fact, Temple's mortality rate (just 1.4 percent of bypass surgery patients) was considerably lower than the state's expected range. Nevertheless, the two largest HMOs in Philadelphia, U.S. Healthcare and Keystone, continued to send more than 100 heart cases per year to Hahnemann, which charged lower fees than Temple (Anders 1996a: 102–103). It is interesting to note that U.S. Healthcare and Keystone, like PacifiCare and FHP International, are for-profit HMOs. Forced to choose between quality and cost, many for-profit HMOs have emphasized the latter. As businesses in a competitive environment, they cannot ignore the "bottom line."

In contrast to hospital report cards, which were systematically published by the federal Health Care Financing Administration for several years and which are now being produced by state governments in most states, HMO report cards are less well established. They are also more varied in sponsorship and content. The NCQA, which developed the Health Plan and Employer Data and Information Set (HEDIS) rating system, is the leading repository of HMO report cards, but it cannot mandate data submission or data standardization. The NCQA has performed an increasingly important role in recent years, but its weaknesses have allowed for-profit consulting firms to flourish.

The NCQA has two data bases that qualify as report cards or report card equivalents. The first consists of HEDIS data submitted voluntarily by nearly one-half of the nation's health plans (Kim 1996). Because these data have not been independently audited, they do not measure up to the high standards the NCQA itself established in a landmark pilot report card that assessed 21 HMOs (NCQA 1995). However, plans are underway to upgrade this data base by insisting on independent auditing. The second data base consists of assessments of HMOs performed by NCQA's accreditation staff. Accreditation results, which range from full accreditation (three years) to temporary accreditation (one year) to no accreditation, might be regarded as de facto report cards. Because only 42 percent of applicants receive full accreditation status (NCQA 1996), variation is high enough to send meaningful signals to consumers. However, accreditation, though popular, is strictly voluntary and is based on flexible truncated versions of HEDIS, which reduces comparability.

Perceiving a gap to be filled, some consulting firms and local business groups have prepared report cards that focus on a particular metropolitan area. Most of these use some—but not all—of the pertinent HEDIS criteria. It is widely believed that consulting firms select the indicators that are likely to cast their clients in a favorable light. Also, local business groups sometimes select measures that assuage the fears of participating health plans (Whipple 1996). So long as participation is voluntary, the sensitivities of health plans are likely to be given some weight.

Do HMO report cards have any positive impacts on HMO practices? Some report card advocates believe that they do. For example, George Isham, the medical director of Health Partners, a Minneapolis HMO, argues that the inclusion of preventive and screening measures in every version of HEDIS has resulted in greater utilization of sound and sensible preventive medicine practices. At Health Partners, the percentage of children immunized against childhood disease climbed from 54 percent to 89 percent in a recent four-year period—an increase Isham attributes to the HEDIS system (Morrissey 1996: 3). This sharp increase in child immunizations is probably a very good thing, although some critics question whether child immunization rates are good proxies for child health (Olson 1996).

More generally, observers have noted pressure from HMOs on physicians to conduct more frequent screening for breast cancer, heart disease, and other illnesses. Of course, some of these trends would have occurred with or without report cards. Nevertheless, one reason for the rapid shift toward greater emphasis on preventive medicine is probably the expectation that this will improve the HMO's overall showing in various report cards (Anders 1996b: A3).

Additional evidence that HMOs take report cards seriously can be found in advertising campaigns. In the Philadelphia area, U.S. Healthcare, a large HMO that fared well in the HEDIS sweepstakes, included a reference to its performance in its newspaper advertisements (Hoadley 1996). In the Washington, D.C. area, Kaiser Permanente, which received full accreditation from NCQA and a favorable report card from *U.S. News & World Report,* made direct references to these accolades in television and radio advertisements. Their marketing manager believes that a "third party endorsement strategy" will enhance Kaiser Permanente's appeal among consumers (Woods 1996).

HMOs that receive poor report cards also adopt strategies and react, sometimes aggressively. When Wellpoint, a Blue Cross spin-off in California, failed to pass NCQA accreditation, it threatened to file a lawsuit (Anders 1996a: 229). The dispute was resolved, at least tentatively, when NCQA agreed to reexamine the plan fairly soon. As discussed in Chapter 3, a Florida health plan, the Physicians Corporation of America, actually filed a suit against the Florida Agency for Health Care Administration to prevent it from disclosing data on any HMO's performance. Although the State Legislature eventually allowed the release of considerable data gathered after July 1, 1996 (Berger 1996), the Physicians Corporation of America was successful in preventing the disclosure of older data as well as NCQA accreditation reports.

Both of these episodes illustrate a common organizational dysfunction—blaming the messenger. Instead of accepting responsibility for their own shortcomings, some health plans have lashed out at report card producers. When such behavior occurs, it limits the capacity of report cards to improve organizational performance.

The principal impact of HMO report cards has probably been on prevention and screening, which have been featured prominently in HEDIS since its inception. But there is also reason to believe that data on the number of major operations have also had some impact. For example, U.S. Healthcare, a division of Aetna Life & Casualty, decided that too many expensive hysterectomies were being performed. After gathering monthly data on 86 gynecologists in its network, it produced and disseminated charts full of red and orange dots showing how often each physician had conducted a biopsy that might rule out the need for a hysterectomy. The impact on physician behavior was dramatic. Within four years biopsy rates for U.S. Healthcare members more than doubled, while hysterectomy rates dropped more than 30 percent (Anders 1996a: 39).

Whether this change is a good development is, of course, debatable. While many experts believe that the number of hysterectomies performed in the United States is excessive, it is easy enough to imagine hysterectomies not being performed, in order to save money, with deleterious consequences for patients. Thus, a great deal depends on how businesses and HMOs interpret report card data. With HMOs, as with hospitals, quality will be defined and weighed differently by different observers. If companies simply select HMOs with low prostatectomy rates, low hysterectomy rates, and low Cesarean section rates in order to lower costs, then their employees may suffer. If HMOs simply reduce prostatectomies, hysterectomies, and Cesarean sections, in order to lower costs and attract corporate customers, then additional patients may suffer.

Report cards may also have negative consequences on the quality of services provided by publicly-traded HMOs if stockholders do not believe that investments in quality contribute to greater profitability. In view of the fact that 69.5 percent of HMOs accounting for 55.7 percent of total enrollments are now run by for-profit firms (InterStudy 1995: 26–27), stockholders' perceptions of the relationship between quality and profitability are likely to be important in shaping the industry's response to report cards.

Airline Punctuality and Safety

Every air traveler can recall a long-delayed flight that resulted in an untimely arrival to attend a meeting, deliver a speech, or visit a long-lost friend. Such delays are aggravating and inconvenient at best. Pressured by angry consumers and impatient members of Congress, the federal Department of Transportation (DOT) adopted a rule in 1987 requiring major air carriers to provide information on the percentage of flights that arrived "on time" so that this information might be shared with consumers. The hope was that this would encourage airlines to improve their performance.

The DOT rule was fairly specific. It applied to airlines receiving more than 1 percent of total domestic service revenue (14 carriers in 1987, 10 today) and required them to furnish the information on a monthly basis. It defined "on time" as a flight that departs from, or arrives, at its gate within 15 minutes of the scheduled time. As noted in Chapter 4, the overall rating for each airline is based on a weighted average of its on-time percentages at each airport. The rule also required computerized reservation system vendors to include the information on their primary schedule and availability displays within ten days after receiving it.

Although the nation's airlines swiftly complied with the new rule (indeed, they supplied more information than required by law), they also took advantage of a major loophole by "padding" their flight schedules to make it easier to arrive on time. By increasing the predicted length of a flight, airlines were able to improve their official statistics without actually improving their performance (U.S. GAO 1990). Although more conservative schedules may provide some benefits in terms of travel planning, the padding of schedules is a classic example of "gamesmanship" in which organizations guarantee better report cards for themselves without providing consumers substantially better results. In this instance, as in others, outputs can displace outcomes.

Fortunately, there are some built-in checks on such dysfunctional incentives. Because pilots are paid based on scheduled flight times, as opposed to actual flight times, airlines that artificially inflate their scheduled flying times wind up paying pilots more. Also, pilots are limited to so many flight hours per month, which means that if scheduled flight times burgeon, pilots may be unable to fly toward the end of each month. Ironically, this may require airlines to cancel profitably-booked flights (Greenberg 1991), which no airline likes to do.

Another loophole has proved more vexing. Under DOT's rule, airlines may exclude flights with mechanical problems from the on-time data. The rationale is that DOT does not wish to encourage airlines to take risks with mechanical difficulties in order to improve their on-time report card. While this undoubtedly makes sense, DOT does not verify that excluded flights involved genuine mechanical problems (U.S. GAO 1990). Thus, an airline bent on deceiving the public could do so by exaggerating the number of mechanical problems.

Despite these difficulties, the DOT's report card has had some positive results. For example, the GAO found that some airlines "tried to improve on-time performance by shifting frequently late flights to less-congested time slots, streamlining baggage handling, and reducing the time required to fuel and prepare their aircraft." (U.S. GAO 1990: 5). These are precisely the sorts of things DOT hoped to encourage. Indeed, even adjustments in estimated flight times could be viewed as a step in the right direction. As one DOT official puts it, "The regulations have achieved their desired result, which was to urge the carriers to do more realistic scheduling. You might say that they've inflated their estimates. But you could also say that they're just a little less optimistic and more realistic" (Bright 1996).

On-time departures and arrivals, though important, do not encompass the full range of indicators of interest to air travelers. Of equal or greater concern is flight safety. Interested consumers can also obtain relevant information on that subject by contacting the National Transportation Safety Board's (NTSB) Data Analysis Division. Upon request, the NTSB furnishes data on the number of accidents and the number of scheduled flight hours per airline for a recent four-year period. By dividing accidents by scheduled flight hours, one can compute a rough measure of each airline's safety record. The data also reveal the number of pilot "deviations" or actions that could result in a violation of an FAA regulation or a North American Aerospace Air Defense Identification Zone tolerance. Such deviations may help to predict the risk of future accidents.

A major accident can have a devastating financial impact on an airline by deflating public trust and investor confidence. Following the Valujet air crash that killed 110 people on May 11, 1996, Valujet's stock plummeted 23 percent within a single day (Griesing 1996). Can a report card documenting safety records have similar, if more muted, effects? It would be interesting to know whether airlines with a large number of accidents or fatalities take a double hit—first after the accident, second after the report card. Conversely, it would be interesting to know whether airlines with an enviable safety record fare better in the stock market after a report card appears.

Employment and Training

Every year the federal government spends billions of dollars aimed at educating and training unemployed adults and youths. State and local governments also spend a great deal of money on similar initiatives, often in conjunction with federal programs. The hope is that these expenditures will enable clients to find steady, gainful employment. In the case of welfare recipients, the additional hope is that they will be weaned off welfare for good.

In 1982 Congress established a new employment and training program that included mandatory performance standards. Known as the Job Training Partnership Act (JTPA), the statute established approximately 600 service delivery areas (SDAs), each of which was to establish a private industry council whose members (mainly drawn from business) were to be selected by the SDA's chief elected official. Federal funds flow through state governments to SDAs, which administer the performance standards subject to federal guidelines.

The performance measures required in 1982 were not unprecedented. The ill-fated Comprehensive Employment and Training Act had also established some crude performance measures. However, the JTPA performance measures focused more on outcomes than on processes and included financial incentives to improve performance. In implementing JTPA, the Department of Labor (DOL) identified several indicators aimed at measuring "gross outcomes" including job placement, earnings levels and wage rates, the elimination of welfare receipt, and the attainment of educational credentials. DOL gave states the choice of measuring performance by using national standards or by using optional adjustment models (essentially, regression models) that take local conditions and types of participants into account.

In certain respects, the JTPA performance standards were very successful. Without coercing the states, the federal government encouraged them to adopt policies that directed attention at hard-to-serve clients. Additionally, state policies definitely shaped the allocation of resources by SDAs (National Commission for Employment Policy 1988). Performance standards also encouraged effective employment and training strategies. Good performers received additional funding, with fewer strings attached; bad performers received additional technical assistance and ran the risk of being dropped from the program if they failed to improve. Above all, SDAs paid attention to program outcomes (Barnow 1992: 297), which was JTPA's stated goal.

On the negative side, there was some evidence of "cream skimming" during JTPA's early years (Donahue 1989). In particular, states that used national standards (as opposed to the optional adjustment models) could improve their performance by focusing on "easier" cases and by shunning "harder" cases (Barnow 1992; Doolittle 1996). DOL compounded this problem initially by focusing on termination measures, as opposed to post-program measures. This encouraged states to stress short-term training techniques that got clients immediate jobs but that failed to equip them with the skills to keep that job.

Over time DOL improved its measures and streamlined its system of incentives. In addition to including post-program measures as dependent variables, DOL added explanatory variables that better reflect earnings capacity. This discouraged cream skimming and encouraged SDAs to provide more services to more disadvantaged clients (Barnow 1992: 299).

Although analysts have generally applauded such steps, they nevertheless have expressed concern that DOL's performance measures tap gross outcomes, not net outcomes. In effect, SDAs are being rewarded for good results, not for value added. In theory, of course, the two may go hand in hand. However, a study by the Manpower Demonstration Research Corporation found weak correlations between JTPA performance measures (gross outcomes) and actual program impacts (net outcomes) in 16 jurisdictions. For example, there was virtually no relationship between how well a site did on the adult standards of "entered employment rate" and average wage at placement compared to site impacts for adults (Manpower Demonstration Research Corporation 1993: 3–6). In a more recent study, Barnow (1996) found only a 0.2 correlation between impact findings and simulation models for the performance standards for adults. Thus, if SDAs adjust their employment and training strategies to improve their JTPA performance measures (gross outcomes), they are not necessarily improving their program impacts (net outcomes).

School Report Cards

How are report cards received by school superintendents, principals, teachers? Telephone interviews with state officials involved in the design and implementation of school report cards suggest that report cards are generally favorably received by parents and school boards, but that they tend to be greeted initially with complaint or skepticism by a majority of school administrators and teachers. With increased familiarity and occasional adaptations, such as giving districts a chance to preview information and providing computer software to reduce the costs of gathering and reporting data, complaints generally subside.

Surveys conducted by the Louisiana Department of Education support these impressions. In one study, a random sample of parents and teachers were asked about their reactions to the 1991–92 school-level report cards. Parents had more favorable reactions and were more optimistic about the potential of report cards for improving education than teachers. Only 21.7 percent of parents, as compared to 39.5 percent of teachers, responded that the report cards were "a waste of time and money" (Kochan et al. 1993: 4). A survey of parent association participants, teachers, and principals revealed that majorities of parents and teachers agreed that the report cards provide useful information and have potential for improving education; principals generally viewed the report cards as ineffective and they objected to their distribution to parents and newspapers (Caldas and Mossavat 1994).

Although several states have substantially modified their report cards, only Idaho scrapped a mandatory school-level report card—some small school districts were spending thousands of dollars preparing report cards that were requested by only a few parents, and other districts that distributed report cards by mail were accused by parents of using them to promote tax levies ("School Report Card Law May Be Dumped" 1996: 11). The Idaho Department of Education continues to distribute district-level reports to school boards, legislators, business and real estate organizations, education reports, and other elites (Kohler 1997).

Not surprisingly, there seems to be considerable variation among school administrators in their use of report cards as a device for establishing or reinforcing mission. A 1995 study of how Nevada school districts responded to reporting requirements concerning exemplary or problematic programs at the school-level found that nine out of seventeen districts identified programs needing attention, but that only four of these conveyed them in the context of a plan for improvement (D. Smith 1996: 16–17). In Oklahoma, where school-level report cards are now distributed to all parents, principals have an opportunity to provide up to a page of comments. Some principals write no more than "Have a nice summer," while others provide detailed discussions about programs and plans (Buswell 1996).

The strong set of educational rewards and sanctions introduced in Kentucky since the adoption of the Kentucky Educational Reform Act in 1990 shows evidence of both functional and dysfunctional responses. The rewards are based on a report card that combines information from the Kentucky Instructional Results Information System, which covers reading, mathematics, social studies, science, and writing through a variety of assessment tools including open response and portfolio components as well as more standard multiple choice tests that are currently administered in grades four, five, seven, eight, eleven, and twelve. Scores in these five subject areas, and a noncognitive component based on measures such as student attendance, dropout, and retention rates, are used to rate students on a zero to 140 point scale where those with less than 40 points are labeled "novice," those with 40 to 99 points are labeled "apprentice," those with 100 to 139 points are labeled "proficient," and those with 140 points are labeled "distinguished." The 20-year goal is to have all students reach proficiency.

Every two years schools are classified in terms of their progress toward reaching the 100 point standard. Each school is given an improvement goal of closing the gap between its current average score and 100 points by 10 percent. For instance, a school that enters the two-year cycle with a 40 point average would be assigned an improvement goal of $(100-40)/10 =$ 6 points. Its threshold for assessment at the end of the two-year cycle would thus be $(40+6) = 46$. A school qualifies for a minimum financial award if it exceeds its threshold by one point and moves 10 percent of its students in the novice category to apprentice. A school qualifies for a maximum award if it exceeds its threshold by twice the improvement goal plus one point and moves 10 percent of its novices to the apprentice category. Schools that just achieve their thresholds are classified as "successful," and receive neither rewards nor sanctions. Schools that achieve average scores between their baselines and thresholds are classified as "improving," and must submit a transformation plan to the state that outlines plans for reaching the threshold in the cycle. Schools whose average scores fall less than 5 points below their thresholds are classified as "in decline," and, in addition to submitting a transformation plan, are assigned a distinguished educator and given additional funding to help reverse the decline. Schools whose average scores fall 5 or more points below their thresholds are classified as "in crisis," and in addition to filing a transformation plan and receiving additional funding, they are assigned a distinguished educator with broad powers including the authority to fire teachers.

The financial awards are substantial. In the 1993–94 cycle, for example, the state gave out $26.1 million in total awards at the rate of $2,600 per teacher in maximum award schools and $1,300 per teacher in minimum award schools (Kelley and Protsik 1996: 7). Currently, teachers in the award schools vote on the disposition of funds and have generally used the awards to fund bonuses for themselves. Divisive controversy in many schools over the use and distribution of the funds, however, prompted a review panel appointed by Governor Wallace Wilkinson and the Kentucky State Legislature to recommend that in the future funds be used for school purposes rather than salary bonuses (Stecklow 1997).

Preliminary research suggests that the Kentucky system of rewards and sanctions has had strong behavioral impacts. Interviews and surveys suggest that Kentucky students wrote more and better as a result of the emphasis the incentive system placed on writing portfolios (Elmore, Abelmann, and Fuhrman 1996: 78). Interview studies suggest that fear of sanction more than expectation of monetary reward was the prime factor in motivating efforts to perform well under the system (Drummond 1997). The desire to avoid the negative consequences associated with sanctions appeared strongest in rural Kentucky where news about schools receives extensive coverage in local newspapers (Kelley 1997). Additionally, it appears that state interventions in schools in decline (transition plan requirements, assignment of distinguished educators, and additional funding) create favorable conditions for improvement (Kelley 1997).

The powerful incentives also have inspired considerable cheating. For example, a 1993 review of portfolio grades, which are assigned by teachers, found that grades in 101 out of 105 schools audited were too generous by an average of 35 points out of 140; a similar study in 1996 downgraded portfolio scores in 78 out of 98 schools audited (Stecklow 1997: A5). Anecdotal evidence abounds about teachers rewriting portfolios for students, principals asking parents to help their children with the portfolios, and claims by some teachers that students of their colleagues cannot read the material in the portfolios that they supposedly wrote (Stecklow 1997). In addition to teachers putting more effort into teaching students how to take tests (Kelley and Protsik 1996; Koretz et al. 1996), there have also been numerous complaints about teachers reviewing tests in advance and providing tips and other aids to help their students score better (Stecklow 1997).

Charles Clotfelter and Helen Ladd (1996: 45–46) provide some illustrations of the manipulation and cheating that have occurred in connection with the South Carolina School Incentive Reward Program (discussed in Chapter 4) and the Dallas Independent School District's incentive program. For example, a former South Carolina high school principal noted that big gains that would qualify for rewards could be manufactured in alternate years by giving examinations in poor environments in "off" years and in comfortable environments in the following "on" years. Teachers giving screening tests for first grade could try to classify a larger number of entering students as unready, and principals could make extra efforts to enroll students in the free and reduced-price lunch program, so as to move the school into a weaker cohort of competing schools. In Dallas, there have been at least two cases in which school staff were caught tampering with test results in an effort to improve ratings, and the district pays close attention when classes show dramatic improvements in test scores.

Clotfelter and Ladd (1994) investigated the impact of the report card used in North Carolina in the 1989–90 and 1991–92 academic years. The report card rated school districts as above, at, or below par through an elaborate statistical procedure. First, data on 27 tests were combined into four subject area averages. Second, these subject area averages were regressed on district characteristics. Third, par values for each subject area for each district were predicted from the regression equations. Finally, par ranges of fixed width were set around each par value and district scores in the subject area, and overall, were determined to fall above, within, or below the range.

Clotfelter and Ladd hypothesized that if the report card were effective as a wake-up call to poorly performing schools, then schools rated below par in 1990 should show larger relative gains in test scores between 1990 and 1992 than schools rated at or above par. To test this hypothesis they estimated a model of average gains in test scores between 1990 and 1992 by subject and grade level. They found that schools rated below par in 1990 did indeed show larger gains than other schools rated at or above par. Although they acknowledge that their method may not adequately control for regression toward the mean, they believe that considering all of the statistical evidence suggests that the report card designation of below par did indeed contribute to larger than average gains.

Additional evidence from North Carolina is consistent with that proposition. If report cards are to have a long-term impact on student performance, one might expect that schools with poor report card ratings would change principals more often than other schools. Clotfelter and Ladd (1994: 14–16) investigated that possibility and found that the post-report card average principal turnover rate for school districts performing below par exceeded that for other school districts. While these findings were not statistically significant, they at least suggest that a theorized mechanism for change is more prevalent when a report card produces negative evaluations.

Estimating the impact of report cards introduced statewide is complicated because other factors, such as contemporaneous changes in other aspects of educational policy that might explain observed changes, cannot be easily taken into account. Clotfelter and Ladd (1996: 49–53) avoid some of these methodological difficulties by using a statistical model that compares pass rates on seventh grade scores in reading and mathematics in the Dallas school district, which introduced a report card with strong financial incentives, to rates in the Austin, El Paso, Fort Worth, San Antonio, and Houston school districts, which introduced neither report cards nor financial incentives but were subject to the same statewide policy changes as Dallas. Interpretation of their results is complicated because relative improvements in pass rates in Dallas seem to begin prior to the actual introduction of the report card. If one is willing to attribute the prior improvement to anticipation of the implementation of the report card, then it appears that the report card was quite effective in increasing pass rates for white and Hispanic students. However, if one rejects this announcement effect, then it would appear that some other factor was responsible for these increases. The fact that some school officials have been motivated to cheat suggests that the report card is strongly influencing behavior, which in turn makes the assumption of anticipation and, therefore a positive impact, more plausible.

The Tennessee Value-Added Assessment System (TVAAS) appears to have had a substantial positive impact on how district administrators, principals, and teachers assess their curriculum and teaching methods. As described in chapter 4, the TVAAS annually produces estimates of student gains in five subject areas for school districts, individual schools, and teachers. Student gains are also reported by grade level and for students grouped into thirds according to their prior-year scores. Created initially primarily as a mechanism for educational accountability, it has become a widely-used diagnostic tool within Tennessee school districts. One director of testing in a school district, referring specifically to information tracing gains over time, volunteered that the TVAAS is "one of the best ways we have ever had to evaluate what we do" (Cherry 1997).

Although there have been no comprehensive studies of TVAAS use within school districts, Ben Brown (1997), the Director of Testing and Evaluation for the Tennessee Department of Education, estimates that 80 percent of districts actually make use of TVAAS data as a diagnostic tool. He bases his estimate partly on the dramatic increase in requests the Department has received from school districts for assistance in use of assessment information since the introduction of TVAAS.

The experiences in a few school districts illustrate the various ways that

TVAAS information is used. In the Wilson County schools, teachers use the reports in a variety of ways (Duncan 1997). Many teachers look at average gains made by students who enter with low, middle, and high achievement levels as a rough gauge of where they have directed their instruction. Principals refer to teacher scores in their evaluations, and sometimes use the scores when making decisions about teacher assignments. Although the teacher scores are available only to the teachers and their principals, teachers sometimes share them voluntarily. Some teachers with low scores in specific subjects have asked to be observed in an effort to find ways of improving. In one school, fifth grade teachers who were dissatisfied with their gains in science decided to reorganize so that the teacher with the largest gains would teach science to all the classes.

Teachers in the Jackson/Madison County School District also often voluntarily exchange their scores with colleagues to try to find out and learn from those who seem to be doing particularly well with specific groups of students (Butler 1997). The grade level scores have been especially useful in providing a focus for coordination across grades. The observation of consistent fall-offs in gains from fifth grade to middle school prompted the formation of a transition committee to look for ways of reducing the disruption that occurs when students change buildings.

One criticism of TVAAS raised by school officials in several districts indirectly speaks to its utility: the November release of TVAAS results by the Department of Education is out of sync with curricular planning, which is done in most districts in August for the upcoming academic year. Release in late-July would enable districts to use the most recent gain scores in their planning. Indeed, teachers in a number of districts use the raw test scores for their students, which they typically receive in May, to estimate their own approximate gain scores for use before the beginning of the next academic year. This is the case in McNairy County, for example, where teachers make extensive use of gain scores when discussing their teaching strategies (Stover 1997).

Overall, the behavioral responses to the TVAAS appear functional: school district administrators, principals, and teachers seem to be using the various forms of gain information largely to identify areas where more improvement is necessary. As long as the tests comprising the Tennessee Comprehensive Assessment Program (TCAP) are reasonably well correlated with state curricular goals, then efforts by districts, schools, and teachers to improve their scores are likely to be socially desirable. With the exception of concerns raised by a few district officials about the second grade tests, which are read to students so that returning teachers have access to specific questions from previous years (Vick 1997), critics of the TVAAS are not concerned with narrow teaching to the test. Rather, they generally raise concerns about whether TCAP appropriately tests higher-order learning skills. That many schools generally recognized as having especially creative programs, such as those around Oak Ridge and the Nashville magnet schools, also do well in terms of their TVAAS scores substantially counters this line of argument (Sanders 1997b).

EPA Toxics Release Inventory

Right-to-know laws requiring employers to notify workers about health risks that might arise from exposure to hazardous chemicals were implemented by the federal government and many state governments during the 1970s and 1980s. The 1984 chemical disaster in Bhopal, India and a near disaster the following year at another Union Carbide plant in West Virginia fed demands from environmental groups for laws that would give citizens access to information about industrial releases of toxic substances in their areas. Amid complex and heated debate, and with unusual parliamentary maneuvers to bypass a key House subcommittee chair (Selcraig 1997), right-to-know provisions for industrial toxic releases were adopted through the Emergency Planning and Community Right-to-Know Act (EPCRA), which became Title III of the Superfund Amendments and Reauthorization Act of 1986 (PL 99–499).

EPCRA requires the Environmental Protection Agency (EPA) to establish a toxics release inventory (TRI). The inventory initially covered 320 listed substances. Over time political pressure and legal challenges led to a few de-listings, but EPA added 286 chemicals and chemical categories to the list through regulations in 1994, so that the number of listed substances currently stands at 643. Reporting requirements initially applied only to manufacturing, but were extended to federal facilities in 1995 by executive order and to most other industries (except services and agriculture) in 1997 by regulation. Facilities with more than ten employees in covered industries must file a report if they manufacture or process more than 25,000 pounds of listed chemicals and chemical categories, or 10,000 pounds of any one of them. The reports must indicate the route of release—air, land, underground (mainly deep wells), surface water, public sewage, or offsite.

Firms are allowed to use material balance, engineering, or direct monitoring methods to estimate emissions. Although firms self-report, EPA had conducted over 4,400 compliance and data quality inspections by 1995, and it routinely cross-checks data with reports made by firms to state agencies (U.S. EPA 1997). Failure to report a listed substance carries a $25,000 fine; falsifying reports is punishable by both fines and criminal sanctions. Early use of fines by EPA, and several large criminal prosecutions, including one leading to a $2 million fine against Consolidated Edison Company in 1994 for providing misleading information about the release of asbestos (McMorris 1994), have helped establish the credibility of reporting enforcement.

EPA makes public the TRI data on an annual basis with a two-year lag due to the timing of reporting and processing—EPA receives about 80,000 reports annually from more than 20,000 manufacturing and 200 federal facilities. Interested parties can access the TRI data on an EPA Internet web page (www.epa.gov/opptintr/tri/access.htm) by facility (name or EPA identification number), location (zip code, city, county, or state), or chemical name. A number of organizations have used TRI data as the basis for rudimentary report cards. Each year the consumer and environmental group Citizen Action/Citizens Fund produces a list of the 50 firms and the 100 sites with the largest poundage of total toxic releases. The National Environmental Law Center and the U.S. Public Interest Research Group (PIRG) have also issued comparative reports based on total releases. *USA Today* (1990), the *Associated Press* (1995), and other news media not only cover reports issued by private organizations, but also have published their own comparisons of firms and regions based on TRI data.

The TRI also serves as the basis for a number of other EPA programs. For example, in 1991 the EPA began the so-called 33/50 program, which involves its entering into agreements with firms to encourage their voluntary reductions of releases of 17 substances listed in the TRI (O'Toole et al. 1997).

Report cards based on TRI data have been very crude. They typically sum the pounds of different emissions to arrive at an output measure. This simple procedure obviously ignores the fact that a pound of one toxic substance may pose very different health and environmental risks than another. To be valid, collapsing this multidimensional output into a single dimension requires weights based on the relative risks of the substances. Beyond the simple problem of adding apples and oranges, there are more subtle problems in interpreting total poundage as a measure of risk that are related to the differences in risks posed by different time patterns and routes of release. Reasonable comparisons of firms should also adjust for the value of product produced and the nature of the industry. For example, one might reasonably compare the ratio of toxic risk per dollar of sales for firms within, say, the chemical industry.

The EPA has recently proposed the Sector Facility Indexing Project, which would attempt to provide at least rudimentary performance measures for five selected industries—oil products, steel, other metals, autos, and paper (Cushman 1997: 1). Specifically, it would create toxicity weights for constructing a hazard index for chemical releases and it would take account in some way of production levels at facilities. It would also provide information on inspections, fines, and other enforcement activities.

Despite the poor quality of the report cards that have been produced from TRI data, some evidence suggests that the availability of TRI data has had some impact on the total toxic waste emissions of firms. James Hamilton (1995) investigated the question of whether or not the release of the first TRI data in June 1989 represented new information to the print media and stockholders. He found that firms with higher total volumes of toxic air, land, underground, or offsite releases had higher probabilities of having stories about their pollution in the print media. Firms with larger numbers of submissions (one submission per toxic substance release per site) showed negative abnormal stock market returns on the day that the TRI data were made public. These findings indicate media and investor attention to the TRI that might be expected to induce reductions in total toxic emissions by firms.

Indirect investigation of whether or not these reductions have occurred takes advantage of the fact that not all states have funded right-to-know programs related to the TRI. EPCRA required all states to establish Local Emergency Planning Committees to prepare plans for dealing with toxic hazards and to make information about toxic risks public, but implementation has varied considerably across states in terms of the resources available to the committees (Rich, Conn, and Owens 1993; Grant and Downey 1995/6). Specifically, only 22 states have funded right-to-know programs related to the TRI. Donald Grant (1997) estimated the effect of a funded right-to-know program and other variables on the annual percentage changes in the ratio of total poundage of toxic chemicals released by manufacturing facilities in a state to the real value of the state's manufacturing shipments. If one assumes that states with funded right-to-know programs have greater dissemination of TRI information, then his finding that states with such programs showed greater percentage reductions over the 1989 to 1991 period at least suggests that TRI information has induced adaptive responses in firms. Yet the focus on total emissions means that some caution is needed in interpreting these induced reductions as functional.

Conclusion

Although more research on the organizational impacts of report cards needs to be done, it is possible to draw some broad but tentative conclusions from research done to date.

First, report cards based on organizational outputs are likely to trigger some type of organizational response. Because outputs can be measured and are subject to the organizations' direct control, organizations have strong incentives to improve their outputs over time. The catch is that organizations' responses may be either functional or dysfunctional. Measured outputs closely aligned with social goals and not vulnerable to deceitful manipulation, such as child immunization rates achieved by HMOs, promote functional responses. Measured outputs only weakly related to social goals, such as certain regulatory enforcement actions, or easily vulnerable to deceitful manipulation, such as portfolio grades in Kentucky schools, increase the chances that some organizational responses will be dysfunctional as well as functional.

Second, report cards based on organizational outcomes are less likely to trigger some type of organizational response, but are more likely to trigger a positive response if the organization reacts. Report cards that focus on an authentic bottom line are less subject to dysfunctional responses, such as cream skimming and teaching to the test. But report cards only reveal what an organization has accomplished, not how or why the accomplishment has occurred. The quest for better outcomes is more likely to achieve success in organizations that routinely engage in systematic self-examination. For example, surgery departments at major hospitals regularly conduct case reviews aimed at quality control. When outcome-based report cards are combined with a strong internal review system, the consequences can be both striking and positive.

Third, report cards that are well publicized or tied closely to tournaments are more likely to have an organizational impact, either good or bad. Without publicity or an explicit link to the availability of resources, report cards appeal primarily to the desire of managers to find ways of helping their organizations do better, especially at government agencies and nonprofit organizations. With publicity or explicit links to the availability of resources, report cards appeal to the material incentives of managers and organizational members as well. An organization that ignores a well publicized report card with unfavorable findings runs the risk of retaliation by public officials, consumers, or both. Report cards that create strong incentives for organizational members, such as salary bonuses or fear of embarrassment, risk dysfunctional responses, especially when monitoring by managers is difficult.

Fourth, the desire to have an impact on target organizations often leads to extensive conversations between report card designers and organization managers. Such conversations can be constructive if they promote reasonableness without undermining functionality. As a side-benefit, they may also promote validity and comprehensiveness, as certain organizations have strong incentives to bring measurement problems to the attention of report card designers. Conversations, however, can also lead to unfortunate concessions, such as allowing the use of inferior or unaudited data. Conversations may also result in optional participation agreements or survey design promises that soften distinctions among organizations. Such concessions undermine functionality by giving poor performers opportunities to disguise their poor performance or to opt out of the process altogether. The quest for reasonableness becomes unreasonable when it allows poorly performing organizations to avoid public identification.

7

Public and Private Roles in Report Card Design

The provision of information through an organizational report card can be a tool of public policy, private policy, or both. In the preceding pages, we have identified report cards produced by government agencies (for example, hospital report cards, public school report cards, airline report cards) and by private organizations (for example, HMO report cards, higher education report cards, economic development report cards, insurer solvency report cards). Thus far, however, we have simply noted each report card's lineage, without addressing the merits of alternative institutional sponsorships.

Is there a "best" way to produce report cards? Should report cards be produced by the public sector or the private sector? Are there creative ways through which the public and private sectors can work together to produce better report cards? Are certain tasks better handled by the public sector? Are other tasks better handled by the private sector? Are there situations that call for a stronger government role? Do other contexts call for a stronger private role? Which government actors are best suited to produce report cards (for example, federal, state, or local officials)? And which private actors are best suited to produce report cards (for example, for-profit versus nonprofit organizations, advocacy groups versus research institutes)?

Early in this book we addressed the first-order question of whether organizational report cards are desirable policy instruments. In this chapter we address a fundamental second-order question: If a report card is to be produced, who should produce it? We begin by considering the general strengths and weaknesses of the public and private sectors in providing report cards. Then we develop a functional (or task-oriented) approach to public-private collaboration. Next we develop a contextual approach that can help determine if the level of government involvement should be ratcheted up or down in any application. Finally, we consider the advan-

164

tages and disadvantages of particular public and private actors as candidates for producing report cards.

Is There Failure in the Report Card Market?

In a well-functioning market economy the decentralized decisions of private economic actors yield efficient production, distribution, and consumption of the vast majority of goods and services valued by people. Government need only specify and enforce property rights and other rules that comprise the frameworks for efficient private decisionmaking and exchange. Various distortions can arise, however, that lead decentralized decisionmaking to be inefficient in the sense that alternative decisions could increase the value of consumption for some people without reducing it for others. These distortions, or market failures, provide rationales for more active government involvement in economic decisions such as the production of organizational report cards.

Turning things around, one might be suspicious of a government role in promoting report cards if there are no apparent market failures. Measuring the actual value of the information provided by report cards poses a difficult task for policy analysts. If a well-functioning market for the information a report card would supply exists, and no private organization produces it, then one should wonder if a report card yields an excess of benefits over costs. If not, then it should not be produced unless some distributional goal not valued by the market contributes to social benefits.

Under what circumstances will markets fail to create socially efficient organizational report cards? One circumstance that may justify government involvement is restriction of consumer choice that reduces the willingness of people to pay for information that they cannot use as individuals. A second circumstance that may justify government involvement is self-selection that operates to limit participation in report cards by poorly performing organizations, or induces private report card suppliers to avoid providing information that presents organizations negatively. A third circumstance arises in connection with the nature of information as a public good.

Inadequate Consumer Demand

A market will provide a good only if someone is willing to pay for it. Consumers willingly pay for information that will inform important decisions—they hire engineers, architects, and termite inspectors to help them assess the quality of houses; they buy, or bear the time and interpersonal costs of borrowing, *Consumer Reports* and similar publications that provide comparative information about appliances, automobiles, and other costly goods; and they pay a bit more for products that bear respected brand names or certifications from organizations like Underwriters Laboratories. If consumers have no decisions to make, however, then they will generally not be willing to pay for information.

American education shows the polar cases of consumer demand for information. At one extreme is higher education, which is characterized by extensive consumer choice in a highly competitive national market. Several commercial publications provide annual comparisons of undergraduate programs at U.S. colleges and universities: *Lovejoy's College Guide, Peterson's Guide to Four-Year Colleges,* and *Barron's Profiles of American Colleges.* These comparisons provide a great variety of detailed information about costs, programs, and facilities that are valued by prospective students and their parents in the search for appropriate alternatives for undergraduate study. Coverage is almost universal, as intense competition for students and their tuition dollars forces colleges to participate. These sources provide primarily input, process, and output information with only very general overall assessments of the colleges' overall performance. For over a decade, however, *U.S. News & World Report* has provided rankings of colleges and universities in its guide to *America's Best Colleges,* as well as report cards on graduate study in a number of academic and professional fields.

The *America's Best Colleges* ranks schools in categories such as national universities and liberal arts colleges, regional universities and liberal arts colleges, and undergraduate engineering and business programs. Its rankings within these categories combine information from surveys of schools' reputations among college administrators with information collected from schools in the categories of selectivity, faculty resources, financial resources, retention based on six-year graduation rates for enrolled freshmen, and alumni satisfaction as measured by the fraction of living undergraduate alumni who make financial contributions to their alma maters (Morse 1995). Although some colleges and universities have attempted to improve their rankings by such tricks as not including verbal SAT scores for their foreign students (Stecklow 1995), the fact that *America's Best Colleges* has entered its second decade attests to its perceived value and viability as a commercial enterprise. It is a clear example of a rather substantial organizational report card with near universal coverage that is produced without any government involvement.

Although primary and secondary education are every bit as important to parents as higher education, circumstances in the United States typically do not generate sufficient consumer demand for information to facilitate market supply of public school report cards. Parents choose their public school districts by virtue of their residential choices, and within a district their children often must attend schools designated by the district. This restricted choice with respect to publicly funded education limits the demand for comparative information to such an extent that almost all school report cards are either mandated or directly supplied by state governments.

The few privately supplied school report cards, such as those produced by the Taxpayers' Federation of Illinois (Stout, Eisenberg, and Nowlan 1996) or local newspapers, rely almost exclusively on data collected and made available by state governments. For example, "Grading Our Schools," which is produced annually by the *Democrat and Chronicle/ Times-Union* and provides information on both public and private schools in the Rochester, New York metropolitan area, relies on data collected by New York State that was not directly disseminated to parents until the introduction of school report cards on the Internet (http:\www.nysed.gov) in 1997. The "Grading Our Schools" insert has proven quite popular. In 1996, over 18,000 inserts were sold, including 2,800 copies to real estate companies and organizations that deal with employee relocation (Lesda 1996). A 1996 telephone survey of the 30 largest Rochester area real estate offices found that 18 make use of the insert in helping clients select school districts (Roghman 1996).

In some markets involving third-party payers, it is the payers, rather than consumers, who create market demand for report cards. For example, firms that provide their employees with health insurance have a financial incentive to choose plans that economically provide valued services. They may be willing to pay for report cards that provide comparative information that they can use in deciding which plans to include in the menu of employee options. As we discuss in the next section, their monopsony power and the competitiveness of the local health insurance market will be important factors in the extent of participation of insurers in privately supplied report cards.

Consumer or third-party payer demand for information may be adequate to support the market supply of some report cards, but at levels or in forms that fall short of efficiency. To the extent that organizations improve the quality of their goods and services in response to report card ratings, the social value of the report cards exceeds the sum of the values derived by individual consumers from better choices. In other words, report cards may provide positive externalities that extend beyond those who are willing to pay for them. The presence of positive externalities in a market generally leads to too little supply of a good from the social perspective, and often serves as a rationale for public subsidies to increase supply.

Self-Selection and Inadequate Supply

Market demand for information will not always elicit the supply of effective organizational report cards. Organizations that fear unfavorable comparisons may be unwilling to provide report card suppliers with proprietary information, or they may provide information that is inaccurate or misleading. When participation is voluntary, self-selection may operate so that only organizations that expect to be rated favorably are covered in report cards. Report card producers, whose revenues typically depend on the number of organizations covered, may attempt to increase participation by refraining from reporting information that invites unfavorable comparisons.

The degree of competition that organizations face in their product markets is likely to be an important determinant of their willingness to cooperate with report card suppliers. In highly competitive product markets, organizations may fear that not participating will be interpreted as a confession of poor performance that will drive customers to competitors. In product markets with less competition, organizations may be less fearful of being stigmatized—being the only nonparticipant among ten or even a hundred competitors conveys a more negative image than being one nonparticipant among two or three competitors. Once a high level of participation is established in a competitive market, it is likely to be an equilibrium in the sense that no organization would want to stop participating as long as all the others are participating.

Consider, for example, A. M. Best's ratings of insurer solvency. Insurance markets, which have relatively low barriers to entry, are highly competitive and participation in ratings is nearly universal. As firms must file information with state insurance commissioners, A. M. Best is able to identify all insurers and therefore would be able to make at least a partial assessment of any insurers who did not participate voluntarily. Participation has become so much the rule that many contracts involving the purchase of insurance make explicit reference to the ratings, and insurers are willing to pay A. M. Best and several of the other major raters to be included.

In contrast to A. M. Best's solvency ratings, recall the HMO report card prepared by *Health Pages* in Pittsburgh. In 1995, only three out of six plans agreed to participate. The leverage of the firms that purchase *Health Pages* to help their employees choose among group health insurance options would probably be greater if there were substantially more HMOs. With a larger number of HMOs from which to choose, the threat by firms to exclude plans that do not participate in the report card would be more credible. It is also possible that a few large employers willing to act in concert would have sufficient monopsony power to force all the HMOs to participate.

Report card suppliers can attempt to get around organizational resistance to participation in three ways. First, they may try to induce demand for report cards among those who purchase services from the organizations, who in turn may exert pressure on the organizations to participate. This strategy is most promising when one or more purchasers account for large fractions of demand, as in the case of third-party payers for health services.

Second, they can base report cards solely on publicly accessible data. By avoiding reliance on proprietary data, they are free to include all the organizations within relevant comparison groups. The effectiveness of the resulting report cards, however, will depend on whether government agencies require organizations to make certain data available. Indeed, such regulations may be explicitly adopted as a policy instrument for inducing the creation of private report cards.

Third, private suppliers of report cards can alter their evaluative methods to soften negative assessments that discourage participation. The success of this strategy inevitably results in some loss of information of potential value to consumers. In the extreme, the report card may become no more than advertising.

Where consumer demand for information is strong, however, report card suppliers who attempt to soften negative assessments may invite competition. For example, concerns in the late 1980s that A. M. Best and the other major insurance raters who derived most of their revenues from the insurance industry might have become too lenient in their ratings in light of poor investment practices, similar to those that affected the savings and loan industry, opened the door for competition from Weiss Research, which derives the majority of its revenues from insurance consumers (Montague 1991).

Information as a Public Good

Information is nonrivalrous in consumption. Once information has been created, its consumption by one person does not interfere with its consumption by others. If the supplier of the report card cannot restrict access to the report card (in other words, it is nonexcludable), then the report card has the characteristic of a pure public good and market supply will generally be less than efficient from the social perspective. Indeed, unless the number of consumers is small so that they can coordinate to contract for supply, or there is one consumer with a sufficiently high level of demand who finds the information sufficiently valuable to bear all the costs of supply, there will be no supply at all (Olson 1973; Weimer and Vining 1992: 41–57). Thus, markets with a small number of third-party payers, or with a larger number but with one payer who accounts for a large share of purchases, are likely to be "privileged" in the sense of having some private supply of the pure public good.

If nonpayers can be excluded from access to the report card, then it will be supplied as a "toll good." Suppliers will produce report cards because they can charge for access to them. Unless suppliers of the report cards are able to discriminate among consumers and charge each no more than his or her willingness-to-pay for the information, there is likely to be inefficiency in the sense that the social costs of providing the information to some consumers would be less than the benefits they would derive from it. Efforts to discriminate among consumers might take the form of offering the report card in more or less convenient forms, and its information on a more or less timely basis. So, for example, insurance ratings are offered virtually free to those who can wait until reports appear in volumes held by libraries, or get by with summaries provided on a more timely basis through web sites. Other consumers, however, may pay substantial fees for online access to the most recent information.

A Functional Approach

In thinking about who should be responsible for report cards, it is useful to recognize that the preparation of a report card is a multifaceted task and that the public and private sectors have different strengths and weaknesses in handling particular assignments. Before deciding who should do what, it is useful to decompose the preparation of a report card into discrete, manageable stages or functions.

As we see it, the process of producing a report card encompasses five basic functions: (1) *Data Gathering*, or assembling the raw data on the organizations within the purview of the report card; (2) *Data Verification*, or testing and establishing the validity of the data; (3) *Data Analysis*, or converting data into valid information useful for assessing organizational performance; (4) *Information Presentation*, or packaging information about organizational performance so that it is attractive and easily understood; and (5) *Information Dissemination*, or distributing report cards, or their contents, to their intended audiences.

Although the specific context of a report card will ultimately determine the feasible and effective ways to combine these functions, we believe that the public sector generally is in a better position to handle the earliest functions, while the private sector generally is in a better position to handle the latest functions. Government intervention is often needed to secure the cooperation of reluctant organizations, to reduce the costs of report card production, and to establish the legitimacy of the report card enterprise. Private participation is often needed to handle certain technical, logistical, and outreach assignments. When problems arise, it is often because either the public sector or the private sector has been miscast.

In the sections that follow we consider appropriate public and private roles in each of the functional areas summarized above. We seek to identify important contextual factors relevant to the choice of the second-order policy instruments that governments can employ to bring about each of the functions (see Table 7.1).

Data Gathering

A report card poses a potential threat to organizations whose performance is being reviewed. For this reason, many organizations, understandably nervous about how they will fare, may decline to participate if they can. Even organizations that expect to be rated relatively well may decline to participate if they perceive providing data as costly or inconvenient. When markets fail to produce report cards, or private report card producers rate organizations overly generously to induce participation, then a strong government role will be necessary to introduce and sustain an effective report card. A great variety of policy instruments can be used to encourage par-

Table 7.1 Government Roles in Report Card Production

Functional area	Important public sector roles
Data gathering	Mandate participation where necessary Direct or support private efforts to develop and obtain appropriate data
Data verification	Regulate to support reporting requirements where necessary Facilitate development of reporting standards
Data analysis	Contract for analysis when market demand for report card information is weak Fill gaps in coverage with respect to interests of specific groups
Information presentation	Contract for design work when market demand for report card information is weak
Information dissemination	Provide information to mass media

ticipation and cooperation in data gathering. *As governments ultimately enjoy a major advantage over private report card producers in data gathering by virtue of their regulatory powers, they often must play a central role in extracting data from reluctant organizations.*

One of the most prominent examples of government-mandated reporting is the financial disclosure requirements of the Securities and Exchange Commission (SEC). The 1933 Securities Act, the 1934 Securities Exchange Act, and subsequent amendments allow the SEC to impose reporting requirements on corporations that issue publicly traded stock and municipalities, utilities, and corporations that issue bonds (Khademian 1992). This information is used directly by individual investors as well as by Standard and Poor's, Moody's, and other companies that rate corporate stocks and bonds. Although private bond and securities rating services predated the SEC disclosure requirements—for example, John Moody began issuing systematic reports on railroads and public utilities in 1913 (Moody 1914: 17), their efforts were hindered by lack of uniformity and comprehensiveness in reporting. Based on a review of the various studies of disclosure conducted between 1927 and 1983, Joel Seligman (1986: 9) concluded: "This evidence persuasively illustrates that without a federal law or government agency mandating minimum standard disclosure requirements, voluntary disclosure practices would be less uniform, more likely to omit information material to investors, and more often employed in securities fraud."

Government-mandated reporting also offers the potential for avoiding duplication of effort. The private sector has a proprietary interest in the data it collects. *Newsweek* is unlikely to share its nursing home data with *Time;* the *New York Times* is unlikely to share its hospital data with the *Washington Post.* In contrast, government agencies are required by law to make most of their data available to interested parties, including the general public. The federal Freedom of Information Act and numerous state-level counterparts place the burden of proof on those who seek to restrict public access to information (Pierce et al. 1985). Consequently, data collected by the government is more likely to be used widely.

Government-mandated reporting typically has the advantage of continuity, increasing the likelihood of organizational comparisons over time. Once a law or administrative order to collect data is adopted, and a bureaucratic structure is built to implement it, the collection will generally continue indefinitely. Political opponents of the data collection are likely to mobilize to fight adoption; once collection has become part of a bureaucratic routine, however, the political costs of stopping or radically changing it are likely to be high, especially if the data have become useful to the media. In contrast, private data collectors are likely to continue to face pressure from organizations to stop collecting data that facilitates embarrassing comparisons.

Not all the advantages lie with the government, however. Private data collectors generally enjoy greater flexibility than public agencies in several areas. First, they are more adaptable in that they can more easily change what data are being collected in response to changes in the service markets they are covering or to changes in knowledge relevant to measuring organizational outcomes—this is the flip side of greater vulnerability to pressure from organizations. Second, they are free of civil service and budgetary rules that restrict the rates at which public agencies can hire individuals with relevant expertise and adopt new innovations in information technology. Third, they can collect qualitative data that government agencies could not because of concerns for procedural fairness. For example, it is hard to imagine state insurance commissioners collecting the sort of information on the managerial effectiveness of insurers gathered by A. M. Best.

In considering alternative policy instruments for bringing about the gathering of data necessary for report cards, we can usefully distinguish among several contexts that depend on the extent of participation by organizations and the quality of the information that they provide. Specifically, we begin by considering a status quo characterized by full participation and appropriate data. We then consider in turn the problems of incomplete participation and inappropriate data.

Full Participation and Appropriate Data.   In some contexts, market forces operating within existing regulatory frameworks result in all relevant organizations providing appropriate data for use by potential report card producers. Strong market forces, for instance, drive colleges and universities to make a great variety of informative data available to *U.S. News & World Report* and other private report card preparers. In such contexts, government need not play an active role in data gathering.

The current availability of appropriate data may be the consequence of previously established reporting requirements. Consider, for example, the case of report cards on insurer solvency. Firms currently face extreme market pressure to participate in the gathering of information for report cards. They routinely provide qualitative information requested by A. M. Best and other report card providers. Yet one can wonder if A. M. Best would have been able to launch insurer report cards at the turn of the century if the National Association of State Insurance Commissioners had not developed reporting requirements for insurers and encouraged its members to implement them. The insurance commissioners of individual states might very well have adopted reporting requirements for the insurers operating within their jurisdictions. While this would have facilitated state-level report cards, lack of uniformity across states would have hindered the realization of the economies of scale and scope that gave a near monopoly position to A. M. Best that greatly insulated it from pressure from individual insurers. Further, the ready availability of standardized data on insurers allowed the easy entry of competitors when insurance buyers became concerned that A. M. Best might have become too soft in its ratings. The strong market demand for insurer report cards probably means that insurers would continue to collect and report solvency information even if they were not legally required to do so by state insurance commissions, but they might not be willing to provide it to all potential report card producers.

More generally, it is important to understand the implications of the existing regulatory framework for the availability of appropriate data for report cards. Although reporting requirements tend to remain in place by virtue of policy inertia, they may become ineffective as new organizational forms arise within industries. For example, the shifting of medical procedures from hospitals to outpatient provision by independent physician practices may mean that these services are no longer included in data reported by hospitals. Efforts to reduce the administrative costs of government agencies may threaten the availability of data for report cards through either the outright elimination of data collection functions or reductions in resources that increase the lag between the time data is collected and reported by organizations and the time it is available to report card producers.

In summary, when highly appropriate data for all relevant organizations are readily accessible, no active government role in data gathering is necessary. Yet attention should be given to the maintenance of existing reporting requirements or government data collection activities that contribute to ongoing report cards.

The Problem of Incomplete Participation. As previously noted, some organizations may decline to provide data because they want to avoid costs, inconvenience, or the risk of embarrassment. To focus on the issue of participation, let us assume that the government agency with regulatory power over the relevant set of organizations has sufficient expertise to know what data would be required to provide an adequate basis for an effective report card. It is then possible for legislatures, or the regulatory agencies themselves, either to mandate or to undertake data collection. The particular policy instrument selected will depend on the strength of market demand for report card information, and the extent to which effective report cards require data on individuals.

Consider first situations in which there is strong demand for report card information and organizational, as opposed to individual-level, data are required for appropriate report cards. Strong demand means that private report card producers have an incentive to gather available data. Government can facilitate universal coverage of industries in private report cards by requiring that the organizations in the industry make essential data available to report card producers. For the reporting requirements to be effective in supporting report cards, they must be clear as to the content, timing, and format of data reporting, and they must be supported by credible penalties for noncompliance.

With respect to format, it is becoming ever more feasible to require that reporting be done through a World Wide Web homepage on the Internet rather than through hard-copy documents. Such electronic postings would allow for low-cost and timely access to the data by report card producers. Except in particular industries, such as home day care provision, where large numbers of organizations lack the immediate capacity for such reporting, electronic posting is likely to be the most effective instrument for facilitating private report card supply.

Compliance can be achieved in a variety of ways. Common approaches, such as requiring organizations to certify compliance in their annual reports, grant applications, and licensing applications, can be used. Where the government is a purchaser of services, it may also tie financial rewards to timely reporting. For example, the Tennessee Medicaid program withholds 10 percent of monthly payments until acceptable encounter data for the month have been reported, and the Arizona Medicaid program limits its reinsurance for exceptionally high cost cases to patients for whom encounter data have been previously submitted on a timely basis (Physician Payment Review Commission 1997: 169).

Private report card producers, who seek to use data that organizations are supposed to make public, can generally be relied upon by government agencies as a source of information about noncompliance because the report card producers have an incentive to report organizations that are not meeting requirements. Nevertheless, an administrative mechanism would still be needed to investigate complaints about noncompliance and impose penalties for those that are sustained.

Consider next situations in which there is strong market demand for report card information, but effective report cards require data on individuals. For example, the most valid methods for assessing the effectiveness of many medical treatments, such as cardiac surgery, require risk adjustments based on the characteristics of individual cases (Hannan et al. 1992). Protecting the privacy of individuals requires strict standards of confidentiality that usually cannot be sustained in systems of public self-reporting by organizations. Removing names, addresses, and other sources of direct identification before posting might be sufficient to protect the identity of most organizational clients, but there would always be the risk that someone might take advantage of the open access to match individuals on the basis of other case data. Consequently, the high degree of confidentiality that must accompany individual-level data calls for a direct government role in collection, storage, and oversight of use.

Finally, consider situations in which there is only weak demand for report card information. Simply requiring organizations to make data publicly available is unlikely to be sufficient to induce the private production of effective report cards. Anticipating a strong governmental role in other phases of report card production leads naturally to a strong governmental role in data gathering. Perhaps the most common approach, which is used most commonly in the areas of primary and secondary education, involves direct reporting of information to state agencies that organize the data into useable form. Agencies may be able to save money and improve timeliness by contracting out for the actual construction and maintenance of the data bases built from organizational reports. Such contracting, however, requires sufficient agency capacity for effectively monitoring the performance of contractors (Globerman and Vining 1996).

The Problem of Inappropriate Data. Sometimes organizations are either induced by market competition or compelled by regulations to make data available, but these data are inadequate for the production of effective report cards. The policy design problem in such circumstances is to find ways of increasing the appropriateness of the routinely available data.

The problem has a straightforward solution if the legislature or the agency with regulatory jurisdiction knows exactly what data should be collected. In such cases, these data can simply be included in a public reporting requirement or agency data collection as discussed above. For example, concern over the safety of college campuses prompted adoption of the 1990 Crime Awareness and Campus Security Act (PL 101–542, Title II), which requires institutions of higher learning that receive federal funds to provide statements of their security policies and campus crime statistics to students, potential students, employees, and other interested parties. Newspapers now commonly print stories about annual changes in crime statistics on campuses in their markets, and these data could be easily incorporated into report cards.

The more challenging problem arises when the agency with regulatory authority does not know exactly what data should be collected. Consider, for example, the complex issues that arise in deciding what data HMOs should report: Should reporting requirements be based on administrative data that is routinely collected, but perhaps not fully adequate for such purposes as risk adjustment, or should they be based on clinical data that would require more costly collection, but would offer more effective risk adjustment? Within either of these broad categories, what specific data are required to support various process, output, and outcome measures? In what format should the data be provided? To whom? How frequently? Not only are these questions difficult to answer, but the answers themselves are likely to change as more is learned and HMOs evolve.

Two broad strategies can be followed to discover appropriate data for report cards. Centralized strategies keep decisionmaking largely within the relevant government agency. For example, the agency may undertake its own research, issue contracts with various private research organizations, or convene expert panels to inform its decisions. Nevertheless, the agency ultimately makes a decision about what data are to be collected. In contrast, decentralized strategies allow, encourage, or induce various organizations in the private sector to develop the information necessary for specifying report card data. For example, government may provide exemptions from anti-trust laws to allow firms within an industry to share information, give grants to encourage research and development, or create an expectation that it will adopt privately developed reporting requirements to induce industry participation. Rather than impose requirements top-down, government allows the industry to set its own data standards through a bottom-up process.

The choice between the centralized and decentralized strategies is very complex. Almost the same choice arises in the context of product safety standards that are developed both by government regulatory agencies and by private organizations such as Underwriters Laboratories, American National Standards Institute, National Fire Protection Association, and the American Society of Mechanical Engineers. Ross E. Cheit (1990) provides a detailed comparison of the development of safety standards in the public and private sector. In terms of rational models of decisionmaking, he finds that private standard-setting generally enjoys an advantage in terms of technical know-how such as production processes, while public standard-setting generally enjoys advantages in terms of gathering information about real-world experience such as accident rates and organizing applied research and development relevant to answering unresolved technical questions (Cheit 1990: 196–202).

In the context of gathering data for report cards, technical know-how is needed to handle the logistics of data collection. Anticipating the cost, accuracy, and timeliness of data generally requires the sort of detailed institutional knowledge that can be best obtained from people experienced in the day-to-day workings of the industry. Such knowledge is likely to be especially important when the industry is characterized by great heterogeneity in terms of organizational size, production and administrative processes, and existing information processing capabilities. For example, the increasing use of various sorts of capitation payments to health care providers by group health plans renders the claims data generated by fee-for-service systems incomplete unless so-called dummy claims are submitted for services provided under capitation (Physician Payment Review Commission 1997: 164).

Yet research and development may also be important in the identification of appropriate data for report cards in complex situations. For example, mammography rates are often used as an indicator of the quality of preventive care provided by HMOs. But what is the appropriate denominator for computing the rate? All adult women? Women over 40 years old? Women over 50 years old? The answer will eventually be found from research into the risks and benefits of mammography for different age groups that is being conducted independently of efforts to design report cards. In other cases, however, the questions are sufficiently narrow that focused research must be done to find adequate answers, and government is likely to be in a better position for organizing it.

Public and private standard-setting also differ from an "evolutionary perspective." Cheit (1990: 202–207) offers the following general characterizations: Public standard-setting tends to take the form of one-shot substantial interventions that are followed with few revisions; private standard-setting tends to involve early intervention with frequent adjustments that are usually in the "right" direction. Although the political context differs in that safety standards, because of their direct implications for product availability and cost, legal liability, and safety, are likely to be more salient to various stakeholders than reporting requirements, Cheit's characterizations probably provide a reasonable basis for predicting the general tendencies of the centralized and decentralized approaches to the development of data standards for report cards.

Two examples related to health care report cards illustrate the tendencies. California law has mandated the collection and public release of hospital discharge abstracts since 1982. As major changes in the content of the abstracts require legislation, various stakeholders have been able to block changes that would facilitate the collection of more appropriate data for risk adjustment. Harold Luft (1996: 35) notes that the California Health Care Association has been able to block collection of physiological data, and the California Medical Association has been able to prevent the collection of license numbers for physicians and surgeons, as well as the extension of reporting to procedures performed on an outpatient basis. Thus, initiation of data collection by legislation moved decisionmaking to the

legislative arena where organized interests could block further development of the data requirements.

In contrast, recall the evolution of the Health Plan and Employers Data
Information Set (HEDIS). The nonprofit National Committee for Quality
Assurance (NCQA) released the first version of HEDIS in 1991. Successive versions, including most recently HEDIS 3.0, which was released in
March 1997, have refined, deleted, and added new items. With funding
from both public and private sources, the NCQA assembled the broadly
representative Committee on Performance Measurement (CPM) in September 1995 to develop more outcome-oriented measures that cover the
full range of health care provided by health plans. The CPM took as its
starting point measures included in HEDIS 2.5, which was already widely
in use for commercial health plans, and Medicaid HEDIS, which had been
developed by NCQA with funding from the Packard Foundation. In addition to forming a technical advisory committee, the CPM issued a public
call for suggested measures to over 1,700 organizations that generated
over 800 submissions (NCQA 1997). The result was an expansion of
HEDIS to 71 measures in eight general categories: effectiveness of care,
access and availability of care, satisfaction with experience of care, health
plan stability, use of services, cost of care, informed health care choices,
and health plan descriptive information. The measures range from specific
data items, such as eye exams for diabetics, to multiple questions on member satisfaction surveys. As a clear indication that participants view the
development of HEDIS as an ongoing evolutionary process, version 3.0
includes 32 additional items, mainly in the effectiveness of care category,
that comprise a "Testing Set" of candidate measures for inclusion in future
versions.

The HEDIS evolution has been driven by strong demands for comparative information on quality of care, especially from large corporations that
make major purchases of group health plans, but also from coalitions of
smaller firms, the Medicaid and Medicare programs, and private founda-
tions. HMOs must increasingly participate to some extent in HEDIS to
satisfy these demands. A 1994 survey of managed care plans sponsored by
the Physician Payment Review Commission (1997: 150–151) found that
three-quarters of HMOs used at least some HEDIS measures, either on
their own initiative or in response to demands from the purchasers of their
services. With the inclusion of measures designed for Medicaid and Medicare patients in HEDIS 3.0, the demands of private purchasers will be
further augmented by regulations associated with these public programs.

The Foundation for Accountability (FAcct), which was founded in 1995, is a coalition of major corporations (including many that specialize in information technology and therefore have a general interest in supplying medical data systems as well as concerns about the quality of managed care), labor unions, public employee pension plans, and various consumer groups that will undoubtedly contribute to greater HEDIS use—and spur further development of HEDIS outcome measures through the development of its own, and potentially competing, performance measures. Consequently, one can reasonably hope that the reporting of most HEDIS measures will eventually become standard practice for HMOs.

The history of HEDIS illustrates the weaknesses as well as the strengths of decentralized development. HEDIS has evolved slowly, still includes relatively few outcome measures, has allowed HMOs to be selective in their choices of measures, and has so far not achieved full participation of HMOs. Still, HEDIS has not triggered the fierce political and scientific backlash that ultimately destroyed the Health Care Financing Administration's (HCFA) more centralized hospital report card system. Despite its faults, HEDIS has contributed to incremental improvements in quality assessment without risking a major legislative battle that might have prematurely locked-in a particular system. Overall, the complexity of quality assessment in the health area, coupled with strong market demand for information about quality, suggests that a HEDIS-like evolutionary process probably offered better long-run prospects than a more centralized approach would have.

More generally, the key consideration in the choice between the centralized and decentralized development of adequate data for report cards is the existence of strong market demand for information about quality. When market demand is strong, then the best long-run role for government is likely to be in facilitating a decentralized process that relies on private organizations to develop data standards through an evolutionary process. Where market demand is weak, then a centralized process is likely to be necessary despite its vulnerability to political stasis.

Data Verification

Data gathered and submitted by targeted organizations, in response to a government directive or a private sector request, should be verified before being used in report cards. Inaccurate data may arise from the generic problems that tend to plague policy implementation (Bardach 1977: 98):

organizations may not have the capacity to deliver accurate data (incompetence), especially if the data are not routinely used for internal purposes (Weimer 1980b); organizations may undermine the entire process by not paying attention to the accuracy of the data they provide (token response); or, in extreme situations, organizations may simply refuse to comply on a timely basis (massive resistance). Specifically with respect to report cards, incentives to try to look better by cheating (deliberate distortion) or to reduce the costs of compliance by being sloppy (reckless disregard) are too great for accuracy to be assumed. Unless some verification process is instituted, the validity of the data may be suspect. As President Reagan once put it in the context of nuclear disarmament data, "Trust but verify!"

Both the government and the private sector have considerable experience with and expertise in data verification. The U.S. General Accounting Office has been conducting audits since 1921, and almost all federal executive agencies are subject to monitoring by their own offices of inspectors general (Light 1993). Most state governments have significant auditing operations within the executive branch, the legislative branch, or both. The private sector is also replete with highly-regarded accounting firms, such as Deloitte & Touche and KPMG Peat Marwick, as well as various organizations, such as the Insurance Services Office, that verify data used in ratings and certifications.

The regulatory power of government enables it to require organizations to submit to data verification. *As a general rule, specification of data verification procedures should go hand-in-hand with any reporting requirements set by government.* The procedures themselves, however, can be quite varied.

Three types of commonly used verification systems show the broad range of options available: attestation with legal liability for falsification by either organizations or their members; periodic direct auditing by a government agency or its designee; and the establishment of requirements for verification by third parties.

Attestation systems establish penalties for failure to report accurate data. The liability for inaccurate reporting is usually assigned to the organization as a corporate body, but it can also be assigned to specific individuals. For example, under the Medicare prospective payment system, attending physicians must attest to the correctness of patients' narrative diagnoses and acknowledge that they know that they are subject to criminal and civil penalties for false attestation. In either case, however, the effectiveness of the system depends on the perception of the risk of falsification by the bearer of the liability. For the system to be effective in deterring cheating, the perceived risk, which is likely to be closely related to the objective risk, must be larger than the perceived gains from cheating. The objective risk is the product of the probability of detection and the penalty resulting from detection. Other things being equal, more frequent and effective auditing and larger and more credible penalties increase the perceived risk of cheating.

In situations in which the organization perceives small benefits from cheating, say because the report card using the data is aimed at consumers with little choice, low rates of auditing can deter cheating so that an effective attestation system is likely to involve relatively low costs. Not all data errors result from cheating, however. Low frequencies of monitoring mean that these "honest" errors are less likely to be detected and corrected. Consequently, a system adequate for deterring cheating may not be very effective in contributing to accuracy more generally.

The calculus of deterrence differs between the organizational and individual levels. Because any individual typically receives only a fraction of the total benefits the organization derives from cheating, and because personalized penalties are likely to be perceived as highly threatening, assigning liability to individuals may produce higher levels of deterrence at lower auditing rates than assigning liability to organizations. There is a danger, however, that the threat of sanctions may lead individuals to become overly conservative when data collection involves uncertainty. A study of the accuracy of Medicare reimbursement, for example, attributes a shift in the distribution of errors made by attending physicians in patient narratives between 1985 and 1988 from 62.8 percent to 43.2 percent favoring over-reimbursement to the introduction of attestation by physicians (Hsia et al. 1992).

Periodic direct auditing by a government agency or its designee combines deterrence against cheating with more general possibilities for improving the accuracy of data. In addition to giving organizations an assessment of the accuracy of their data, auditors often have experience and expertise that enable them to provide advice about how to improve data collection procedures. Auditing each reporting cycle would be a highly effective way of improving accuracy. Except in the rare circumstance when the number of reporting organizations is small, such frequent auditing is likely to be too costly to be a practical part of a report card system design, and, unless the potential social benefits from eliminating report card errors are very high, undesirable. Instead, direct auditing is likely to be more appropriately used on a less frequent basis through which it maintains deterrence value but loses some of its potential for contributing to more accurate data overall.

The potential for direct auditing to contribute to improved data quality may also suffer when the deterrent function creates an adversarial relationship between organizations and auditors that interferes with constructive communication. Eugene Bardach and Robert A. Kagan (1982) identify this problem as the "regulatory ratchet" that plagues the relationship between regulated firms and government health and safety inspectors. Firms and inspectors tend toward a legalistic view that focuses on violations of rules rather than a common effort to solve problems so that the experience and expertise of inspectors do not contribute as much to improvements as they potentially could. Third-party certification systems, which permit more constructive communication between organizations and external auditors, may avoid the regulatory ratchet problem.

A third-party certification system requires organizations to obtain verification from specified auditors who certify that reported data meet minimal standards of accuracy. A single auditor, such as a professional organization, or a class of auditors, such as public accounting firms, can be specified by government. As the organization has less incentive to conceal information from these auditors than from auditors with the authority to impose penalties, it is likely to be more open to sharing information about its problems and seeking advice about how to correct them. In situations in which organizations can choose from among a large number of auditors, there is some danger that competition among them will make them too accommodating. An important element of the design of third-party certification systems, therefore, is careful specification of qualified auditors.

Accrediting bodies in various fields often train and certify auditors. For example, in 1996 the NCQA established an audit committee to develop standards for the auditing of HEDIS data. The NCQA expects to license auditing organizations and certify members of their staffs as qualified to use its standardized audit methodology. As the audit methodology focuses on the adequacy of the process of data collection rather than explicitly on data accuracy per se, it emphasizes capacity building rather than deterrence.

A private report card producer, acting on its own authority, can request that data be audited. To strengthen such a request, the private organization might use an asterisk or some other device to distinguish between organizations whose data have been audited by some outside party and organizations whose data have not been audited. It may also seek to put pressure on organizations indirectly through major purchasers. However, only government can require universal participation in audits and directly punish organizations that evade them. For example, the NCQA has encouraged HMOs to audit their HEDIS data for many years. The results were disappointing. Finally, in 1996 the HCFA announced that all HMOs with Medicare contracts must have their data audited by a peer review organization. By the end of 1998, all HMOs serving Medicare patients will have audited data.

There may be subtle differences between the sort of monitoring provided by for-profit and nonprofit organizations. Both types of organizations currently provide third-party utilization review services to private health insurance providers. These reviews most commonly cover screening of hospital admissions and reviews of lengths of stay in hospitals (U.S. GAO 1992a). Mark Schlesinger and colleagues (1996) conducted a national survey of utilization reviewers to see if nonprofits differed from for-profits in terms of the provision of public goods, positive and negative spillovers, community orientation, and trust. They found that nonprofits were more likely to engage in grant-funded research and to make public information about the review process (public good measures) and that they were more likely to be influenced by local boards of directors and to incorporate local norms of treatment into their evaluations (community orientation measures), but that they showed no clear patterns of differences with for-profits in the other areas (Schlesinger, Gray, and Bradley 1996: 730–733). The apparently greater willingness of nonprofits to share information about their review process suggests that there may be a rationale for encouraging their use when verification requirements are introduced and there is potential for learning across organizations.

Data Analysis

Report cards require that raw data on inputs, processes, outputs, and outcomes be converted into useful information about organizational performance. Important decisions must be made about how various dimensions of performance are to be measured, whether they are to be aggregated into an overall rating or ranking, and how any aggregation is to be done. Appropriately taking account of important inputs that differ across organizations, such as clientele characteristics, typically requires the sophisticated application of multivariate statistical techniques that raise many difficult questions: how to handle missing data, how to operationalize the dependent variable, what covariates to employ, what estimation techniques to use, how many alternative models to develop, and so forth. These decisions require technical skill, good judgment, creativity, and the ability to handle deadline pressure. They also require courage in the face of pressure from the organizations being rated. For all these reasons, organizing data analysis presents report card designers with a complex task.

The desirable role for government in data analysis depends critically on the nature of report card supply by the private sector. If private sector supply of report cards is vigorous, then the appropriate role for government is likely to be limited to oversight and, perhaps, support for research and development. If private sector supply is absent or weak, then a more active government role in data analysis will be required to ensure provision of an adequate report card.

Consider first the case of vigorous private sector supply. Oversight by the government agency with regulatory authority in the market involves reviewing the various measures used in the report cards to determine if they effectively distinguish among organizations in terms of performance. When the organizations enjoy stronger market positions vis-a-vis report card producers than do the demanders of performance information, competitive pressures may lead to the selection of soft measures. By developing and demonstrating the use of more discriminating measures, government may be able to give consumers a focus for their information demands that will be heeded by private report card producers. Continuing attention to the content of private sector report cards may also make the possibility of the introduction of a government report card more credible. The greater the extent to which private sector report card producers perceive a threat of a government produced report card, the more likely they will be to embrace more discriminating performance measures.

There may also be an appropriate role for government in research and development more generally. If there are many report card producers, either competing directly in the same market or serving similar markets in different geographic areas, then research conducted by one report card producer directed at developing better performance measures may be under-supplied because it has the characteristics of a public good in the sense that other report card producers could not be excluded from using the new measures. Government investments in research and development can counter this under-supply. For example, the HCFA has contributed financially to HEDIS development, and it has contracted with RAND to conduct a four-year project to refine and test Medicare performance measures developed by FAcct (Physician Payment Review Commission 1997: 151). Government may also enjoy an advantage in terms of access to data from many sources that would not be readily available to independent researchers.

When the private sector fails to produce report cards, or produces report cards that are grossly inadequate, government has three broad options: directly produce a report card itself; induce private sector supply with some form of subsidy or other intervention; and contract with a private party to produce it.

A purely public solution avoids time-consuming transaction costs if the government gathered and validated the data in the first place. The government's historic and legal commitments to fairness and due process help to ensure that rated organizations will be treated fairly; its concern with the distribution of important services makes it potentially more attentive to the information needs of specific types of consumers, such as the old and the poor. The government is also more likely to share its data with outside critics than a proprietary firm would be. Unfortunately, government agencies often lack the in-house expertise needed to design effective performance measures and the resources to produce them on a timely basis.

A purely private solution also has advantages. A private firm or a non-profit organization can move more quickly to undertake and complete an assignment than a government agency hampered by strict hiring and procurement rules (Bretschneider 1990). Also, a private firm or a nonprofit organization may have specialized in related sorts of data analysis, giving it valuable experience and expertise. The major problem in implementing a private solution is finding an appropriate policy instrument for inducing the private production of report cards. When there is some market demand for report card information, government may be able to induce private sector supply by lowering the costs of data collection so that report cards become profitable. For example, a government agency might make the data it collects on organizations available in electronic format to potential report card producers. Of course, market demand may be so low that even lowering the cost of data collection to zero may not be enough to induce private sector supply.

Because both the public and private sectors have advantages in data analysis, there is much to be said for contracting-out as an approach that harnesses the distinctive strengths of both sectors. *In principle, government contracting can take advantage of the expertise that a private supplier has to offer without forfeiting the government's commitment to fairness among organizations and concerns about special groups of consumers.* Much depends, however, on how contracts are designed and executed.

A good contract is clear, specific, easy to honor, and easy to monitor. It specifies deadlines, work products, payment schedules, allocations of responsibility, and mechanisms for supervision. The government must be a smart buyer, which requires doing some homework in advance and observing the contractor's behavior after the contract is awarded. The ABCs of contracting for many types of services are simple and straightforward; yet, sadly, they are often neglected (Schlesinger et al. 1986; Kettl 1993; Wallin 1997).

Contracting for the development or production of performance measures raises some special problems. In order for government to write and implement an effective contract for the development of report card performance measures from scratch, it must have at least some minimal level of relevant expertise in-house (Vining and Weimer 1990). If in-house expertise is very scarce, then contracting first for design specifications might be a valuable intermediate step for developing it. Other approaches include "borrowing" expertise through professional review panels and involving nonprofit and professional organizations with relevant substantive interests in the design process. As a misstep by the agency may make it vulnerable to political attacks by interests opposed to the report card, building capacity, even at the cost of delay, may be the best long-run strategy.

Contracting agencies should also anticipate the possibility of opportunism on the part of contractees. The development of sophisticated data analysis procedures by contract winners typically gives them an advantage relative to potential future bidders. As a consequence, government may become locked-in to a specific supplier with an accompanying loss of control over quality and cost. Governments can try to counter lock-in by writing various provisions into contracts "by specifying hand-over procedures, obliging contractees to use common standards, and requiring transparent procedures and detailed system documentation" (Globerman and Vining 1996: 584). Building capacity within the contracting agency for doing data analysis also reduces the risk of lock-in by increasing the feasibility of handling the function in-house.

Information Presentation

The packaging or presentation of information can facilitate or undermine utilization (Jaeger et al. 1993). An appealing format is especially important for lay persons or casual readers, who are not occupationally required to pay attention to a report card. If the format is attractive and comprehensible, then the report card is more likely to have an impact on the choices that consumers make. An appealing format may also facilitate use by busy policymakers, benefits managers, and other elites.

As a general rule, the private sector has much greater capacity for presenting information in a lucid, riveting way. It is no accident that our metaphor for adroit public relations is Madison Avenue and not Pennsylvania Avenue. The private sector, disciplined by market forces, has learned how to sell a product, whether that product is a deodorant, a beer, or a report card. Although the government is getting better in this area, the private sector still has a decisive edge.

To cite one example, the private sector is much more likely than the government to use a magazine format for a report card. *Health Pages,* a private-sector organization which produces HMO report cards for particular metropolitan areas, publishes a magazine with diagrams, pictures, and contrasting colors to facilitate use. Another private-sector publication, the *Washington Consumers' Checkbook,* evaluates both products and services for Washington-area consumers. Including cartoons and diagrams in its magazine to break up the monotony of text and charts has paid off for the *Washington Consumers' Checkbook:* it now reaches 60,000 subscribers.

To cite another example, the private sector is more likely than the government to use letter grades for its report cards. The Corporation for Enterprise Development, a private-sector organization which rates the states on their economic performance, business vitality, and development capacity, uses letter grades for each index and for components of indexes as well. Similarly, the newspaper *Education Week* recently used letter grades to assess state educational performance across several dimensions. The day may come when government agencies also use letter grades. Until now, however, government agencies have been reluctant to do so. To some government officials, letter grades seem like attention-grabbing gimmicks; to most private firms, attention-grabbing gimmicks require no apology.

Although there is little potential for government to improve information presentation in report cards produced by the private sector, potential exists for private sector contributions to the effective communication of information presented in report cards produced by government. One way to tap this potential is to contract out for the design of report card formats. Because less specialized knowledge is needed to judge the quality of work, government agencies will generally find it easier to write and monitor contracts for formatting design than for data analysis. If there is some market demand for report card information, then another alternative for tapping the presentational expertise of the private sector is simply to make the analyzed data available to private sector report card producers. In other words, rather than contracting for design work, government would try to induce private-sector supply by lowering the overall cost of report card production by fully subsidizing data gathering, verification, and analysis through in-kind provision. The school report card produced annually by the *Democrat and Chronicle/Times-Union* illustrates this approach—it selects among various measures provided by New York State to provide a rich comparison of schools in the Rochester metropolitan area.

Information Dissemination

The final test of a report card is whether it actually reaches consumers and policymakers and affects their behavior. Some report cards do; many do not. The difference between the two depends in part on the content (credibility) and the presentation (comprehensibility); it also depends on what techniques are used to distribute report card results to a broader audience.

In theory, many techniques are available: mass or targeted mailings, press conferences, exclusive interviews, newspaper, radio, or television advertising, CD-roms, or web sites. One level of government can mandate distribution by a lower level of government—some states require local school boards to distribute school report cards, and the federal government requires states to create local emergency planning committees to gather and distribute information on toxic substances. The appropriateness of a given technique will depend in part on the audience. Policymakers will respond more favorably to a personal interview or a press conference resulting in a news story. Ordinary citizens will respond more favorably to a web site or to television advertising. Certain elites, with a keen interest in the subject, will respond well to a targeted mailing or a CD-rom that may be purchased.

When it comes to disseminating information, the private sector has a decisive edge. *The most effective communicators in modern society are journalists, advertising executives, and public relations experts, most of whom work for the private sector.* While government officials have scored some occasional coups in distributing information (for example, in public health campaigns), they have usually done so in tandem with the private sector.

The mass media are especially important sources of information for both consumers and political elites. The mass media have helped to publicize report cards and to bring them to the attention of a wider audience. Indeed, in some instances, the mass media have prodded government officials to release information that they preferred not to release. Hospital and surgeon report cards, for example, were made public because of persistent mass media inquiries backed up by legal threats.

The mass media also have the potential to help equalize the information possessed by the rich and the poor, the well-educated and the poorly-educated. Television in particular has the capacity to reach citizens whose socioeconomic status is low. Of course, television can seldom capture the nuances of a complex report card. But newspapers can do this, and newspaper summaries of report card findings are extremely helpful to nonprofit organizations that assist the poor and the poorly-educated to make better choices for themselves and their loved ones. For example, the *Detroit Free Press* published a detailed and comprehensive report card on Michigan's nursing homes, based on inspection records from a recent four-year period (Young 1996). Armed with that report card, nursing home advocacy groups can assist disadvantaged citizens in making sensible nursing home choices.

The mass media, though important, are not the only private organizations that are well-equipped to distribute information to consumers. Child care resource and referral agencies, which assist parents who are seeking child care, are in a unique position to distribute performance-based information to parents at precisely the time when they are making child care choices. Although resource and referral agencies have not yet figured out how to extract quality-relevant information from state licensing agencies and how to distribute it to parents without upsetting providers (Gormley 1995), they are, in principle, well-suited for that task. Indeed, the impact of report cards is probably enhanced when real people actually explain the statistical tables to potential users.

Although no particular strategy for facilitating private sector dissemination of report cards produced by government will be generally applicable, some general principles apply. First, lower the cost of media access to report cards as much as possible. Routinely sending advance copies to newspapers and television news departments, posting complete copies of report cards on web pages, and providing summaries that can be easily translated into news stories are good strategies. Second, make it easy for interested parties to obtain complete report cards. Providing media with accurate information on how to obtain copies can help. So too can making sure that agency personnel are aware of report cards so that they can channel requests for report cards to the proper place. Third, communicate with groups that can help reach specific populations of interest or specialized media. Appropriate personnel in these groups should receive copies of report cards along with advice about who might benefit from the information that they contain.

Who Should Tie the Functions Together?

Our discussion of public and private sector roles in the functional areas of report card design has used the term "government" generically. Yet in the U.S. federal system, government could refer to a federal, state, or local entity. Within each of these categories of government, different types of executive, or perhaps even legislative, agencies could take the lead in organizing the production of a report card. What are the general considerations in deciding which government agency should play a lead role in tying the report card functions together?

One obvious consideration is whether the geographic jurisdiction of the government entity encompasses the entire market. The more completely a report card covers a market, the more effective it will be in informing consumers' choices. For example, nursing homes usually draw from areas that extend beyond the borders of local governments. Consequently, a state-level report card would probably be more useful than one produced by a single local government.

Another consideration is the substantive jurisdictions of the various levels of government. Does the level of government have a constitutional and legal basis for concerning itself with the market? Broadcast media, for example, operate in local markets but they are regulated by the federal government. As local and state governments would have no legal basis, and little, if any, leverage in seeking cooperation from broadcasters in data gathering and verification, they would be unlikely to produce effective report cards. In contrast, the federal government does not play a direct regulatory role in day care and therefore would be an unlikely producer of report cards on day care providers.

Jurisdictional considerations rule out specific levels of government. When more than one level satisfies jurisdictional constraints, then additional considerations become relevant. For example, both state and local governments regulate day care. As day care markets often extend beyond municipal boundaries, counties would probably best match the geographic market; yet the inclination of residents to contact city officials suggests that report cards might best be produced at the municipal level (Gormley 1991).

Jerry Mashaw and Susan Rose-Ackerman (1984: 115–122) set out a number of normative criteria for deciding where to locate regulatory authority as between states and the federal government: the presence of externalities; the possible existence of Prisoners' Dilemmas among states that prevent redistribution; economies and diseconomies of scale in administration; substantive benefits of variety and uniformity; and citizen participation in regulatory choice. Of these considerations, economies and diseconomies of scale in administration and the substantive benefits of variety and uniformity are most relevant to locating authority for report cards.

Governments with smaller geographic jurisdictions, such as municipalities and counties, often enjoy more knowledge about the specific characteristics of local markets that might enable them to better target them in terms of presentation and dissemination. Yet they often lack resources, such as technical expertise, data processing capabilities, and discretionary funds, that are required to produce sophisticated report cards. In addition to advantages in many of these resource areas, more geographically extensive governments often can exploit economies of scope: the development costs of a report card may not differ much whether it is done for one geographic market or many. Such economies of scope are likely to be very important in terms of facilitating standardization of data formats. Subtitle F of the Health Insurance Portability and Accountability Act of 1996 (PL 104–191), for example, seeks to simplify the collection and electronic sharing of health data by requiring the Secretary of Health and Human Services to adopt standards for unique identifiers for individuals, employers, health plans, and health care providers. Implementation of Subtitle F should facilitate the production of health care report cards by both private groups and states.

Variety, which results from state or local authority, and uniformity, which results from federal authority, offer different substantive benefits. Vesting authority for report cards with state and local governments not only allows them to use their local knowledge to design report cards to fit market conditions, but also creates an opportunity for experimentation that can potentially lead to the identification and diffusion of better report cards in the future. Unfortunately, however, state and local discretion discourages standardization, which is extremely important for policy analysts, policymakers, and citizens who wish to make comparisons across jurisdictions. For example, each state environmental protection agency is now free to measure water quality as it sees fit (by focusing on compliance with federal regulations, on citizen complaints, on the health of fish, or on improvements over time). The result is a mishmash of data of little value to anyone (Hunter and Waterman 1996: 205–216). Vesting authority at the federal level facilitates interstate comparisons. It also makes compliance with reporting and verification requirements easier for firms doing business in more than one state.

But within any government, which agency should have responsibility? Regulatory agencies generally have the most direct connection to specific markets, and therefore considerable substantive knowledge of potential use in report card design. They also follow procedures and develop norms consistent with maintaining confidentiality, often an important consideration in data gathering and analysis. They may not have the capacity for organizing research, contracting with private organizations, or dealing effectively with large volumes of individual-level data, however. Consequently, it does not necessarily follow that the agency with the most direct connection to the policy area will be best able to orchestrate report card design.

A legislature with concerns about the capacity of the agency most directly concerned with the relevant policy area can consider alternative agencies. It can even consider writing fairly strict specifications that effectively require an agency to turn over implementation of the report card to a third party. For example, in 1992 the Tennessee legislature specified the Tennessee Value-Added Assessment System in such a way that the state's department of education had no real alternative to turning over its design and operation to the University of Tennessee.

In discussing the private sector, we have also thus far not been very specific. If the private sector should take the lead in gathering data, analyzing data, or distributing information, which type of private organization is most suitable for such tasks? A newspaper or magazine? A consumer advocacy group? A think-tank or research institute?

Each of these organizational types has advantages and disadvantages. They differ in their commitment, expertise, objectivity, skills, and credibility. Some of them have ready-made audiences, while others do not. Some of them have ready-made data bases, while others do not. Private organizations thus differ markedly in their goals, resources, and outlooks.

In general, advocacy groups are least suitable for producing report cards. Although they possess considerable knowledge and a strong commitment to the subject matter, they lack objectivity. This handicaps them at the data analysis stage in particular, but it is a weakness at other stages as well. A group with known biases is unlikely to secure cooperation from targeted firms. Nor is such a group credible enough to command the mass media's respect when presenting findings. If other groups do nothing, then an advocacy group may play a useful interim role by producing a flawed report card and demonstrating the obvious need for someone else to assume responsibility. Otherwise, advocacy groups serious about the introduction of effective report cards should leave their development to groups that possess greater objectivity.

At the opposite end of the spectrum, research institutes are best equipped to produce report cards. Their objectivity tends to be strong, their knowledge and technical skills impressive. They have the capacity to handle some of the more sophisticated tasks of producing a report card with discretion, delicacy, and precision. They are especially good choices to handle difficult data analysis assignments. Although we have found many examples of research institutes that analyze data under contractual arrangements with government agencies, we have found few examples of research institutes that handle all five phases of report card production. The reticence of research institutes may reflect an awareness of the government's comparative advantage in handling certain report card tasks. It may also reflect frustration with some of the imperfections of report cards or fear that targeted firms may punish those who portrayed them unfavorably in a report card.

The mass media fall somewhere in between advocacy groups and research institutes in their suitability for producing report cards. Their strengths include objectivity and a ready-made audience with at least a passing interest in report cards. Their weaknesses include limited technical skills and a limited attention span. Few newspaper or magazine reporters are in a position to judge the merits of scientific disputes concerning risk adjustment, estimating techniques, or the measurement of dependent variables. Also, with a few notable exceptions, such as *U.S. News & World Report,* which routinely publishes report cards on higher education and health care, their interest in the subject matter of report cards is ephemeral. More specialized journals, such as *Health Pages,* have longer attention spans but also suffer from limited technical skills. In the final analysis, the mass media are excellent choices for presenting and distributing information, but prior tasks are best handled by other organizations, whether public or private.

Conclusion

The appropriate role for government in the production of report cards depends critically on the nature of market forces affecting private-sector supply. When market demand for report card information is strong, typically the case when consumers have choice over important goods, and report card producers have a strong market position relative to the organizations whose performance they are assessing, then, unless important values other than efficiency are at stake, the private sector is likely to produce effective report cards without an active government role. When market demand for report card information is weak, or report card producers are not able to secure relevant data, then government will have to play a role if effective report cards are to be available.

Government can play different roles in each of the functional areas of report card design. Strong roles, involving regulatory powers or direct government production, are most likely to be justified in the prerequisite functions of data gathering and verification; they are least likely to be justified in the subsequent functions of information presentation and dissemination. A strong government role in earlier functions may make the ultimate supply by the private sector feasible. In some situations government success in increasing access to data and reducing the cost of access may be sufficient to induce private report card supply. In other situations government provision of data analysis, whether in-house or through contracting, may suffice. If not, government should look for ways of tapping private sector expertise in information presentation and dissemination.

8

Conclusion

As social problems, proposed solutions, and political developments converge, policy innovation becomes possible. In education, health care, and other policy domains, the convergence of key factors has created opportunities for using organizational report cards as policy instruments. If "policy entrepreneurs" design and promote them well (Kingdon 1984) and "fixers" monitor their implementation and utilization (Bardach 1977), then report cards could become permanent and desirable features of our public policy landscape.

In this chapter, we assess organizational report cards as policy instruments, both in comparative terms and on their own merits. We also offer some comments and recommendations on three key elements of report cards: their content (substance and technique), their presentation (medium and format), and their impact (on organizational behavior). Our intent is not to summarize what we have already said but rather to offer some new observations on how to improve report card design and use.

Organizational Report Cards versus Other Policy Tools

The organizational report card is only one of several techniques that policy entrepreneurs may employ in the quest for accountability or quality. To place report cards in perspective, it is useful to compare them with other techniques or tools. Such comparisons reveal that report cards possess unusual strengths.

Promoting Accountability

To achieve greater accountability it is possible to pursue either of two paths. The first leads to "top-down accountability" which holds organizations accountable to their legal sovereigns within government. Legislative oversight is a classic example. The second leads to "bottom-up account-ability" which holds organizations accountable to customers or clients outside of government. Consumer choice arrangements, such as vouchers, illustrate the second approach.

Both top-down and bottom-up accountability have their advantages and disadvantages. Legislative oversight enables elected representatives to gather information relevant to organizational performance, to confront leaders of organizations with poor track records, and to demand reform in a public setting. Consumer choice enables those who purchase services to "vote with their feet" by patronizing superior performers and rejecting inferior performers. Legislative oversight can be potent, constructive, and democratic, but it can also degenerate into legislative freelancing, when an individual committee chair pursues causes of greater relevance to him or her than to the general public (Gormley 1989: 194–197). Consumer choice can replicate the virtues of the marketplace, but it can also reward the information-rich at the expense of the information-poor.

A striking advantage of organizational report cards is that they facilitate both top-down and bottom-up accountability. Organizational report cards can be used by public policymakers, including legislators, political executives, and civil servants. Even judges may use them from time to time (a federal district court judge responsible for managing a public school system, for example). Organizational report cards can also be used by con-sumers, who may choose a different school or hospital or health plan after reviewing comparative information. Alternatively, report cards can be used by advocacy groups, who generate pressure for systemic reform by noting widespread weaknesses in organizational performance.

Of special importance in a democracy, organizational report cards pro-vide individual citizens with information that may help them to participate in politics intelligently. Unlike citizen participation requirements, organ-izational report cards ensure that voice is tempered to some degree by relevant information. Report cards do not guarantee an informed citi-zenry, but they tend to enhance the quality of public debate. In short, report cards make a distinctive contribution to both politics and markets by facilitating both top-down and bottom-up accountability.

Promoting Quality

Among the many mechanisms for enhancing the quality of services deliv-ered by public or private organizations, three stand out: regulation, self-regulation, and subsidization. Regulation was the preferred approach of the Progressives, who regarded it as direct, efficient, and effective. It was revived and transformed during Franklin Roosevelt's New Deal and once again during the 1970s (Eisner 1993). It is still widely used today, at all levels of government, but it has fallen out of favor because it is often coercive, costly, and unreasonable (Bardach and Kagan 1982; Howard 1994; U.S. GAO 1996d).

Self-regulation is a natural alternative to regulation. By definition, it is not coercive, and, by inclination, few organizations impose costly or unreasonable restraints on themselves. But self-regulation seldom goes far enough. Sometimes, it is more of a public relations exercise, involving what Edelman (1967) calls "symbolic politics," than a meaningful attempt to enhance quality. Consider, for example, self-regulation by the tobacco, the motion picture, and the firearms industries. Further, when it takes the form of certification or licensing by industry associations, self-regulation may be used by established firms to restrict competition by raising the cost of entry into the industry by new firms.

Well targeted subsidies can be more effective than self-regulation, less coercive than regulation. By tying financial rewards to various dimensions of quality, subsidies induce organizations to improve along these dimensions. But effectively targeting subsidies poses severe measurement problems. Subsidies not well targeted to dimensions of quality may fail to produce desired effects, or do so only indirectly by giving organizations more resources with which they can buy all sorts of things, including perhaps quality-enhancing innovations. But whether or not they are effectively targeted, subsidies are expensive. With voters increasingly sensitive to higher taxes and fearful of ballooning budget deficits, the politics of distribution, once so popular in legislative bodies, has become much more muted in recent years. Thus it is natural that we turn to other alternatives.

Another striking advantage of report cards is that they provoke a response from targeted organizations without straitjacketing them. In this sense, report cards are "catalytic controls" (Gormley 1989) that apply enough pressure to ensure a response but which also preserve discretion so that organizations can respond creatively and cost-effectively to demands for greater quality. Report cards covering firms in markets with consumer choice are typically stronger than self-regulation, less coercive than direct regulation, less expensive than subsidies. It is easy to understand their contemporary appeal.

Versatility

Depending on the problem, a report card may not be enough to turn an organization around, much less to turn an industry around. Health maintenance organizations have sufficiently strong incentives to cut costs that they need much stronger incentives to promote quality than report cards alone can provide. Public schools can ignore a report card's implicit demand for higher quality more easily than they can ignore a teacher's union's demand for higher wages. Often a catalytic control is not enough.

Yet another advantage of report cards, however, is their versatility. An organizational report card may have a modest impact on its own but a substantial impact when used in conjunction with some other policy instrument, such as regulation, endorsements, accreditation, and tournaments.

Should Report Cards Cover Individuals?

Most of the criteria that we specified for assessing report cards push the appropriate focus toward subunits of corporate organizations. By focusing on subunits, greater comprehensiveness (of the report card itself) can typically be achieved because the subunit produces only one, or a few, organizational services; greater validity for the report card's measures can often be achieved because they are more likely to be based on appropriate risk adjustment. For example, moving from a hospital to a cardiac surgery report card isolates one from among many medical services and, by restricting attention to a more homogeneous group of patients, facilitates the use of more appropriate methods and data for risk adjusting. The more narrowly focused report card may also have greater comprehensibility simply because it covers less ground, and it offers greater relevance to the extent that it concerns specific decisions that actually confront consumers. While the focus on one service might be dysfunctional by leading the larger organization to give the covered service too much attention, it might also be more likely to contribute to a functional response by capturing the attention of a manager closer to the production of the service of interest. These considerations do not always favor report cards for surgery units over those for hospitals, or report cards for schools over those for school districts, but they do suggest that focusing on organizational subunits, either exclusively or in addition to their larger organizations, is often desirable. But how far does this logic carry? Specifically, should report cards focus on individuals?

In several important contexts the quality of the services delivered depends on the skill and effort of identifiable individuals. Elementary school children typically spend the vast majority of their time in school with a single teacher over the course of an academic year, and research indicates that variation in the effectiveness of teachers is substantial, generally exceeding variation in the effectiveness of schools (Hanushek 1994: 78). Patients receive operations from surgical teams directed by particular physicians whose knowledge, experience, skill, and procedural preferences can affect outcomes. Considerable evidence shows that the propensity to use surgery as a treatment for many medical conditions varies greatly across local areas and that at least some of the variation results from disagreements among physicians about the proper use of medical interventions (Phelps 1992, 1995).

Primary education and specialized medical treatment share two prerequisites for individual-level report cards: First, individuals play sufficiently important roles to be reasonably held accountable for outcomes or outputs. Second, substantial variation in the quality of service provided by the individuals makes information about their performance valuable to consumers or overseers. Yet moving from an organizational subunit to the individual as the reporting unit dramatically increases the importance of fairness. Organizations and their subunits shield individuals to a considerable extent from the consequences of adverse report cards. Even their managers typically maintain some anonymity, share accountability with other staff, and can usually draw upon organizational resources to fight back against unfair assessments. Individuals face more immediate threats to their reputations and livelihoods from adverse individual-level report cards. Not only are they singled out for attention, but they are likely to have fewer resources available for challenging unfair assessments. At least from the perspective of relative harm, therefore, it seems appropriate to be more concerned about fairness to individuals than to organizations.

Concerns about fairness immediately bring to the fore the normative criteria of validity and comprehensiveness. Validity is clearly important: poorly measured contributions to outcomes provide an inadequate basis for fair comparisons. Comprehensiveness is also relevant to fairness when there are several important outcomes, and different trade-offs by individuals in producing covered and uncovered outcomes are reasonable. Reporting on contributions to a single subject, for example, may unfairly compare those who teach several subjects.

It is not surprising, then, that several of the report cards that provide individual-level comparisons stand out as particularly sophisticated in terms of data and methods used for assessing performance. The New York State cardiac surgery report card uses specially collected clinical data for all patients undergoing coronary artery bypass graft (CABG) surgery in a logistic regression model that permits the reasonable estimation of risk-adjusted mortality rates for surgeons. The Tennessee Value-Added Assessment System (TVAAS) applies several models that make sophisticated use of five years of data for each student in five subject areas to estimate the relative effectiveness of teachers within school districts in producing student gains. Each of these report cards has strong validity for the outcomes it measures. Although not fully comprehensive, each emphasizes one or more important outcomes that provide a reasonable basis for comparison of individuals.

Each report card started off recognizing the risks and limitations of individual-level assessment. The New York state cardiac surgery report initially withheld comparative information on surgeons, releasing it only after losing a lawsuit brought under the Freedom of Information Act. The legislation that established the TVAAS required that three years of data be accumulated before teacher effects were estimated and reported. It also limited distribution of teacher information to confidential reports to teachers, their principals, and their school boards as well as stipulating that the reports not be the sole basis for teacher evaluation. (Strictly speaking, these restrictions on distribution mean that the teacher effects component of the TVAAS does not qualify as a report card unless one views school board members as overseers rather than organizational heads.) Many parents would be interested in knowing the teacher effects, and one can imagine the pressures they would exert on principals to move their children to more highly rated teachers.

Each report card deals in its own way with the trade-off between inclusiveness and the precision of individual ratings: On the one hand, it is desirable to cover all individuals providing the service so that consumers have information about all possible choices. On the other hand, ratings for individuals with few clients are imprecise—small sample sizes lead to large standard errors. The New York cardiac surgery report presents risk-adjusted mortality rates by name of surgeon only for those who have performed at least 200 isolated CABG operations over the most recent three-year period at the same hospital—other surgeons at the hospital are grouped together into the category "all others." The TVAAS takes a different approach. Rather than setting a lower limit on the number of student scores a teacher must accumulate before receiving an effectiveness rating, it incorporates a "shrinkage measure," which can be thought of as a form of Bayesian updating, that takes account of the amount of information available for estimating the effect of each teacher. Teachers start with priors equal to the average effect for all teachers in the district. As more test scores accumulate, the teacher effect moves away from the district average and toward the mean gains for the set of students actually taught by the teacher. With this procedure, it is possible to provide reasonable estimates of effectiveness for all teachers within a school district.

A Bayesian approach similar to the one incorporated within the TVAAS could also be used by the New York cardiac surgery report card and other report cards that provide information directly to consumers about specific individuals. More generally, report card designers should consider using a Bayesian approach whenever the units being compared include some with extremely small sample sizes.

Content

It is axiomatic to say that report cards seek to measure organizational performance. But should they measure it directly or indirectly? Should quality be defined in terms of outcomes, outputs, processes, inputs, or some combination of the above? Should quality be treated as a multidimensional or unidimensional variable? Should quality be regarded as something that exists or something that is perceived? We have already spoken of the need for validity and comprehensiveness. But how valid and how comprehensive must a report card be? At what point does an obsession with validity become unreasonable? At what point does the pursuit of comprehensiveness pose a threat to understanding? In the real world, report cards are produced with limited amounts of time and money. Thus we confront the practical question: How do we design report cards that are scientific enough to be credible but simple enough to be understandable and cheap enough to be acceptable?

The Ambiguous Legacy of Survey Research

Faced with a limited budget and limited experience in measuring quality, many organizations have opted for a customer satisfaction survey as a first step in constructing a report card. For some organizations, that has been both the first step and the last step. For others, the survey has been one technique among many.

A survey is popular for three reasons. First, it is relatively cheap. A mail survey of approximately 2,000 HMO consumers, for example, can be administered for between $10,000 and $12,000 (Torda 1997). Developing a new survey instrument might double that cost, but the overall expense would still be reasonable. Second, it is relatively simple and straightforward. To conduct a survey, it is not necessary to hire a team of statisticians; to explain a survey, it is not necessary to translate technical terms or numbers. Third, it is relatively palatable to evaluated organizations. Customer satisfaction responses tend to be strikingly positive, which makes everyone look good. If a particular organization looks bad, then it can usually figure out how to boost its rating during the next round. Meanwhile, it can blame its showing on question wording, temporary management problems, or something else.

There are, however, reasons to be cautious about customer satisfaction surveys. First, they are sometimes based on a skewed sample of respondents. Persons who recently joined or recently left a health plan may be excluded, for example, leaving a sample of relatively comfortable customers (Anders 1996d). Second, surveys are based on the premise that consumer preferences over specific quality margins are exogenous. Yet as Hibbard et al. (1997: 9) have pointed out, consumers are frequently constructing preferences while they respond to a survey rather than reporting on preexisting preferences. If so, surveys are really tapping what social scientists like to call "nonattitudes" or responses that are not particularly reliable. Third, survey responses lend themselves to manipulation. A frequent ploy is to collapse positive responses to a Likert-scale question so that all the rated organizations look alike. By merging good/very good/ excellent responses, report card designers may secure the cooperation of targeted organizations, but they may also eliminate distinctions among organizations that could be informative to consumers.

Despite these limitations, customer satisfaction surveys are useful components of many report cards. In thinking about health care quality, Avedis Donabedian (1988) has argued that quality has three distinct elements: structure (resources and institutional arrangements); process (what is actually done by health care professionals and their patients); and outcome (the effects of care on the health status of patients and the wider community). Customer satisfaction surveys offer considerable insights into the process of health care, especially interpersonal interactions between health care professionals and patients. Short of actually observing how physicians, nurses, and patients interact, there is no better way to know whether patients are treated with courtesy, dignity, and respect.

Of course, we also want to know whether the outcomes of these interactions are favorable. A physician with a good bedside manner is not enough when a patient's life is at stake. A teacher with a winning smile is not enough if challenging subjects are being taught. And all the resources in the world are not enough if those resources are ineptly utilized. As Donabedian (1988: 1746) puts it, "As a general rule, it is best to include, in any system of assessment, elements of structure, process, and outcome."

Surveys can play a role in outcome measurement, but to do so they must ask questions about people's physical, employment, or other condition rather than their satisfaction with the way services were delivered to them. Health researchers have developed indicators in the general health domains of social function, psychological function, physical function, and impairments that can be used to construct quality-of-life measures (Gold et al. 1996: 94–96). With respect to report cards on cardiac surgery, for example, one might imagine surveying those who survived cardiac surgery with instruments that assess their conditions in one or more of these health domains. Answers to these survey questions could be used to construct an outcome measure that could be used in parallel with mortality to assess hospitals and surgeons. Surveys, if thought of more broadly than simply instruments for assessing consumer satisfaction, can potentially offer report card designers a source of data on outcomes that could otherwise not be measured.

Certain HMO report cards will soon be including the results of such surveys. In December 1996 the NCQA, prodded by the Health Care Financing Administration, incorporated a new survey into its Health Plan Employer Data and Information Set (HEDIS) requirements for Medicare HMOs. The new survey, to be administered by independent contractors, attempts to measure the functional status of senior citizens. Known as SF36, it covers such items as whether each senior can bend, climb stairs, bathe, dress, and so forth (Kim 1996). In contrast to customer satisfaction surveys, which focus on process, the SF36 survey focuses on the actual health of senior citizens, as reported by the seniors themselves. With appropriate risk adjustment, and in conjunction with other data, it can be used eventually to assess the effectiveness of Medicare HMOs.

The Importance and Difficulty of Risk Adjustment

Effective report cards compare organizations in terms of their performance. Measuring performance generally requires that some outcomes, or their proxies, be adjusted to take account of the difficulty of bringing them about. The task, commonly referred to as risk adjustment, ranges from the relatively simple calculation of ratios (for example, finding airline fatality rates by dividing the outcome of total crash fatalities by a measure of exposure such as the number of revenue passenger miles) to the complex construction of counterfactuals (for example, calculating risk-adjusted fatality rates for hospitals by comparing gross mortalities with the predicted number of mortalities based on the health status of admitted patients). How well have outcome measures in report cards been risk adjusted?

Consider first the case of primary and secondary education. Two factors have contributed to the development of fairly sophisticated risk-adjustment methods. First, despite their limitations, standardized test scores are widely accepted as legitimate proxies for educational outcomes. As a consequence, researchers have accumulated considerable experience using similar sorts of data. Second, concerns about the fairness of state funding across school districts, especially in light of *Serrano v. Priest* (1971) and subsequent legal challenges to school finance systems, and the search for ways of improving school effectiveness in response to the ongoing educational "crisis," have encouraged researchers to formulate educational production functions that model test scores as dependent on various educational inputs including the socioeconomic backgrounds of students.

The major limitation in educational risk adjustment is the common unavailability of test scores for individual students in successive grades. As a consequence, models often explain levels, rather than gains, in test scores, which places an immense burden on researchers to take account of all the factors that should explain students' current levels of achievements. Further, as data on important covariates, such as family socioeconomic status, are usually not available at the individual-level, models must often be reformulated in terms of school averages that can be related to such proxies for the student body socioeconomic status as the fraction of students participating in subsidized school lunch programs.

The risk-adjustment methods incorporated in the South Carolina and Tennessee school report cards show how multi-year data can be used to construct gain measures for schools based on the scores obtained by individual students in successive years. Indeed, the experience with TVAAS suggests that estimating models based on multi-year student test score data obviates the need to include the various covariates commonly employed in less data-rich models. Data collection need not be expensive—the five-subject area tests administered in Tennessee cost only $3.59 per student per year in 1995 (Bratton, Horn, and Wright 1996: 30). Relatively small investments in building such longitudinal data bases of student test scores can create an extremely valuable resource for producing more valid report cards. *States serious about developing appropriately risk-adjusted performance measures for schools should implement multi-grade testing programs in important subject areas.* Although it is important that the selected tests be appropriate for measuring achievement in terms of state curricula, also participating in testing developed for the National Assessment of Educational Progress (NAEP) allows for comparisons across states. And, as recommended by Diane Ravitch (1995: 183), Congress should remove restrictions it has placed on the use of NAEP tests to assess student performance at the school district level.

Turning to health care, one finds great variety in types of medical services and the institutional arrangements used to deliver them. It is not surprising that this variety has given rise to a great diversity of risk-adjustment practices.

Thus far most of the progress in risk adjustment has resulted from attempts to take account of differential costs of treatment rather than variations in the quality of care. In 1983 the federal government switched from fee-for-service reimbursement of hospitals for Medicare patients to prospective payments based on the diagnosis-related group into which patients fall by virtue of their medical condition upon admission. Since then, researchers have developed indexes of expected patient costs for prospective payment systems in a variety of other applications such as Medicare beneficiaries in HMOs (Ellis and Ash 1995–1996) and the disabled in Medicaid group health plans (Kronick et al. 1996). With large sums of money at stake, refinements in risk adjusting patient populations for purposes of prospective payment systems will undoubtedly continue. These applications are only indirectly related to quality of care—they attempt to set payments so that the funded health care providers do not have an incentive to engage in cream skimming. But research attention is increasingly being given to measuring health outcomes (Siu et al. 1992) and risk adjusting them in their application to such services as nursing home care (Kane and Kane 1988; Mukamel 1997) and home health care (Shaughnessy et al. 1994).

The most advanced uses of risk-adjusted outcome measures have been made in specific acute care areas where focusing on a single outcome, mortality, is reasonable. The CABG surgery report cards produced by New York and Pennsylvania, as well as the acute myocardial infarction study produced by California, for example, illustrate well-focused and sophisticated methodologies.

In contrast to these selected areas of acute care, little progress has been made in developing risk-adjusted outcome measures for HMOs. Perhaps one reason is that measuring maintained health is much more difficult than measuring mortality. HEDIS has a few output, but mainly process, measures as proxies for outcomes. Process measures may seem relatively easy to risk adjust. For example, breast cancer screening might seem appropriately expressed in terms of the fraction of women within targeted age groups who have mammograms. As Harold Luft (1996: 31) notes, however, the age-adjusted mammography rate may not be a good measure of organizational performance if HMOs enroll women with very different education levels—achieving a high rate may be easier with better educated women.

Risk adjusting typically becomes more important with respect to measures that are closer proxies for health because health results from many factors, with most not directly under the control of an HMO. Consider the rate of low-weight births, one of the few HEDIS measures that might be interpreted directly as an outcome. Arnold Epstein (1995: 60) notes that research has not conclusively established the link between low birth weight and the quality of routine prenatal care. Many other factors, including socioeconomic status, almost certainly play some role. Failing to risk-adjust for these other factors could lead to incorrect assessments of the relative quality of HMOs serving different populations. The same concerns apply to asthma, which appears to be related to socioeconomic status.

Although some of the obstacles to effective risk adjustment are technical, many are clearly political. Naturally, targeted organizations prefer econometric models that make them look good to those that make them look bad. In practice, advances in risk adjustment have often been combined with pragmatic political concessions. Some of these concessions have been sensible, while others have achieved consensus at the expense of standardization or validity.

After experimenting with different models as predictors of heart attacks, the California Office of Statewide Health Planning and Development (OSHPD) opted to present the results of two very different models in its hospital report card. The first model, Model A, includes as predictors only clinical risk factors that were almost certainly present when the patient was admitted to the hospital (or comorbidities); the second model, Model B, also includes factors that may have developed after admission (or complications). In a useful preamble, the report explains to readers that the first model is more conservative, while the second is more comprehensive

(California OSHPD 1996: 7–9). Readers are free to choose the model they prefer, and astute readers are free to consult a technical appendix. Also, hospitals have fewer reasons to complain about mistreatment, because the state has explicitly recognized that reasonable people may disagree about the most appropriate way to adjust for risk.

A less appropriate compromise has been reached by the federal Department of Labor (DOL) in its implementation of the Job Training Partnership Act (JTPA). After carefully developing separate econometric models for different outcome variables (placement rates, earnings levels, and so forth), DOL invited each state to use the national model or some other model of its own choosing. A modicum of consistency is achieved by insisting that every service delivery area within a given state must be evaluated based on the same set of risk factors. But state discretion, in this instance, means that interstate comparisons cannot easily be made, except for states that have agreed to use the national model. In this case, a misplaced commitment to federalism has extended from flexibility in program implementation (where it is entirely appropriate) to flexibility in program evaluation (where it is far less appropriate). In its attempt to defuse political opposition, DOL has made it difficult to judge which states are performing better. As a result, risk-adjusted state performance measures are currently unavailable.

Taking Account of Multidimensionality

Occasionally, a baseball team appears with razor-sharp pitching, red-hot hitting, and a leak-proof infield. Such a team has a good chance of making it to the World Series, because most opposing baseball teams have at least one fatal flaw that stands as a barrier to excellence. The same is true of other organizations. For example, a study of colleges found that those whose students scored high in academic achievement were not necessarily those with high student morale (Cameron 1978). As the author, Kim Cameron, observed, organizational effectiveness is a multidimensional variable.

Unfortunately, many organizational report cards treat quality as if it were unidimensional. Certainly, this is true of hospital report cards, which have tended to focus on mortality alone as if it were the only dependent variable (or outcome) that mattered. Yet, as critics have noted, the quality of life after surgery is arguably as important as whether the patient survives (Green et al. 1997: 1154). A patient's mobility, cognitive functioning, and general disposition are all important outcomes that, in principle, ought to be measured.

Death has figured prominently in hospital report cards because it is easily measured and because it is undeniably important. But what about the surviving patient's functional status? Although such measures are now readily available and are relatively easy to administer, they have seldom been used in hospital report cards. Another conspicuous failure is the absence of systematic efforts to measure the quality of death. Some deaths are slow, painful, and undignified; others are not. Upon closer examination, even death is a multidimensional variable!

Although measurement problems and cost considerations account for some unidimensional approaches to quality, others may reflect concern about the average consumer's capacity to process large amounts of information. In fact, both decisionmaking theory and empirical research support the proposition that consumers make poorer choices when they receive a surfeit of information (Hibbard et al. 1997). However, comprehensibility does not require the use of a single dependent variable, such as death, or a quality index that merges distinct dimensions of quality. An alternative approach would be to collapse multiple indicators into three or four broad areas of performance. Consumers who are particularly interested in one of these dimensions could then explore that dimension in greater detail (Hibbard et al. 1997: 11). In short, the competing demands of validity and comprehensibility can be reconciled if report cards are designed with both in mind.

Presentation

Presentation matters. A catchy jingle (Snap / Crackle / Pop) or slogan (Where's the Beef?) can attract interest and customers. Bright colors and clever graphics can lure newspaper readers, as *USA Today* has discovered. Special features (Your Health and You) can lure television viewers. Special effects (kinetic creatures from Outer Space) can attract moviegoers. It is important to remember, however, that report cards seek to inform consumers, not to manipulate them. *The goal is to help consumers, not to ensnare them.* It is also important to remember that report cards seek to improve the functioning of markets of special public importance—markets for education, health care, child care, and employment, among others. The stakes are high and they are public stakes even if some of the services in question are provided by the private sector. In this section, we consider how best to reach consumers with information that they find relevant and comprehensible.

Which Formats Are Best?

Most report cards begin with paper—sometimes lots of paper. To do justice to a complex statistical model, it is often necessary to provide a detailed explanation of how the model was derived and how its coefficients should be interpreted. Some report cards include a separate technical appendix to satisfy the curious reader with some quantitative skills. This is a sensible strategy, though it does not eliminate the need for some brief discussion of the methodology directly before or after the heart of the report card.

The heart of the report card is normally a table or chart or, more commonly, a series of tables or charts. In preparing such materials, report card producers must decide whether to present raw numbers, bar graphs, icons signifying better or worse than average, or some combination of the above. The advantage of raw numbers (and, to a lesser degree, bar graphs) is their precision. The advantage of icons is their capacity to condense a large body of information. Arrows pointing upward tell you instantly which health plans are better than average; but if the two plans you're thinking of both feature arrows in the same direction, then you may be the victim of too much condensing.

After conducting focus groups to determine which formats Medicaid consumers prefer, the Oregon Consumer Scorecard Project eventually opted for bar graphs with numbers, followed by icons signifying above average/below average/average performance (Hanes and Greenlick 1996). This approach would seem to offer the best of both worlds. But sometimes the numbers in question are not simple percentages (the percentage of HMO customers who are very satisfied with a particular plan) but estimates based on logistic regression results (measuring the difference between a particular hospitals's expected and observed mortality rate). Whether consumers have the capacity to grasp statistical estimates such as these is unclear. Indeed, that depends in part on how cleverly and tenderly report card producers explain their methodology in the narrative that precedes or follows the numbers.

The problem, however, with complementary techniques for presenting the same information and narratives that carefully describe report card methodology, is that they may yield an overly bulky report card. Is there some optimum length for a report card? In a study of school report cards, Jaeger et al. (1994: 28) actually found that parents prefer longer report cards. However, in their study, "long" was defined as four pages while "short" was defined as two pages. Some observers might say that they were in fact studying the difference between short and very short report cards. In any event, the more common finding is that consumers complain about getting too much information. For example, a 16-page booklet comparing 38 health plans on 20 performance measures left Minnesota consumers gasping for relief (Hibbard et al. 1997: 1–4). More precisely, consumers complain about both too much and too little information (Hanes and Greenlick 1996). Although this might appear contradictory, consumers are actually saying that they would like to have greater control over what information they receive. A good table of contents provides some measure of control, saving consumers from the laborious task of leafing through a lengthy document. Another solution, described more fully below, is to rely more extensively on the Internet, which enables users to ignore irrelevant information and retrieve more detailed information on selected topics of interest.

Do the same rules of thumb concerning format apply to both mass and elite audiences? Because elites, such as public policymakers, have a professional interest in many public issues and appear to be conversant with many topics, it is tempting to assume that elites can handle longer and more technical reports. However, many members of Congress have notoriously short attention spans, thanks to a daily schedule that is punishing at best. More broadly, Congress seems to suffer from an information overload that once prompted the Senate chaplain to pray for relief. As David Whiteman (1995: 39) has reported, the Rev. Richard Halverson apparently concluded that divine intervention was needed to solve the Senate's information glut: "Like an avalanche, data inundates the Senate and its committees, so that however long and hard staffs work and Senators try to process the material, they face an impossible task which would challenge the most sophisticated computers. Gracious Father, give all who are involved in this information overkill Thy wisdom and discernment."

It is also natural to assume that policymakers and other elites prefer print to video formats. Certainly, policymakers at both the federal and state levels use considerable amounts of written information (Mooney 1992; Whiteman 1995). But elites also respond to video presentations, such as televised reports. For example, a study of an NBC special on fraud and abuse in home health care found that government officials who saw or heard about the broadcast were more likely to change their views on the seriousness of home health care problems (Cook et al. 1983). A report card that served as the basis of a hard-hitting investigative story on television could have a dramatic effect on both public policymakers and the viewing public.

Role of the Internet

Older readers probably share our inclination to think of report cards as paper documents. Recent and projected growth in the use of the Internet, however, calls for a more technologically astute perspective.

Disseminating Information. A number of organizations have established World Wide Web sites on the Internet, where consumers can access report card information. In some instances, the web site is a substitute for printed information; in others, it supplements information available in a newspaper or magazine. In some instances, the web site presents ratings or rankings; in others, the web site presents raw data, which consumers must massage and analyze to extract meaning.

The Internet has some natural advantages as a source of information for consumers. As one study shows (Hanes and Greenlick 1996), consumers like the idea of gaining access to precise, detailed information that answers very specific questions without having to slosh through copious amounts of information that does not directly meet their information needs. In general, a web site fits that description. Also, its marginal cost of access is very low for Internet users, and, with commonly available search engines, it greatly increases the chances that interested persons will find the report card even if they were unaware of its existence.

Admittedly, not every consumer has access to the Internet. A report card that is available only through the Internet may not directly benefit such consumers, many of whom are already disadvantaged because they lack wealth. As Vice President Al Gore has warned (quoted in Shenk 1997: 210), "If we allow the information superhighway to bypass the less fortunate sectors of our society, even for an interim period, we will find that the information rich will get richer while the information poor will get poorer with no guarantee that everyone will be on the network at some future date."

Nevertheless, the proportion of Americans with access to the Internet is growing rapidly. As of 1997, 40 percent of all American households own a computer and 28 percent of all adults regularly use the Internet (Samuelson 1997: 63). Moreover, the latter figure will surely and quickly increase, thanks to governmental and private initiatives to supply computers to schools and libraries. Thus while the information gap between the rich and the poor is an appropriate cause of concern, it should not discourage utilization of the Internet for report cards. A better solution to the information gap is to ensure that poor citizens have access to the Internet as well, whether at home, at work, or at a local library.

A key question that report card producers face when they choose to showcase their product through the Internet is whether to provide an explicit rating of organizations or raw data only. The former approach facilitates comprehensibility and relevance by reducing or eliminating computation costs to consumers. But ratings do imply a certain confidence in the validity of the underlying data and in the computational techniques employed. If organizations lack that confidence, then they may prefer to present raw data only, inviting consumers to design their own do-it-yourself report cards.

Confronting that choice, the Federal Aviation Administration (FAA) decided to furnish only raw data when it added an airline safety category to its web site on February 28, 1997. One of the FAA's reservations is that "accident" and "incident" data are defined rather broadly. For example, accidents include broken bones that result from unexpected turbulence, and incidents include untimely nosebleeds that require a pilot to cancel a flight (Toenniessen 1997). Most observers would probably agree that neither should be blamed on the airline in question. Another reservation is that reasonable people may disagree about the most appropriate denominator when calculating safety records. A common approach is to divide accidents or incidents or both by the number of flights, but this ignores the length and the distance of each flight. On the other hand, four short flights are probably more treacherous than one flight that exceeds all four combined in revenue flight hours or revenue passenger miles. The FAA's solution to these quandaries is to let the consumer decide how safety should be measured.

The FAA's rationale is clear enough but it imposes an intolerable burden on the average consumer. The FAA's web page (www.faa.gov) requires consumers to (a) choose the most appropriate numerator; (b) choose the most appropriate denominator; (c) select a suitable time frame; (d) download the data; and (e) calculate ratios by hand. These tasks are time-consuming and a bit tricky. A newspaper or magazine could accomplish them easily enough and produce a helpful article or two, but few consumers are likely to do it themselves. In fact, the main benefit derived from the FAA's failure to rate airlines based on their safety records is that it insulates the FAA from criticism from airlines with bad safety records and from public criticism should a horrible catastrophe befall an airline with a good safety record. The main cost is that ratings published by industry critics, such as former inspector general Mary Schiavo (1997: 248–250), will not be as rich or as nuanced or as up-to-date as ratings that the FAA could have published.

Another question that organizations confront when using the Internet to showcase a report card is whether to make comparisons using interval or ordinal data. In its web site, the Pacific Business Group on Health (PBGH) uses colored arrows (based on an ordinal scale) to signify HMOs whose customer satisfaction scores are above average, well above average, below average, well below average, or average (www.healthscope.org). The biggest advantage of this system is that it is highly user-friendly. At one glance, consumers can discern which health plans stand out from the rest, in both positive and negative directions. The use of multiple satisfaction measures (for the doctor seen most frequently, the quality of the specialist, attention to what you have to say, explanation of medical procedures and tests, etc.) is an added bonus.

The major limitation of the ordinal approach, however, is that it may be unfair to certain HMOs and misleading to consumers. For example, there may be no statistically significant difference between an organization whose satisfaction rating places it at the upper edge of the "average" category and one whose rating places it at the lower edge of the "above average" category. Yet the arrows (or icons), based on the ordinal-level scale, imply a significant difference. Concerned about this, the board that sets policy for the PBGH's web site has decreed that interval-level data must be presented in the future (Castles 1997). When the demands of comprehensibility conflict with those of fairness, such trade-offs may well be appropriate. An alternative approach, currently under consideration, would be to present both interval-level and ordinal-level data on the same screen. Such a strategy could facilitate comprehension without undermining fairness.

Do report cards presented on the Internet actually reach consumers? The answer thus far is a qualified yes. During the open enrollment season, when consumers choose their HMO, the PBGH web site receives approximately 2,000 visits per week; during other time periods it averages about

200 visits per week (Castles 1997). The FAA's airline safety data, daunting though they may be, have also generated some interest. After the initial flurry of excitement, visits to the airline safety web site have stabilized at approximately 4,000 visits per week (Toenniessen 1997). These are certainly respectable figures. Also, it is important to remember that visits by journalists and advocates may result in articles and charts that reach an even greater number of consumers. Thus the direct and indirect effects of Internet access could be significant indeed. On the other hand, visits to Internet sites do not guarantee that consumers actually change their behavior. Nor do they guarantee that airlines or HMOs or other organizations improve their performance as a result.

An Aside: Role of the Internet in Data Gathering. The Internet has obvious potential as a medium for disseminating report cards. Though perhaps less obvious, its potential use in data gathering is also great. As noted in Chapter 7, requiring organizations to report data as postings on web pages offers several advantages over more standard reporting formats. First, it is likely to make data publicly available much sooner than do systems that involve centralized collection and processing by a government agency or contractor. Second, it increases the pool of potential report card producers by facilitating accessibility to data. Especially if web pages are required to carry a distinctive code, anyone with capabilities in net surfing would have the raw materials for making report cards. Concern for reasonableness would limit this approach to organizations that have, or could easily procure, the capability for producing web pages—today school districts, hospitals, and health maintenance organizations, but not in-home day care providers, could be reasonably expected to post data on web pages.

One application in which web-page data posting would almost certainly be superior to the traditional approach is in the reporting of contributions received and expenditures made by political campaign organizations (candidate committees). Campaign organizations in federal elections must report to the Federal Election Commission (FEC) all contributions received from political action and party committees and contributions amounting to more than $200 from any individual per year. The campaign organizations must also report expenditures made to any individual or vendor that exceed $200 per year. In nonelection years, presidential campaign committees must file monthly or quarterly as well as annually, while House and Senate campaign committees must file semiannually and annually, respectively. More importantly, in election years, House and Senate campaign committees must file quarterly, 12 days before the general election (20 days before a primary election), and 30 days after the general election.

Once the FEC receives the reports, it makes hard copies of them available to the public within 48 hours at its Washington, D.C. headquarters. In 1996 it was able to enter all the reports into its electronic data base within 30 days. Nevertheless, only reports filed for the first six months of the calendar year are generally available on congressional campaign committees at the time of the election.

In 1997 the FEC began allowing, but not requiring, campaign committees to file data in electronic format in an effort to speed up the process. It also has introduced online access to help the media and researchers make more timely use of its data bases, and it now requires copies of reports to be filed in each of the states in which campaign expenditures are made. Despite these efforts, the current reporting schedule guarantees that voters will have a very incomplete picture of the sources of campaign contributions to candidates before they cast votes. Consequently, the data collected by the FEC has little value as a resource for timely report cards.

Imagine a change in the campaign finance law that required congressional candidates to establish web pages on which they posted information about campaign contributions within a specified number of days after receiving them (for example, two business days). The FEC would monitor these pages to ensure that they are kept up to date, and routinely extract data for its various data bases. Report cards that listed campaign contributions from various types of sources, however, would be produced by newspapers and public interest groups. Such reports might very well stimulate some voters to investigate the web pages themselves. Web-page posting would certainly give meaning to disclosure, and would be an attractive component from the public's perspective of any campaign finance reform.

People Who Need People

Although the World Wide Web presents exciting possibilities for augmenting report card use, another more old-fashioned approach also has much to commend it—real advice from real people. Report cards seldom speak for themselves, and consumers often experience difficulty interpreting tables and text. For example, focus groups with Medicaid recipients in Oregon found that even user-friendly report cards presented problems for persons comparing HMOs. As Pamela Hanes and Merwyn Greenlick (1996:

26) concluded, "A consistent theme that emerged was the need to have a live person available, either by phone, at an orientation meeting, or located elsewhere."

The need for personal assistance is particularly strong for certain segments of the population. Persons with low literacy levels, poor eyesight, poor technical skills, or low self-confidence may be unable to digest report cards on their own. Welfare recipients and senior citizens, for somewhat different reasons, are likely to derive special benefits from personal assistance. But personal advice can benefit others as well, including parents of preschool children who must choose a child care facility and parents of school-aged children who have the opportunity to choose a school.

As we have noted, parents who wish to choose a public school have access to useful report cards in most states and superb report cards in some. In some metropolitan areas, such as Rochester, New York, report cards are available for private schools as well. The report card revolution has proceeded more rapidly in education than in other policy domains. However, many states and school districts currently report test score results for different schools that have not been adequately risk adjusted for students' demographic characteristics. In such states and school districts, parents could learn a great deal from educational advisors equipped to clarify the difference between a school with good test scores and a school with effective teachers. If we were to move toward a system of more extensive school choice (encompassing both public and private schools), then the need for "parent information centers" would be even greater.

Child care presents an interesting contrast to elementary and secondary education. In recent years, several hundred resource and referral agencies have sprung up with the express purpose of providing personal assistance to parents seeking child care. Thus the intermediary organizations already exist. Unfortunately, the report cards do not! Throughout the country resource and referral personnel offer generic advice on what to look for in a day care center or a family day care home but lack the information to tell parents what they can expect to find at a particular facility. Among state child care licensing agencies, only the state of Colorado makes systematic information on child care quality (based on each facility's regulatory history) available to parents through local resource and referral agencies (Gormley 1995).

The child care case also reveals an important limitation of advisory bodies. As resource and referral agencies have considered the most appropriate way to help parents, most have reservations about sharing quality-relevant information about particular facilities with parents. Surprising as it may seem, these advisory bodies shrink from dispensing strong advice for legal and political reasons (fear of a lawsuit from a provider or parent, and reluctance to upset providers who provide the lion's share of their fees). As resource and referral agencies develop in other policy domains, such as health care and education, we are likely to see the same phenomenon. Thus the combination of a report card and an advisory group does not guarantee that consumers will get candid appraisals from persons who understand how a particular industry works.

Report card producers can take at least a small step toward providing personal assistance by establishing toll-free numbers that can be used by interested persons to contact people capable of answering questions about the report card. Commonly asked questions may indicate presentational weaknesses that can be corrected in future editions. They may also identify people who require other sorts of assistance offered by the report card producer.

Impact

Reaching consumers is an intermediate goal—not an end in itself. The end is to improve the quality of social services that affect our lives—education, health care, employment and training, mass transportation, and so forth. Such changes will not take place unless report cards are functional—in other words, until they give the right kinds of incentives to targeted organizations. *The goal is not simply to have an impact but to have a positive impact.* A report card that encourages cream skimming or deception or other dysfunctional behavior is one that substitutes results for good results. It is also important that report cards be reasonable. Costs imposed on targeted organizations will eventually be borne by consumers, employees, and taxpayers. In this section, we consider whether report cards should be linked to tournaments or regulatory sanctions in order to enhance their effectiveness.

Should Tournaments Be Tied to Report Cards?

Profit-seeking organizations that generate revenue by selling services to informed consumers in competitive markets face powerful incentives to deliver the services consumers want at the lowest possible cost. Yet many important services, such as primary and secondary education, are currently supplied predominantly by organizations that face very attenuated competition for customers. By providing a basis for comparing organizations that provide similar services, report cards open the possibility of creating competition through tournaments, which employ administrative mechanisms that tie rewards to relative performance.

With the exception of some procurement programs (Fong 1986) and some state use of federal funds under the JTPA (Heckman, Heinrich, and Smith 1997), pure tournaments have had relatively little application as policy instruments in the public sector. More commonly, however, tournaments have been grafted onto more traditional funding systems, such as lump-sum budgets for bureaus or capitation payments for service providers, in an effort to induce specific types of performance improvement. For example, the tournaments established by the Dallas Independent School District, South Carolina, and several other states tie rather modest financial rewards to the relative performance of schools.

The absence of pure tournaments as funding mechanisms for publicly supported social services should not be surprising. Strongly rewarding the successful and penalizing the unsuccessful would certainly create strong incentives for improvement, but penalties would likely lead to further reductions in performance by the organizations already performing poorly, risking a downward spiral ending in extinction. While punishments and extinctions of poorly performing organizations might very well promote efficiency in the long run if they were allowed to proceed, they would have undesirable, and very politically unpalatable, short-run consequences. In particular, they would effectively punish those who happened to be receiving services from the unsuccessful organizations. Such punishment would strike most observers as extremely unfair.

Pure tournaments greatly increase the importance of the validity and comprehensiveness of the measurement of performance. It is important that the strong financial incentives provided by tournaments be aligned closely to true performance. Any significant mismatch between measured and true performance could result in reductions in true performance for even winning organizations. Again, concerns about fairness would arise when measurement is imperfect.

Pure tournaments also raise concerns about collusion and sabotage (Dye 1984). If there are a small number of contestants in the tournament, then it may be possible for them to reach an agreement to limit their responses to relatively low cost actions. Active sabotage is unlikely in most contexts. Passive sabotage taking the form of withholding information about beneficial innovations is more likely, however. While managers of organizations deriving revenues from noncompetitive sources may have little incentive beyond professional prestige to share information about how to lower costs or improve quality, they have no particular incentive to withhold it. In a pure tournament, however, they have a clear incentive to withhold information that might raise the relative performance of other organizations in the competition.

Making tournaments minor accessories to more traditional funding systems softens their effects, both positive and negative, so that they are more likely to be politically feasible. With respect to school tournaments, for example, prizes given to winners do not come at the direct expense of losers. In some cases, competition is made very indirect by giving payments to all contestants who achieve some minimal performance level. Competition in these cases only arises in the sense that the total prize pool must be split more ways as more contestants achieve the minimum standards. Indeed, such systems are generally referred to as "quality incentive payment systems" rather than as tournaments.

Growing federal expenditures on nursing home care through the Medicaid program, coupled with concern about the capacity of those who receive such care for assessing and responding to its quality, have prompted interest in quality incentive systems for nursing facilities. Several states have adopted quality incentive systems in response to the federal Omnibus Budget Reconciliation Act of 1987 (PL 100–203), which encourages states to reward nursing homes that provide the highest quality of care to Medicaid recipients with incentive payments or public recognition (Chapin and Silloway 1992). Is there any evidence indicating that quality incentive systems actually contribute to quality improvements?

From 1980 to 1983 the National Center for Health Services Research conducted an experiment in San Diego to determine the effects of incentive payments on the quality and cost of nursing home care. Thirty-six facilities were randomly assigned to either traditional flat-rate daily reimbursement financing or an incentive package that tied the daily reimbursement rate to case mix and provided lump-sum bonus payments for patients whose health improved while in nursing care and for patients promptly discharged. In a reanalysis of the experimental data that explicitly modeled health changes of nursing home residents, Edward Norton (1992) found that the incentive package had beneficial effects on both the quality and cost of nursing home care.

The only state effort that has been evaluated to date is the Quality

Incentive Program in Illinois. The program sets minimum standards for nursing facilities in six areas: structure and environment, resident participation and choice, community and family participation, resident satisfaction, care plans, and specialized intensive services. Nursing facilities that volunteer to be evaluated (about 90 percent of facilities) can earn slightly higher per diem reimbursement rates for meeting standards, which have been gradually tightened over time to control costs. A facility also earns a "star" for each of the standards that it meets. An evaluation of the program found quality improvements over time that are at least consistent with a positive impact (Geron 1991).

In a budget-constrained world nonmonetary prizes offer the possibility for rewarding winners without penalizing losers. For example, the exemption from certain regulations and the trophy flags awarded by South Carolina to winning schools through its School Incentive Reward Program do not come at the expense of losing schools. When the nonmonetary awards are based on achieving minimum standards rather than relative performance, they are more like certification systems than tournaments. Nevertheless, the nonmonetary awards may be significant to organizations, especially if they perceive them as signaling quality to important external audiences.

Consider again the Illinois Quality Incentive Program. Scott Geron (1991: 299–300) found considerable anecdotal evidence that the "star system" was an influential component of the program. Nurses who conducted onsite visits for the program often reported comments from facility managers suggesting that they cared much more about the number of stars they received than the financial incentives—incentive payments are small and only apply to patients paid for by Medicaid, while the number of stars makes a statement to all potential clients. Indeed, some facilities dropped out of the program rather than bear a reduction in their number of awarded stars.

What do these theoretical and practical observations suggest about the appropriateness of enhancing report cards with tournaments? Most of the industries in which report cards are likely to be considered—health, education, insurance, public services—involve neither common shocks to production costs nor relative ease of ranking over rating, conditions necessary to make pure tournaments theoretically superior to other reward systems (McLaughlin 1988). Consequently, there would be no strong efficiency rationale for pure tournaments even if they were practical. Grafting tournaments onto more traditional reward systems may have some value in shaping incentives in situations in which consumers have little choice. Consider, for example, federal bonuses to states under the Personal Responsibility and Work Opportunity Reconciliation Act of 1996 (PL 104–193). Congress authorized the disbursement of $1 billion in bonuses between 1999 and 2003 to states that perform well in moving people from welfare to work. The difficulty of knowing now what improvements are feasible makes it easier to rank states than to assess them in terms of a preset absolute standard—a circumstance in which a tournament might be attractive. Indeed, there have been proposals discussed within the Department of Health and Human Services to use data from unemployment insurance participation to rank states in terms of levels and gains in employment, job retention, and earnings progression. These measures, along with changes in births among girls from age 15 to 17, would provide the dimensions of competition in a tournament with shares of the federal bonus money as prizes (Havemann 1997).

Of course, the best tournaments are markets in which organizations compete for informed consumers. If creating such markets is feasible, say by combining vouchers or other mechanisms for expanding choice with report cards, then there is likely to be no need for a tournament. Where market competition is unfeasible, tournaments or other quality incentive payment systems are likely to be desirable if they can be tied to report cards that effectively measure performance.

Regulatory Sanctions and Report Cards

A tournament rewards outstanding organizations that perform well in comparison to other organizations within the same class. An alternative approach is to penalize organizations that perform poorly as indicated by their failure to meet some minimum quality threshold, as revealed by a report card. Sanctions may include monetary fines, special regulatory requirements, or, in the worst cases, termination.

Although information is often viewed as an alternative to regulation, it is also the basis of any regulatory compliance system. Thus a report card can, in principle, be used to enhance regulatory tools by specifying with greater precision where regulatory sanctions need to be employed. That will happen, however, only when information systems and regulatory systems are closely integrated and only when regulators have the authority and the will to penalize organizations based on recent performance.

A surprising number of federal and state agencies lack the authority to impose monetary fines on poor performers. The federal DOL, for example, possesses rich data on the performance of approximately 640 service delivery organizations that provide job training services but can only recommend that states sanction poor performers. Although many state child care licensing agencies can impose monetary fines on day care centers with poor track records, 31 cannot (U.S. GAO 1992b).

The bigger problem, however, is a lack of will, which in turn is rooted in a lack of political support. The federal HCFA, for example, can terminate Medicare contracts with HMOs whose quality does not meet a certain threshold. However, the head of HCFA's managed care office in Philadelphia does not recall a single case in which his region has imposed such a sanction (Sayen 1996). Occasionally, HCFA launches an inquiry based on quality concerns, but such inquiries are rare and they usually result in nothing worse than a slapping of wrists (Loen 1996).

In elementary and secondary education, there is growing interest in using report cards (or school test results) as the basis for regulatory sanctions. In the city of Chicago, seven high schools with exceptionally poor records have been ordered to "reconstitute" themselves. All school employees, from principals to janitors, have been told that they must reapply for their jobs; not every person will be rehired (Walsh 1997).

It remains to be seen whether Chicago's tough approach actually works. It is always possible, for example, that schools might respond by blaming the messenger or teaching to the test. In theory, however, information-based sanctions have the potential to upgrade the performance of sanctioned organizations and those that fear sanctions in the future. Some evidence supports that theory. In a study of OSHA, for example, Wayne Gray and John Scholz (1993) found that penalized firms reported fewer safety mishaps during subsequent years.

When does it make sense to link report cards to regulatory sanctions such as monetary fines or even termination? When consumer choice is limited, as in the case of most public school systems, additional information in the hands of consumers does not eliminate market imperfections. Under such circumstances, a regulatory strategy is necessary if report cards are likely to have a strong impact on organizational behavior.

In other situations, consumer choice may prevail in theory but may be undermined in practice. In child care, for example, consumers are nominally free to choose a child care arrangement that meets their needs, but availability constraints (especially for infant care), affordability constraints (especially for the working poor), and time constraints (for all parents) make it difficult for consumers to "vote with their feet." Also, the regulatory histories of licensed child care facilities are almost never made available to parents (Gormley 1995). Until that changes, information-based sanctions (including monetary fines and even terminations) are necessary to protect children from health and safety threats.

Exemplary Report Cards

Some people collect stamps, coins, or campaign buttons. During the course of our research we have collected an assortment of report cards. Indeed, we can confidently assert that we possess more report cards than any of our colleagues, neighbors, or friends. We doubt that our collection is quite as valuable as a set of buffalo-head nickels or vintage plate blocks, but it does permit us to offer some general observations on the state of the art.

We believe that there are some impressive report cards already being circulated today. If such report cards are not as common as white mice, neither are they as rare as purple cows. Some of the impressive report cards we have seen are produced by government agencies; others are produced by private organizations. Many of them are published annually and get better every year. None of them is perfect, but each has several commendable features.

In sorting our exemplary report cards, we have grouped them into three basic categories: *scientific report cards,* or those that are methodologically strong because they have high validity and comprehensiveness; *popular report cards,* or those that communicate effectively because they are highly comprehensible and relevant; and *hybrid report cards,* or those that do an especially good job of blending science and effective communication. We are pleased to report that, as indicated in Table 8.1, some report cards are outstanding in more than one category. Though there are often trade-offs between such values as validity and comprehensibility, some report cards do a good job of achieving both.

Scientific Report Cards

Among the many report cards we considered in the course of our research, the TVAAS strikes us as the one with the strongest scientific basis for several reasons. First, it is based on extensive and appropriate data. Testing in five subject areas provides a reasonably comprehensive basis for measur-

Table 8.1 Report Card on Exemplary Report Cards

	Validity	Comprehensiveness	Comprehensibility	Relevance	Reasonableness	Functionality
Tennessee Value-Added Assessment System	XXX	XXX	X	XXX	XX	XX
New York State Cardiac Surgery Report Card	XXX	X	XX	XX	XX	XXX
U.S. News & World Report Business School Ratings	X	XX	XXX	XX	XX	X
Health Pages (HMO Report Cards)	X	XX	XXX	XXX	XXX	X
Missouri Obstetrical Services Report Card	XX	XX	XXX	XXX	XX	XXX
California Cooperative HEDIS Reporting Initiative	XX	XX	XXX	XXX	XX	XX

Scores: XXX—excellent; XX—good; X—adequate.
SOURCE: Authors' judgment!

ing the appropriate educational outcome of cognitive development. Testing students in five successive years provides an exceptionally strong foundation for estimating student gains that can be interpreted in value-added terms. Second, it employs relatively simple models with intuitive interpretations. Student scores over years and across subjects are modeled in terms of the additive effects of districts, schools, and teachers. The multi-year test data, in which students act as controls for themselves, permit simple model specifications without the numerous covariates required in models based on single-year test scores. Third, the estimation of the models is appropriately sophisticated. It combines fixed district and school effects with random teacher effects that take account of the amount of information available on each teacher. It also allows for the inclusion of test data for students with incomplete records, a problem that often makes use of multi-year data impractical. Extensive data, straightforward models, and sophisticated estimation give the TVAAS very strong validity and make it an exemplar of appropriate performance measurement.

The TVAAS also earns high marks for comprehensibility, reasonableness, relevance, and, as far as we can tell at this point from anecdotal reports, functionality. In terms of comprehensibility, its gain scores can be easily interpreted, though the complexity of its estimation process poses somewhat of a barrier for those wishing to understand how the gain scores are estimated. With a very low cost per pupil, less than one tenth of a percent of per pupil expenditure in 1995 (Bratton, Horn, and Wright 1996: 30), it must be judged very reasonable. In view of choices available to parents, and the interests of public officials in accountability, the TVAAS earns good grades in terms of relevance. Its relevance would be even greater if parents had access to teacher effects data, but such access might undermine its political viability.

The CABG surgery report produced by the New York State Department of Health also deserves praise for its strong scientific basis. The Cardiac Surgery Reporting System provides exceptionally appropriate clinical data for assessing the mortality risks of patients. Its use of in-hospital death following surgery to operationalize mortality shows a reasonable trade-off between construct validity and measurement error—deaths within some period, say 90 days, following surgery would probably be marginally better conceptually but would be much more costly to measure without error. Logistic regression analysis provides a solid basis for predicting the probability of death for patients in terms of their clinical characteristics. Although mortality is not the only relevant outcome of cardiac surgery, it is almost certainly the most important to patients anticipating surgery, so that the lack of comprehensiveness does not seriously undercut the overall validity of using risk-adjusted mortality rates to characterize surgical success.

Unlike the cardiac surgery report produced by the Pennsylvania Health Care Cost Containment Council, the New York report does not provide other information that might be of interest to patients contemplating cardiac artery bypass graft surgery such as average cost per surgery, the names and practice groups of all surgeons, and the average hospital stay broken down by regional insurer. The New York report, however, provides a clearer exposition of its risk-adjustment methodology and is somewhat superior to Pennsylvania's both in terms of data and methodology, and comprehensibility (due to its easy-to-interpret graphics in the accompanying consumer guide). Neither report provides risk-adjusted mortality rates for surgeons who fail to do minimum numbers of operations, thus depriving consumers of potentially valuable (but also potentially misleading) information.

Both states have witnessed declines in actual and risk-adjusted cardiac surgery mortality rates since the introductions of their report cards. Moreover, these declines have been greater than those reported for the United States as a whole (Peterson et al. 1997). Thus, while the precise effects of New York's CABG report card are still being debated, the evidence clearly suggests some positive impact. Any effects that have resulted from the report card have been purchased at reasonable compliance costs for surgical units, which use a standard protocol to capture clinical data and provide it in electronic format to the Cardiac Surgery Reporting System. Admittedly, however, clinical data tend to be more expensive than administrative data.

Popular Report Cards

U.S. News & World Report is one of the pioneers in producing popular report cards. Its business school report card, published annually since 1990, is illustrative of the more visible report cards it produces. Aimed at a mass audience, the guide to the nation's "top 25 business schools" generates considerable publicity in the mass media, substantial interest among students, and some apprehension in the business school community.

As noted earlier, the *U.S. News* business school report card is technically flawed, in that it measures gross outcomes, not net outcomes (Tracy and

Waldfogel 1997). Because it relies on self-reported data, it also runs the risk of rewarding schools that adopt self-serving definitions of key terms. For example, some schools have defined the proportion of students employed at graduation to include students who have received a job offer at graduation, even though they are not supposed to do so (Liptack 1997). The *U.S. News* ranking also relies heavily on a survey of business school administrators and a survey of corporate recruiters when calculating the overall ranking for each school. Even the best reputational measures of quality suffer from a time lag problem, as reputations change more slowly than quality itself.

Nevertheless, the *U.S. News* business school report card is superior to others, such as those produced by *Business Week* and the *Princeton Review*. Although *Business Week* publishes an assortment of interesting statistics, each school's overall score is determined exclusively by surveys of students and corporate recruiters (Byrne and Leonhardt 1996: 122). As for the *Princeton Review*, it relies exclusively on a student survey to calculate an overall score. In contrast, the *U.S. News* rating is based not only on the two surveys it conducts but also on student selectivity (an input measure) and placement success (a gross outcome measure). The median starting base salary for graduates—an indicator of special interest to many students—is one of the indicators of placement success.

The *U.S. News* survey is very readable and is more accessible than ever, now that key findings are available through the Internet (*Business Week* also makes key findings available through the Internet). Also, most of the information requested by *U.S. News* is already gathered by business schools. Thus the marginal costs of supplying information to *U.S. News* are relatively low.

Although business school administrators are reluctant to admit that they pay close attention to magazine rankings, students clearly do. For example, students at the University of Pennsylvania's Wharton School have worn t-shirts proclaiming "We're Still Number One" after receiving *Business Week's* highest accolade in successive "competitions." At Georgetown University, a worse than expected showing in the 1996 *Business Week* sweepstakes led MBA students to demand a "town meeting" with Dean Robert Parker. A subsequent decline in Georgetown's ranking by *U.S. News* added fuel to the fire and contributed to a decision to dismiss the dean in the summer of 1997. The ratings controversy at Georgetown resulted in some finger-pointing and some personal anguish, but it also resulted in some soul-searching and some reform. Thanks in part to the controversy, Georgetown's business school faculty adopted some far-reaching curriculum reforms that would have been unthinkable two years earlier. In the long run, these reforms may be good for students and may help Georgetown to improve not just its rating but the quality of its educational product as well.

Health care consumers in several metropolitan areas are fortunate to have access to HMO report cards prepared by *Health Pages*. The first versions of these report cards, which appeared in the early 1990s, took the form of magazines devoted exclusively to health care choices in a particular metropolitan area (for example, Pittsburgh or Denver). Later versions have been available through the Internet, sometimes in conjunction with a local newspaper or magazine (Cronin 1997).

The printed versions of the *Health Pages* report cards have several attractive features: separate tables and charts on subjects consumers care about, such as member satisfaction and preventive health care screening; liberal use of contrasting colors to enhance visibility and clarity; and succinct, readable summaries explaining each table or chart. They are also embellished by playful cartoons—for example, a newborn who apparently weighs just more than a banana to illustrate low birth weight babies.

One of the most admirable features of the *Health Pages* report cards is that they typically provide enough information to help but not so much as to overwhelm consumers. By focusing on a local market, these report cards avoid excessive clutter. National health care report cards, such as those published by *U.S. News & World Report,* are impressive in many respects but they typically furnish more information about organizations than consumers wish to process. For national markets, such as higher education, a national report card is entirely appropriate; for local markets, such as hospitals or HMOs, a national report card runs the risk of providing more information than consumers can handle.

A weakness of the *Health Pages* report cards is that the data furnished by HMOs are almost never audited. Another weakness is that the *Health Pages* report cards have not yet had a discernible impact on organizational performance. An analysis of trends in three markets—Denver, Pittsburgh, and St. Louis—reveals no consistent pattern in preventive medicine outputs following the publication of the first edition of *Health Pages.* Perhaps that will change as HMO ownership patterns stabilize (it is difficult to hold an HMO accountable for deteriorating performance if it has just merged with another HMO) and as data reporting practices become more standardized and more reliable (it is especially important that data be audited).

In principle, the indicators reported by *Health Pages* should encourage superior performance.

Hybrid Report Cards

We have cited some examples of technically sophisticated report cards; we have also cited examples of user-friendly report cards. Other report cards are unusually well-rounded—they are scientific in their methodology and their standards (though perhaps less so than the very best in this category) and they are user-friendly as well. These report cards might serve as templates for organizations that lack the capacity for applying the latest risk-adjustment techniques but are committed to report cards that possess considerable scientific rigor and consumer accessibility.

In contrast to New York, which has issued outcome-focused hospital report cards derived from risk-adjusted models, Missouri has opted for less technical report cards that address a wider range of consumer concerns. Since 1992 Missouri has issued occasional consumer guides to the state's hospitals, covering such subjects as outpatient procedures, obstetrical services, and emergency departments. The data in each report are quite varied. For example, the obstetrical services guide includes data on the availability of labor, delivery, and recovery beds, the cesarean delivery rate, the vaginal birth after cesarean rate, very low birth weight, neonatal mortality, and patient satisfaction, among other variables (Missouri Department of Health 1994).

Unlike the New York report card on CABG surgery, the Missouri report card on obstetrical services does not take into account differences in client characteristics. Thus to the extent that low birth weight and patient satisfaction depend on demographic variables or prior health conditions, the Missouri report card is measuring gross outcomes, not net outcomes. This detracts from the overall validity of the report. In several other respects, however, the Missouri report card is impressive. Its focus is quite broad, as it includes structural, process, and outcome measures. Its relevance is high, as it addresses issues that consumers care about. It is relatively easy to understand, due to user-friendly icons similar to those used in *Consumer Reports*. It also generated little controversy among hospitals, thanks to a fairly inclusionary report development process and assurances that hospitals could express reservations or criticisms in a supplementary technical report (Land et al. 1995).

Most impressively, the Missouri report card has had an impact on the state's hospitals. A survey of state hospital administrators, conducted in 1994, found that a substantial number of hospitals altered their policies shortly after the obstetrical services guide appeared. For example, one-third of the hospitals that previously did not have nurse educators for breast-feeding arranged for such services within ten months after the guide was published. Cesarean deliveries declined at hospitals reporting relatively high rates, and vaginal birth after c-section rates improved at hospitals reporting relatively low rates. In general, positive changes were more likely in communities with competitive hospital environments than in communities with only one hospital (Longo et al. 1997).

For the past several years, the California Cooperative HEDIS Reporting Initiative (CCHRI), with leadership and administrative support from PBGH, has produced an annual HMO report card that encompasses nearly all health plans doing business in California. Participation is universal among California's large health plans; the same data are collected from all the participants; and the data are audited by Medstat, an independent firm (Hopkins 1997). The last point is particularly important, because it distinguishes the CCHRI effort from many other HMO report cards. One weakness of the report card is that it includes no risk adjustment, despite evidence that senior citizens offer more positive evaluations. In this respect, the CCHRI report card is neither better nor worse than other HMO report cards. In other respects, however, the CCHRI report card is very impressive.

To facilitate access, the PBGH offers both a print version of the CCHRI report card and an Internet version that goes beyond that report card. The print version presents findings on several preventive services, with a circle icon representing above average/below average/average for each service and each plan. The Internet version also includes the results of a customer satisfaction survey, with an arrow icon conveying five different levels of customer satisfaction, for such factors as skill in finding and treating problems, attention to what you have to say, and explanation of medical procedures and tests. In the near future, the printed CCHRI report card will also feature the results of a customer satisfaction survey.

It is difficult to know for sure how much of an impact the CCHRI report card has had on consumers or firms. However, a 1996 survey of HMO consumers found that report cards ranked first on a list of information sources, much higher than health fairs and radio advertisements and even higher than family and friends (Smart 1996). These encouraging findings suggest that the CCHRI report card and another report card developed especially for California public employees may also be having an impact on HMOs themselves, though that remains to be demonstrated. Indeed, one interesting feature of the CCHRI report card is that it is paid for not only by large corporations that purchase health care but also by large HMOs that sell health care. It may well be that HMOs pay more attention to report cards that they have helped to design and finance. Although some California HMOs complain about the cost (approximately $100,000 per health plan), it seems reasonable, given the magnitude and importance of the enterprise.

Concluding Thoughts

Policy researchers often face a trade-off between the certainty and timeliness of their findings. Studying a phenomenon when it is still rare and evolving limits the empirical evidence that can provide a basis for firm conclusions; studying it only after it has become widespread and mature risks irrelevance to the decisions facing policymakers who have opportunities to encourage, discourage, or direct it. We think that our investigation of organizational report cards comes at a time that allows for a reasonable balance between the confidence we can place in our conclusions and the likely relevance of those conclusions to the development and use of report cards in the future. We hope that the conclusions we have offered in this chapter, as well as the advice offered throughout the book, will prove useful to policymakers and report card designers.

Clearly, organizational report cards are here to stay. Demands for systematic performance data from policymakers, citizens, managers, and consumers will help to guarantee that. The content, format, and impacts of report cards, however, will generate considerable debate. Although we have emphasized the importance of six criteria in evaluating report cards, we believe that validity is of special importance. An invalid report card may have an impact on organizational behavior, but that impact may very well be dysfunctional. In contrast, a valid report card that addresses the needs of diverse audiences can contribute to organizational improvement. Surely, that is a worthy goal in a society increasingly dependent on a complex assortment of service delivery organizations.

Selected Guide to Organizational Report Cards

Airlines

Office of Assistant Administrator for
System Safety
Federal Aviation Administration
800 Independence Ave., S.W.
Washington, D.C. 20591
(202) 267-3611
www.faa.gov
    See also Miscellaneous, *Consumer
Reports*

Child Care

Working Mother
135 W. 50th St., 16th floor
New York, NY 10020
(800) 925-0788
www.workingmother.com

Colleges and Universities

U.S. News & World Report
2400 N St., N.W.
Washington, D.C. 20037
(202) 955-2000
www.usnews.com

National Research Council
Guide to Graduate Programs

National Academy Press
2101 Constitution Ave., N.W.
Washington, D.C. 20418
(202) 334-3313

Economic Development

Corporation for Enterprise
Development
777 N. Capitol St., N.E. Suite 410
Washington, D.C. 20002
(202) 408-9788

Employment and Training

Office of Policy & Research
Employment and Training
Administration
U.S. Department of Labor
200 Constitution Ave., N.W.
Washington, D.C. 20210
(202) 219-5487

Hospitals

Office of Statewide Health Planning
and Development
1600 19th St.
Sacramento, CA 95814
(916) 654-1606

Missouri Department of Health
P.O. Box 570
Jefferson City, MO 65102
(314) 751-6279

New York State Department of Health
Box 2000
Albany, NY 12237
(518) 474-7354
www.health.state.ny.us

Pennsylvania Health Care Cost
Containment Council
225 Market St.
Harrisburg, PA 17101
(717) 232-6787
www.phc4.org

Joint Commission on Accreditation of
Health Care Organizations
One Renaissance Blvd.
Oakbrook Terrace, IL 60181
(630) 792-5000
www.jcaho.org
    See also Miscellaneous, *U.S. News
& World Report*

Insurance Companies

A. M. Best Company
Ambest Road
Oldwick, NJ 08858
(908) 439-2200
www.ambest.com

New York State Insurance Department
Agency Building One
Empire State Plaza
Albany, NY 12257
(518) 474-6600
www.ins.state.ny.us/hlthrk95.htm
    See also Miscellaneous, *Consumer
Reports*

Managed Care Organizations

National Committee for Quality
Assurance
2000 L St., N.W.
Washington, D.C. 20036
(202) 955-3500
www.ncqa.org

California Cooperative HEDIS
Reporting Initiative
c/o Pacific Business Group on Health
33 New Montgomery St., Suite 1450
San Francisco, CA 94105
(415) 281-8660
www.healthscope.org

Health Pages
19 Mayo Ave.
Annapolis, MD 21403
(410) 267-7793
www.thehealthpages.com
    See also Miscellaneous, *Newsweek;
U.S. News & World Report*

Miscellaneous

Consumer Reports
101 Truman Ave.
Yonkers, NY 10703
(914) 378-2000

Newsweek
251 West 57th St.
New York, NY 10019
(212) 445-4000

U.S. News & World Report
2400 N St., N.W.
Washington, D.C. 20037
(202) 955-2000
www.usnews.com

Nursing Homes

Agency for Health Care
Administration
Nursing Home Data Section
2727 Mahan Dr.
Tallahassee, FL 32308
(888) 419-3456
www.fdhc.state.fl.us/nurhom/
guide.html
  See also Miscellaneous, *Consumer
Reports*

Public Schools

TVAAS
University of Tennessee Value-Added
Research and Assessment Center

225 Morgan Hall
P.O. Box 1071
Knoxville, TN 37901
(423) 974-7336
www.state.tn.us/education/rptcrd97/
welcome.htm

For Illinois schools:
www.chicago.tribune.com/ws/front/
0,1413,48,00.html

For New York state schools:
www.nysed.gov/emsc/repcrd96.html

For South Carolina schools:
www.state.sc.us/sde/ednews/1997/
reward97.htm

References

Aberbach, Joel. 1990. *Keeping a Watchful Eye: The Politics of Congressional Oversight.* Washington, DC: The Brookings Institution.

Abt Associates. 1978. "National Day Care Study: Preliminary Findings and Their Implications." Cambridge, MA: Abt Associates, January 31.

Adams, James Ring. 1986. "When Is an 'A' Rating Not an 'A'?" *Forbes,* October 20, p. 43.

Allison, Paul. 1982. "Discrete-Time Methods for the Analysis of Event Histories." In Samuel Leinhardt, ed., *Sociological Methodology 1982.* San Francisco: Jossey-Bass, pp. 61–98.

Alonso, William and Paul Starr. 1987. "Introduction." In William Alonso and Paul Starr, eds., *The Politics of Numbers.* New York: Russell Sage Foundation, pp. 1–6.

A. M. Best, Inc. 1995. *Best's Insurance Reports: Life-Health, United States,* Vol. 1. Oldwick, NJ: A. M. Best.

Ambrose, Jan Mills, and J. Allen Seward. 1988. "Best's Ratings, Financial Ratios and Prior Probabilities in Insolvency Prediction." *Journal of Risk and Insurance,* 55(2): 229–244.

Ammons, David. 1995. "Introduction." In David Ammons, ed., *Accounting for Performance: Measurement and Monitoring in Local Government.* Washington, DC: International City / County Management Association.

Anders, George. 1996a. *Health against Wealth: HMOs and the Breakdown of Medical Trust.* Boston: Houghton Mifflin.

—— 1996b. "New Rules Press HMOs to Disclose Data." *Wall Street Journal,* July 16, p. 3.

—— 1996c. Wall Street Journal Washington Bureau. Personal email communication, October 28.

—— 1996d. "Polling Quirks Give HMOs Healthy Ratings." *Wall Street Journal,* August 27, p. B1.

Anderson, Charles. 1979. "The Place of Principles in Policy Analysis." *American Political Science Review,* 73(4): 711–723.

Associated Press. 1993. "Rating of Hospitals Is Delayed on Grounds of Flaws in Data." *New York Times,* June 23, p. 19.

———— 1995. "Study Warns of Chemical Accident Risk." *San Francisco Chronicle,* August 16, p. A6.

Axelrod, Robert. 1984. *The Evolution of Cooperation.* New York: Basic Books.

Bailey, Clifton. 1996. Health Care Financing Administration. Telephone interview, June 3.

Baker, Paige, and Dengke Xu. 1995. "The Measure of Education: A Review of the Tennessee Value Added Assessment System." Nashville, TN: Tennessee State Comptroller of the Treasury, Office of Educational Accountability, April.

Baldwin, Mark. 1986. "Hospital Industry Leaders Criticize Publication of Hospital Death Rates." *Modern Healthcare,* 16(7): 26–27.

Banks, Jeffrey S. 1995. "The Design of Institutions: An Agency Theory Perspective." In David L. Weimer, ed., *Institutional Design.* Boston: Kluwer Academic Publishing, pp. 17–36.

Banks, Jeffrey and Barry Weingast. 1992. "The Political Control of Bureaucracies under Asymmetric Information." *American Journal of Political Science,* 36(2): 509–524.

Bardach, Eugene. 1977. *The Implementation Game: What Happens After a Bill Becomes Law.* Cambridge, MA: The MIT Press.

———— 1989. "Social Regulation as a Policy Instrument." In Lester Salamon, ed., *Beyond Privatization: The Tools of Government Action.* Washington, DC: Urban Institute Press, pp. 197–229.

Bardach, Eugene and Robert A. Kagan. 1982. *Going by the Book: The Problem of Regulatory Unreasonableness.* Philadelphia: Temple University Press.

Barnow, Burt. 1992. "The Effects of Performance Standards on State and Local Programs." In Charles Manski and Irwin Garfinkel, eds., *Evaluating Welfare and Training Programs.* Cambridge, MA: Harvard University Press, pp. 277–309.

———— 1996. "Exploring the Relationship between Performance Management and Program Impact." Baltimore, MD, Johns Hopkins University, May.

Baumgartner, Frank and Bryan Jones. 1993. *Agendas and Instability in American Politics.* Chicago: University of Chicago Press.

Behn, Robert. 1991. *Leadership Counts: Lessons for Public Managers from the Massachusetts Welfare, Training, and Employment Program.* Cambridge, MA: Harvard University Press.

———— 1996. "Linking Measurement and Motivation: A Challenge for Education." Paper presented at Symposium on Financial Management, University of Illinois, Champaign-Urbana, October 16–17.

Bendor, Jonathan, Serge Taylor, and Ronald Van Gaalen. 1985. "Bureaucratic Expertise versus Legislative Authority: A Model of Deception and Monitoring in Budgeting." *American Political Science Review,* 79(4): 1041–1060.

Berger, Sandy. 1996. Florida Agency for Health Care Administration. Telephone interview, December 4.

Berliner, Joseph S. 1957. *Factory and Manager in the USSR*. Cambridge, MA: Harvard University Press.

Berliner, Paul. 1994. *Thinking in Jazz: The Infinite Art of Improvisation*. Chicago: University of Chicago Press.

Bernard, Chester I. 1973. *Functions of the Executive*. Cambridge, MA: Harvard University Press.

Bernstein, Marver. 1955. *Regulating Business by Independent Commission*. Princeton, NJ: Princeton University Press.

Berwick, Donald M. and David L. Wald. 1990. "Hospital Leaders' Opinions of the HCFA Mortality Data." *Journal of the American Medical Association*, 263(2): 247–249.

Bierlein, Louann. 1996. "Charter Schools: Initial Findings." Education Commission of the States, Denver, CO, March.

Blais, Andre and Stephane Dion, eds. 1991. *The Budget-Maximizing Bureaucrat: Appraisals and Evidence*. Pittsburgh: University of Pittsburgh Press.

Blau, Peter M. 1972. *The Dynamics of Bureaucracy*. Chicago: University of Chicago Press.

Bobrow, Davis and John Dryzek. 1987. *Policy Analysis by Design*. Pittsburgh: University of Pittsburgh Press.

Bock, Darrell R. and Richard Wolfe. 1996. "Audit and Review of Tennessee Value-Added Assessment System (TVAAS): Final Report." *Report to the Tennessee Comptroller of the Treasury*. March.

Bogart, Leo. 1989. *Press and Public: Who Reads What, When, Where, and Why in American Newspapers*, 2nd ed. Hillsdale, NJ: Lawrence Erlbaum Associates.

Boroson, Warren. 1991. "Holes in the Safety Net." *The Record,* June 23, pp. B01, B05.

Bowie, Mary Kay. 1997. Joint Commission on Accreditation of Healthcare Organizations. Telephone interview, February 27.

Bratton, Samuel E., Jr., Sandra P. Horn, and S. Paul Wright. 1996. *Using and Interpreting Tennessee's Value-Added Assessment System: A Primer for Teachers and Principals*. Knoxville, TN: Value-Added Research and Assessment Center, University of Tennessee.

Brennan, Troyen and Donald Berwick. 1996. *New Rules: Regulation, Markets, and the Quality of American Health Care*. San Francisco: Jossey-Bass Inc.

Bretschneider, Stuart. 1990. "Management Information Systems in Public and Private Organizations: An Empirical Test." *Public Administration Review,* 50(5): 536–545.

Bright, Donald. 1996. U.S. Department of Transportation. Telephone interview, October 10.

Brown, Ben. 1997. Director of Testing and Evaluation, Tennessee Department of Education. Telephone interview, December 2.

Burton, Scot, Abhyit Biswas, and Richard Nehemeyer. 1994. "Effects of Alternative Nutrition Label Formats and Nutrition Reference Information on Consumer Perceptions, Comprehension, and Product Evaluations." *Journal of Public Policy and Marketing,* 13(1): 36–47.

Buswell, Robert. 1996. Oklahoma Office of Accountability. Telephone interview (by Tamar London), June 3.

Butler, Paula. 1997. Testing Coordinator, Jackson-Madison County School District. Telephone interview, December 2.

Byrne, John and David Leonhardt. 1996. "The Best Business Schools." *Business Week,* Oct. 21, pp. 110–122.

Caldas, Stephen J. and Mark K. Mossavat. 1994. "A Statewide Assessment Survey of Parents', Teachers', and Principals' Perceptions of School Report Cards." Paper presented at the annual meeting of the American Educational Research Association, New Orleans, April 4.

California Office of Statewide Health Planning and Development. 1996. *Report of the California Hospital Outcomes Project, Acute Myocardial Infarction, Vol. 1: Study Overview and Results Summary.* Sacramento, CA: California Office of Statewide Health Planning and Development, May.

California Public Employees' Retirement System. 1995. "Health Plan Quality/ Performance Report." Sacramento, CA, May.

———— 1996. "Health Plan Quality/Performance Report." Sacramento, CA, September.

Calvert, Randall. 1995. "The Rational Choice Theory of Institutions: Implications for Design." In David Weimer, ed., *Institutional Design.* Boston: Kluwer Academic Publishers, pp. 63–94.

Cameron, Kim. 1978. "Measuring Organizational Effectiveness in Institutions of Higher Education." *Administrative Science Quarterly,* 23(4): 604–632.

Carter, Neil, Rudolf Klein, and Patricia Day. 1992. *How Organizations Measure Success: The Use of Performance Indicators in Government.* London: Routledge.

Castles, Anne. 1997. Pacific Business Group on Health. Telephone interview, June 30.

Caulkins, Jonathan P., Arnold Barnett, Patrick D. Larkey, Yuehong Yuan, and Jesse Goranson. 1993. "The On-Time Machines: Some Analysis of Airline Punctuality." *Operations Research,* 41(4): 710–720.

Chapin, Rosemary and Glenn Silloway. 1992. "Incentive Payments to Nursing Homes Based on Quality-of-Care Outcomes." *Journal of Applied Gerontology,* 11(2): 131–145.

Cheit, Ross E. 1990. *Setting Safety Standards: Regulation in the Public and Private Sectors.* Berkeley, CA: University of California Press.

Chernew, Michael and Dennis P. Scanlon. 1998. "Health Plan Report Cards and Insurance Choice." *Inquiry,* 35(1): 9–22.

Cherry, William. 1997. Director of Testing, Stuart County School District. Telephone interview, December 5.

Chubb, John and Terry Moe. 1990. *Politics, Markets, and America's Schools.* Washington, DC: The Brookings Institution.

Church, Thomas W. and Milton Heumann. 1989. "The Unexamined Assumptions of the Invisible Hand: Monetary Incentives as Policy Instruments." *Journal of Policy Analysis and Management,* 8(4): 641–657.

Cibulka, James G. 1991. "Educational Accountability Reforms: Performance Information and Political Power." In Susan H. Fuhrman and Betty Malen, eds., *The Politics of Curriculum and Testing.* New York: The Falmer Press, pp. 181–201.

Clones, Daphne. 1997. Corporation for Enterprise Development. Telephone interview, July 15.

Clotfelter, Charles T. and Helen F. Ladd. 1994. "Information as a Policy Lever: The Case of North Carolina's School 'Report Card'." Paper presented at the annual conference of the Association for Public Policy Analysis and Management, Chicago, October 28.

———— 1996. "Recognizing and Rewarding Success in Public Schools." In Helen F. Ladd, ed., *Holding Schools Accountable: Performance-Based Reform in Education.* Washington, DC: The Brookings Institution, pp. 23–63.

Cobb, Roger and Charles Elder. 1983. *Participation in American Politics: The Dynamics of Agenda-Building,* 2nd ed. Baltimore, MD: Johns Hopkins University Press.

Cohen, David. 1978. "Reforming School Politics." *Harvard Educational Review,* 48(4): 429–447.

Cohen, David and James Spillane. 1993. "Policy and Practice: The Relations between Governance and Instruction." In Susan Fuhrman, ed., *Designing Coherent Education Policy: Improving the System.* San Francisco: Jossey-Bass, pp. 35–95.

Coleman, James S., et al. 1966. *Equality of Educational Opportunity.* Washington, DC: U.S. Department of Health, Education, and Welfare.

Cook, Sir Edward. 1914. *The Life of Florence Nightingale,* Vol. 1. London: Macmillan and Co.

Cook, Fay, Tom Tyler, Ed Goetz, Margaret Gordon, David Protess, Donna Leff, and Harvey Molotch. 1983. "Media and Agenda Setting: Effects on the Public, Interest Group Leaders, Policy Makers, and Policy." *Public Opinion Quarterly,* 47(1): 16–35.

Corporation for Enterprise Development. 1994. *1994 Development Report Card for the States.* Washington, DC: CFED.

———— 1996. *The 1996 Development Report Card for the States.* Washington, DC: CFED.

Council of Chief State School Officers. 1995. *State Education Accountability Reports and Indicator Reports: Status of Reports Across the States, 1995.* Washington, DC: State Education Assessment Center.

Covalaski, John M. 1995. "ISO Carved Out New Market Niche." *Best's Review (Property / Casualty),* 96(6): 58–62.

Crenshaw, Albert. 1997. "Beleaguered IRS Announces Steps to Curb Abuses." *Washington Post,* September 26, p. 3.

Cronin, Carole. 1997. Health Pages. Telephone interview, June 30.

Culyer, A. J. and Adam Wagstaff. 1993. "QALYs versus HYEs." *Journal of Health Economics,* 11(3): 311–323.

Cushman, John H., Jr. 1997. "E.P.A. Is Pressing Plan to Publicize Pollution Data." *New York Times,* August 12, pp. A1, C20.

Cuttance, Peter. 1994. "Quality Assurance in Education Systems." *Studies in Educational Evaluation,* 20(1): 99–112.

Danielson, Michael. 1976. *The Politics of Exclusion.* New York: Columbia University Press.

Darling-Hammond, Linda. 1992. "Education Indicators and Enlightened Policy." *Educational Policy,* 6(3): 235–265.

Delli Carpini, Michael and Scott Keeter. 1996. *What Americans Know About Politics and Why it Matters.* New Haven, CT: Yale University Press.

Deming, W. Edwards. 1982. *Quality, Productivity, and Competitive Position.* Cambridge, MA: MIT, Center for Advanced Engineering Study.

Derthick, Martha and Paul J. Quirk. 1985. *The Politics of Deregulation.* Washington, DC: The Brookings Institution.

Dolan, P., C. Gudex, P. Kind, and A. Williams. 1996. "Valuing Health States: A Comparison of Methods." *Journal of Health Economics,* 15(2): 209–231.

Donabedian, Avedis. 1988. "The Quality of Care: How Can It Be Assessed?" *Journal of the American Medical Association,* 260(12): 1743–1748.

Donahue, John. 1989. *The Privatization Decision: Public Ends, Private Means.* New York: Basic Books.

Doolittle, Fred. 1996. Manpower Demonstration Research Corporation, New York. Telephone interview, November 8.

Downs, Anthony. 1967. *Inside Bureaucracy.* Boston: Little, Brown.

Drummond, Michael, George Torrance, and James Mason. 1993. "Cost-Effectiveness League Tables: More Harm Than Good?" *Social Science and Medicine,* 37(1): 33–40.

Drummond, Steven. 1997. "Bonuses Weren't Prime Reason Schools Worked to Improve, Study in Ky. Says." *Education Week,* April 2, p. 7.

Duncan, Felicia. 1997. Elementary Supervisor, Wilson County Schools. Telephone interview, December 3.

Dunleavy, Patrick. 1991. *Democracy, Bureaucracy, and Public Choice.* Englewood Cliffs, NJ: Prentice Hall.

Dye, Ronald A. 1984. "The Trouble with Tournaments." *Economic Inquiry,* 22(1): 147–149.

Dyer, Henry S., Robert L. Linn, and Michael J. Patton. 1969. "A Comparison of Four Methods of Obtaining Discrepancy Measures Based on Observed and Predicted School System Means on Achievement Tests." *American Educational Research Journal,* 6(4): 591–605.

Edelman, Murray. 1967. *The Symbolic Uses of Politics.* Urbana, IL: University of Illinois Press.

Edgman-Levitan, Susan and Paul Cleary. 1996. "What Information Do Consumers Want and Need?" *Health Affairs,* 15(4): 42–56.

Eisner, Marc. 1993. *Regulatory Politics in Transition*. Baltimore, MD: Johns Hopkins University Press.

Ellis, Randall P. and Arlene Ash. 1995–1996. "Refinements to the Diagnostic Cost Group (DCG) Model." *Inquiry*, 32(4): 418–429.

Elmore, Richard F., Charles H. Abelmann, and Susan H. Fuhrman. 1996. "The New Accountability in State Education Reform: From Process to Performance." In Helen F. Ladd, ed., *Holding Schools Accountable: Performance-Based Reform in Education*. Washington, DC: The Brookings Institution, pp.65–98.

Epstein, Arnold. 1995. "Performance Reports on Quality: Prototypes, Problems, and Prospects." *New England Journal of Medicine*, 333(1): 57–61.

Feldman, Martha. 1989. *Order by Design*. Palo Alto, CA: Stanford University Press.

Fetler, Mark. 1986. "Accountability in California Public Schools." *Educational Evaluation and Policy Analysis*, 8(1): 31–44.

——— 1990. "Refining a Performance Accountability System in California: A Case Study of a Constitutional Initiative." Paper presented at the annual meeting of the American Educational Research Association, Boston, April.

Feuer, Michael. 1997. National Academy of Sciences. Telephone interview, May 18.

Fisher, Thomas H. 1996. "A Review and Analysis of the Tennessee Value-Added Assessment System." Report to the Tennessee Comptroller of the Treasury, January.

Florida Agency for Health Care Administration. 1996. "1996 Guide to Hospitals in Florida." Tallahassee, FL: Agency for Health Care Administration.

Fong, Glenn R. 1986. "The Potential for Industrial Policy: Lessons from the Very High Speed Integrated Circuit Program." *Journal of Policy Analysis and Management*, 5(2): 264–291.

French, Russell L., Gordon Bobbett, and Charles Achilles. 1994. "An Analysis of State Report Cards on Schools Produced in Eleven Southeastern States." Paper presented at the annual meeting of the American Educational Research Association, New Orleans, April.

Fudenberg, Drew and Eric Maskin. 1986. "The Folk Theorem in Repeated Games with Discounting or with Incomplete Information." *Econometrica*, 54(3): 533–554.

Gafni, Amiram, Stephen Birch, and Abraham Mehrez. 1993. "Economics, Health, and Health Economics: HYEs versus QALYs." *Journal of Health Economics*, 11(3): 325–329.

Gaines, Gale F. 1991. "Report Cards for Education: Accountability Reporting in SREB States." Atlanta: Southern Regional Education Board.

Galinsky, Ellen, et al. 1995. *The Study of Children in Family Day Care*. New York: Work and Families Institute.

Gallagher, Alison. 1991. "Comparative Value Added as a Performance Measure." *Higher Education Review*, 23(3): 19–29.

Garwood, Heidi. 1997. Florida Association of HMOs. Telephone interview, June 9.

Gerard, Karen. 1992. "Cost-Utility in Practice: A Policy Maker's Guide to the State of the Art." *Health Policy,* 21(3): 249–279.

Geron, Scott Miyake. 1991. "Regulating the Behavior of Nursing Homes through Positive Incentives: An Analysis of Illinois Quality Incentive Program (QUIP)." *Gerontologist,* 31(3): 292–301.

Ghali, William A., Arlene S. Ash, Ruth E. Hall, and Mark A. Moskowitz. 1997. "Statewide Quality Improvement Initiatives and Mortality after Cardiac Surgery." *Journal of the American Medical Association,* 277(5): 379–382.

Globerman, Steven and Aidan R. Vining. 1996. "A Framework for Evaluating the Government Contracting-Out Decision with an Application to Information Technology." *Public Administration Review,* 56(6): 577–586.

Gold, Marthe R., Joanna E. Siegel, Louise B. Russell, and Milton C. Weinstein, eds. 1996. *Cost-Effectiveness in Health and Medicine.* New York: Oxford University Press.

Goldstein, Harvey. 1984. "The Methodology of School Comparisons." *Oxford Review of Education,* 10(1): 69–74.

———— 1987. *Multilevel Models in Educational and Social Research.* New York: Oxford University Press.

———— 1991. "Better Ways to Compare Schools?" *Journal of Educational Statistics,* 16(2): 89–91.

Gormley, William T., Jr. 1983. *The Politics of Public Utility Regulation.* Pittsburgh: University of Pittsburgh Press.

———— 1986. "The Representation Revolution: Reforming State Regulation through Public Representation." *Administration and Society,* 18(2): 179–196.

———— 1989. *Taming the Bureaucracy: Muscles, Prayers, and Other Strategies.* Princeton, NJ: Princeton University Press.

———— 1991. "Day Care in a Federal System." *Social Service Review,* 66(4): 582–596.

———— 1995. *Everybody's Children: Child Care as a Public Problem.* Washington, DC: The Brookings Institution.

Graber, Doris. 1989. *Mass Media and American Politics,* 3rd ed. Washington, DC: Congressional Quarterly Press.

Granito, John. 1991. "Evaluation and Planning of Public Fire Protection." In Arthur E. Cote, ed., *Fire Protection Handbook,* 17th ed. Quincy, MA: National Fire Protection Association, pp. 10, 37–51.

Grant, Don Sherman, II. 1997. "Allowing Citizen Participation in Environmental Regulation: An Empirical Analysis of the Effects of Right-to-Sue and Right-to-Know Provisions on Industry's Toxic Emissions." *Social Science Quarterly,* 78(4): 859–873.

Grant, Don Sherman, II and Liam Downey. 1995/6. "Regulation through Information: An Empirical Analysis of the Effects of State-Sponsored Right-to-

Know Programs on Industrial Toxic Pollution." *Policy Studies Review,* 14(3): 339–352.

Gray, Wayne and John Scholz. 1993. "Does Regulatory Enforcement Work? A Panel Analysis of OSHA Enforcement." *Law and Society Review,* 27(1): 177–213.

Green, Jesse and Neil Wintfeld. 1995. "Report Cards on Cardiac Surgeons: Assessing New York State's Approach." *New England Journal of Medicine,* 332(18): 1229–1232.

Green, Jesse, Neil Wintfeld, and Mel Krasner. 1997. "In Search of America's Best Hospitals." *Journal of the American Medical Association,* 277(14): 1152–1155.

Green, Jesse, Neil Wintfeld, Phoebe Sharkey, and Leigh Passman. 1990. "The Importance of Severity of Illness in Assessing Hospital Mortality." *Journal of the American Medical Association,* 263(2): 241–246.

Greenberg, Peter. 1991. "U.S. Airlines Lacking Some Timely Truth in their Scheduling." *Seattle Times,* January 20, p. 54.

Griesing, David. 1996. "Managing Tragedy at Valujet." *Business Week,* June 3, p. 40.

"Guide to the College Guide." 1996. *U.S. News & World Report,* September 16, pp. 106–107.

Hadden, Susan. 1986. *Read the Label: Reducing Risk by Providing Information.* Boulder, CO: Westview Press.

Hamilton, James T. 1995. "Pollution as News: Media and Stock Market Reactions to the Toxics Release Inventory Data." *Journal of Environmental Economics and Management,* 28(1): 98–113.

Hanes, Pamela and Merwyn Greenlick. 1996. *Oregon Consumer Scorecard Project, Final Report.* Rockville, MD: Department of Health and Human Services, September 30.

Hannan, Edward L., Harold Kilburn Jr., Michael Lindsey, and Rudy Lewis. 1992. "Clinical versus Administrative Data Bases for CABG Surgery: Does It Matter?" *Medical Care,* 30(10): 892–907.

Hannan, Edward L., Harold Kilburn Jr., Michael Racz, Eileen Shields, and Mark R. Chassin. 1994. "Improving the Outcomes of Coronary Artery Bypass Surgery in New York State." *Journal of the American Medical Association,* 271(10): 761–766.

Hannan, Edward L., Dinesh Kumar, Michael Racz, Albert L. Siu, and Mark R. Chassin. 1994. "New York State's Cardiac Surgery Reporting System: Four Years Later." *Annals of Thoracic Surgery,* 58(6): 1852–1857.

Hannan, Edward L., Michael Racz, James G. Jollis, and Eric Peterson. 1997. "Using Medicare Claims Data to Assess Provider Quality for CABG Surgery: Does it Work Well Enough?" *Health Services Research,* 31(6): 659–678.

Hannan, Edward L., Albert L. Siu, Dinesh Kumar, Harold Kilburn Jr., Mark R. Chassin. 1995. "The Decline in Coronary Artery Bypass Graft Surgery Mortality in New York State." *Journal of the American Medical Association*, 273(3): 209–213.

Hansmann, Henry. 1987. "Economic Theories of Nonprofit Organization." In Walter W. Powell, ed., *The Nonprofit Sector: A Research Handbook*. New Haven, CT: Yale University Press, pp. 27–42.

Hanushek, Eric A. 1972. *Education and Race*. Lexington, MA: DC Heath.

——— 1994. *Making Schools Work: Improving Performance and Controlling Costs*. Washington, DC: The Brookings Institution.

Havemann, Judith. 1997. "Proposed Welfare Bonus Rules Put Emphasis on Jobs, Earnings." *Washington Post*, July 18, p. 10.

Hechinger, Grace and Fred Hechinger. 1974. "Are Schools Better in Other Countries?" *Education Digest*, March, pp. 7–10.

Heckman, James, Carolyn Heinrich, and Jeffrey Smith. 1997. "Assessing the Performance of Performance Standards in Public Bureaucracies." *American Economic Review*, 87(2): 389–395.

Heclo, Hugh. 1977. *A Government of Strangers*. Washington, DC: The Brookings Institution.

Helburn, Suzanne, et al. 1995. "Cost, Quality, and Child Outcomes in Child Care Centers: A Technical Report." Economics Department, University of Colorado at Denver, January.

Hibbard, Judith and Jacquelyn Jewett. 1996. "What Type of Quality Information Do Consumers Want in a Health Care Report Card?" *Medical Care Research Review*, 53(1): 28–47.

Hibbard, Judith, Paul Slovic, and Jacquelyn Jewett. 1997. "Informing Consumer Decisions in Health Care: Implications from Decision-Making Research." *Milbank Quarterly*, 75(3): 395–414.

Hibbard, Judith H., Shoshanna Sofaer, and Jacquelyn J. Jewett. 1996. "Condition-Specific Performance Information: Assessing Salience, Comprehension, and Approaches for Communicating Quality." *Health Care Financing Review*, 18(1): 95–109.

Hirsh, Michael. 1997. "Infernal Revenue Disservice." *Newsweek*, October 13, pp. 33–39.

Hirschman, Albert O. 1970. *Exit, Voice, and Loyalty*. Cambridge, MA: Harvard University Press.

Hoadley, Jack. 1996. Physician Payment Review Commission, Washington, DC. Telephone interview, November 5.

Hofferth, Sandra, et al. 1991. *National Child Care Survey, 1990*. Washington, DC: Urban Institute.

Holmstrom, Bengt and Jean Tirole. 1989. "The Theory of the Firm." In Richard Schmalensee and Robert D. Willig, eds., *Handbook of Industrial Organization*. New York: North Holland, pp. 61–133.

Holthausen, Robert W. and Richard W. Leftwich. 1986. "The Effect of Bond Rating Changes on Common Stock Prices." *Journal of Financial Economics*, 17(1): 57–89.

Hopkins, David. 1997. Pacific Business Group on Health. Telephone interview, February 25.

Hornberger, J. C., D. A. Redelmeier, J. Peterson. 1992. "Variability among Methods to Assess Patients' Well-Being and Consequent Effect on Cost-Effectiveness Analysis." *Journal of Clinical Epidemiology,* 45(5): 505–512.

Howard, Philip. 1994. *The Death of Common Sense: How Law is Suffocating America.* New York: Random House.

Howes, Carolee and Judith Rubenstein. 1985. "Determinants of Toddlers' Experience in Day Care: Age of Entry and Quality of Setting." *Child Care Quarterly,* 14(Summer): 140–151.

Hoxby, Caroline Minter. 1994. "Do Private Schools Provide Competition for Public Schools?" National Bureau of Economic Research, Working Paper 4978.

Hoy, Elizabeth W., Elliot K. Wicks, and Rolfe A. Forland. 1996. "A Guide to Facilitating Consumer Choice." *Health Affairs,* 15(4): 9–30.

Hsia, David C., Cathaleen A. Ahern, Brian P. Ritchie, Linda M. Moscoe, and W. Mark Krushat. 1992. "Medicare Reimbursement Accuracy Under the Prospective Payment System." *Journal of the American Medical Association,* 268(7): 896–899.

Hunter, Susan and Richard Waterman. 1996. *Enforcing the Law: The Case of the Clean Water Acts.* Armonk, NY: M. E. Sharpe.

Iezzoni, Lisa, Arlene Ash, Gerald Coffman, and Mark Moskowitz. 1992. "Predicting In-Hospital Mortality." *Medical Care,* 30(4): 347–359.

Ingram, Robert W., Leroy D. Brooks, and Ronald M. Copeland. 1983. "The Information Content of Municipal Bond Rating Changes: A Note." *Journal of Finance,* 37(3): 997–1003.

Innes, Judith. 1998. "The Power of Data Requirements." *Journal of the American Planning Association,* 54(3): 275–278.

Insurance Services Office. 1997. *Product Spotlight: Public Protection Classification.* New York.

InterStudy. 1995. *Interstudy Competitive Edge: Part 2, Industry Report.* Minneapolis, MN: InterStudy, Spring.

Ippolito, Pauline M. and Alan D. Mathios. 1991. "Health Claims in Food Marketing: Evidence on Knowledge and Behavior in the Cereal Market." *Journal of Public Policy and Marketing,* 10(1): 15–32.

Isaacs, Stephen L. 1996. "Consumers' Information Needs: Results of a National Survey." *Health Affairs,* 15(4): 31–41.

Jaeger, Richard, et al. 1993. "Designing and Developing Effective School Report Cards: A Research Synthesis." Greensboro, NC: Center for Educational Research and Evaluation, University of North Carolina at Greensboro, October.

Jaeger, Richard, Barbara Gorney, Robert Johnson, Sarah Putnam, and Gary Williamson. 1994. "A Consumer Report on School Report Cards." Greensboro, NC: Center for Educational Research and Evaluation, University of North Carolina at Greensboro, August.

Jenkins-Smith, Hank and David L. Weimer. 1985. "Analysis as Retrograde Action: The Case of the Strategic Petroleum Reserves." *Public Administration Review,* 45(4): 485–494.

Jensen, Michael C. and William H. Meckling. 1976. "Theory of the Firm: Managerial Behavior, Agency Costs and Ownership Structure." *Journal of Financial Economics,* 3(4): 305–360.

Jewett, Jacquelyn J. and Judith H. Hibbard. 1996. "Comprehension of Quality Care Indicators: Differences Among Privately Insured, Publicly Insured, and Uninsured." *Health Care Financing Review,* 18(1): 75–94.

Johannesson, Magnus and Ulf-G Gerdtham. 1996. "A Note on the Estimation of the Equity-Efficiency Trade-off for QALYs." *Journal of Health Economics,* 15(3): 359–368.

Johannesson, Magnus, Joseph Pliskin, and Milton C. Weinstein. 1994. "A Note on QALYs, Time Trade-off, and Discounting." *Medical Decision Making,* 12(2): 188–193.

Johnson, Ronald N. and Gary D. Libecap. 1989. "Bureaucratic Rules, Supervisor Behavior, Agency Costs and Ownership Structure." *Journal of Law, Economics and Organization,* 5(1): 53–82.

Judis, John. 1996. "Bad Choice." *The New Republic,* September 30, p. 6.

Kaagan, Stephen S., and Richard J. Colby. 1989. "State Education Indicators: Measured Strides, Missing Steps." Princeton, NJ: Policy Information Center, Educational Testing Service.

Kahneman, Daniel, Paul Slovic, and Amos Tversky, eds. 1982. *Judgment under Uncertainty: Heuristics and Biases.* New York: Cambridge University Press.

Kane, Robert L. and Rosalie A. Kane. 1988. "Long Term Care: Variations on a Quality Assurance Theme." *Inquiry,* 25(1): 132–146.

Kantrowitz, Barbara and Karen Springen. 1997. "Why Johnny Stayed Home." *Newsweek,* October 6, p. 60.

Kaplan, Robert and David Norton. 1996. *The Balanced Scorecard.* Boston: Harvard Business School Press.

Katz, Richard S. and Munroe Eagles. 1996. "Ranking Political Science Programs: A View from the Lower Half." *PS: Political Science and Politics,* 29(2): 149–154.

Katzmann, Robert A. 1980. *Regulatory Bureaucracy: The Federal Trade Commission and Antitrust Policy.* Cambridge, MA: The MIT Press.

Kaufman, Herbert. 1960. *The Forest Ranger: A Study of Administrative Behavior.* Baltimore, MD: Johns Hopkins University Press.

———— 1981. *The Administrative Behavior of Federal Bureau Chiefs.* Washington, DC: The Brookings Institution.

Kelley, Carolyn. 1997. "The Kentucky School-Based Performance Award Program: School-Level Effects." Wisconsin Center for Educational Research, University of Wisconsin at Madison.

Kelley, Carolyn and Jean Protsik. 1996. "Risk and Reward: Perspectives on Implementation of Kentucky's School-Based Performance Award Program." Madison, WI: Wisconsin Center for Educational Research, University of Wisconsin at Madison.

Kershaw, David, and Jerilyn Fair. 1977. *The New Jersey Income-Maintenance Experiment*. New York: Academic Press.

Kettl, Donald. 1993. *Sharing Power: Public Governance and Private Markets*. Washington, DC: The Brookings Institution.

Khademian, Anne M. 1992. *The SEC and Capital Market Regulation: The Politics of Expertise*. Pittsburgh: University of Pittsburgh Press.

Kiesling, Herbert J. 1994. "Reading the Report Cards: What Do 'State of Achievement' Reports Tell Us about American Education? (Review Essay)." *Economics of Education Review*, 13(2): 179–193.

Kim, Nancy. 1996. National Committee for Quality Assurance, Washington, DC. Telephone interview, December 5.

Kingdon, John. 1984. *Agendas, Alternatives, and Public Policies*. Boston: Little, Brown.

———— 1995. *Agendas, Alternatives, and Public Policies*, 2nd ed. New York: Harper Collins.

Kisker, Ellen, et al. 1991. *A Profile of Child Care Settings: Early Education and Care in 1990, Vol. 1* Princeton, NJ: Mathematica Policy Research Inc.

Klinger, Karen. 1995 "Bypass Surgery Ratings Said Flawed." *United Press International, Domestic News*, May 3.

Knowlton, Steven. 1995. "Hyping Numbers at Colleges." *New York Times*, January 8, Sec. 4A, p. 48.

Knutson, David J., Jinnet B. Fowles, Michael Finch, Jeanne McGee, Nanette Dahms, Elizabeth Kind, and Susan Adlis. 1996. "Employer-Specific versus Community-Wide Report Cards: Is There a Difference?" *Health Care Financing Review*, 18(1): 111–125.

Kochan, Susan E., Bobby J. Franklin, Linda J. Crone, and Catherine H. Glasock. 1993. "How do Parents and Teachers 'Grade' Louisiana's School Report Card Program?" Paper presented at the Mid-South Educational Research Association meeting, New Orleans, November 9.

Kohler, Nancy. 1997. Idaho Department of Education. Telephone interview, January 7.

Koretz, Daniel M., Sheila Brown, Karen J. Mitchell, and Brian M. Stecher. 1996. *Perceived Effects of the Kentucky Instructional Results Information System (KIRIS)*. Santa Monica, CA: RAND Corporation.

Krakauer, Henry. 1997. Office of Assistant Secretary for Policy Evaluation, Department of Health and Human Services. Telephone interview, May 20.

Kreps, David. 1990. "Corporate Culture and Economic Theory." In James Alt and Kenneth Shepsle, eds., *Perspectives on Positive Political Economy*. New York: Cambridge University Press, pp. 90–143.

Kronick, Richard, Tony Dreyfus, Lora Lee, and Zhiyuan Zhou. 1996. "Diagnostic Risk Adjustment for Medicaid: The Disability Payment System." *Health Care Financing Review*, 17(3): 7–33.

Ladd, Helen F., ed. 1996. *Holding Schools Accountable: Performance Based Reform in Education.* Washington, DC: The Brookings Institution.

Lagnado, Lucette. 1996. "Grading the Report Cards: There's Plenty of Information Available for Consumers to Rate Health-Care Providers. But Is it Any Good?" *Wall Street Journal,* October 24, p. R15.

Land, Garland, Daniel Longo, Barbara Hoskins, and Judith Fraas. 1995. "The Development of a Consumer Guide on the Quality of Obstetrical Services: The Missouri Experience." *Journal of Public Health Management and Practice,* 1(3): 35–43.

Lehnen, Robert G. 1992. "Constructing State Education Performance Indicators from ACT and SAT Scores." *Policy Studies Journal,* 20(1): 22–40.

Lehnen, Robert G., et al. 1995. "Improving Indiana School District Reporting." School of Public and Environmental Affairs, Indiana University.

Lesda, Sheldon. 1996. Manager / Single Copy Department, *Democrat and Chronicle / Times Union.* Correspondence, July 1.

Levitt, Barbara and James G. March. 1988. "Organizational Learning." *Annual Review of Sociology,* 14: 319–340.

Light, Paul. 1993. *Monitoring Government: Inspectors General and the Search for Accountability.* Washington, DC: The Brookings Institution.

———— 1995. *Thickening Government: Federal Hierarchy and the Diffusion of Accountability.* Washington, DC: The Brookings Institution.

Linder, Stephen and B. Guy Peters. 1989. "Instruments of Government: Perceptions and Contents." *Journal of Public Policy,* 9(1): 35–58.

Lipsky, Michael. 1980. *Street-Level Bureaucracy.* New York: Russell Sage Foundation.

Liptack, Elisabeth. 1997. Georgetown University School of Business. Telephone interview, December 9.

Loen, Rae. 1996. Health Care Financing Administration. Telephone interview, November.

Longo, Daniel, Garland Land, Wayne Schramm, Judy Fraas, Barbara Hoskins, and Vicky Howell. 1997. "Consumer Reports in Health Care: Do They Make a Difference in Patient Care?" *Journal of the American Medical Association,* 278(19): 1579–1584.

Lowery, Robert C. and Brian D. Silver. 1996. "A Rising Tide Lifts All Boats: Political Science Department Reputation and the Reputation of the University." *PS: Political Science and Politics,* 29(2): 161–167.

Luft, Harold S. 1996. "Modifying Managed Competition to Address Cost and Quality." *Health Affairs,* 15(1): 23–38.

Luft, Harold S., Deborah W. Garnick, David H. Mark, Deborah J. Peltzman, Ciaran S. Phibbs, Erik Lichtenberg, and Stephen J. McPhee. 1990. "Does Quality Influence Choice of Hospital?" *Journal of the American Medical Association,* 263(21): 2899–2906.

Lynch, John G., Jr., Thomas E. Buzas, and Sanford V. Berg. 1994. "Regulatory Measurement and Evaluation of Telephone Service Quality." *Management Science*, 40(2): 169–194.

MacRae, Duncan, Jr. 1971. "Scientific Communication, Ethical Argument, and Public Policy." 1971. *American Political Science Review*, 65(1): 38–50.

—— 1985. *Policy Indicators: Links between Social Science and Public Debate.* Chapel Hill, NC: University of North Carolina Press.

Magat, Wesley and W. Kip Viscusi. 1992. *Informational Approaches to Regulation.* Cambridge, MA: The MIT Press.

Mandeville, Garrett K. 1995. "The South Carolina Experience with Incentives." In Thomas A. Downes and William A. Testa, eds., *Midwest Approaches to School Reform.* Chicago: Federal Reserve Bank of Chicago, pp. 69–97.

Mannemeyer, Stephen T., Michael A. Morrisey, and Leslie Z. Howard. 1997. "Death and Reputation: How Consumers Acted upon HCFA Mortality Information." *Inquiry*, 34(2): 117–128.

Manno, Bruno V. 1995. "Educational Outcomes Do Matter." *The Public Interest*, 119(Spring): 19–27.

Manpower Demonstration Research Corporation. 1993. "A Summary of the Design and Implementation of the National JTPA Study." New York: MDRC, January.

Market Research. 1997. "Advertising Awareness and Tracking Study." Bethesda, MD, February.

Mashaw, Jerry L. and Susan Rose-Ackerman. 1984. "Federalism and Regulation." In George C. Eads and Michael Fix, eds., *The Reagan Regulatory Strategy: An Assessment.* Washington, DC: The Urban Institute Press, pp. 111–145.

Mayston, David, and David Jesson. 1988. "Developing Models of Educational Accountability." *Oxford Review of Education*, 14(3): 321–339.

McCombs, Matthew and Donald Shaw. 1972. "The Agenda-Setting Function of the Mass Media." *Pubic Opinion Quarterly*, 36(2): 176–187.

McCubbins, Mathew D. and Thomas Schwartz. 1984. "Congressional Oversight Overlooked: Police Patrols versus Fire Alarms." *American Journal of Political Science*, 28(1): 165–179.

McGee, Jeanne and David Knutson. 1994. "Health Care Report Cards: What About Consumers' Perspectives." *Journal of Ambulatory Care Management*, 17(4): 1–14.

McLarty, Joyce R. and Susan Hudsen. 1987. "Formative and Summative Approaches to Effectiveness Indicators." Paper presented at the annual meeting of the American Educational Research Association, Washington, DC, April.

McLaughlin, Kenneth J. 1988. "Aspects of Tournament Models: A Survey." *Research in Labor Economics*, 9: 225–256.

McMorris, Frances A. 1994. "Legal Beat: Con Ed Enters Guilty Plea in Asbestos-Explosion Case." *Wall Street Journal*, November 1, p. B10.

Merton, Robert K. 1957. *Social Theory and Social Structure.* Glencoe, IL: Free Press.

Meyer, Robert H. 1991. "Educational Performance Indicators and School Report Cards: Concepts." Paper presented at the annual meeting of the Association for Public Policy Analysis and Management, Washington, DC, October.

——— 1994. "Educational Performance Indicators: A Critique." Harris Graduate School of Public Policy Studies, University of Chicago, December.

——— 1995. "Value-Added Indicators of School Performance." Harris Graduate School of Public Policy Studies, University of Chicago, August.

——— 1996. "Value-Added Indicators of School Performance." In Eric A. Hanushek and Dale W. Jorgenson, eds., *Improving America's Schools: The Role of Incentives*. Washington, DC: National Academy Press, pp. 197–223.

Miller, Arthur H., Charles Tien, and Andrew A. Peebler. 1996. "Departmental Rankings: An Alternative Approach." *PS: Political Science and Politics*, 29(4): 704–717.

Miller, G. A. 1956. "The Magical Number Seven, Plus or Minus Two: Some Limitations on Our Capacity for Processing Information." *Psychological Review*, 63(2): 81–97.

Miller, Gary. 1992. *Managerial Dilemmas*. New York: Cambridge University Press.

Missouri Department of Health. 1994. *Show Me Buyer's Guide: Obstetrical Services*. Jefferson City, MO: Missouri Department of Health.

Mitchell, Peter. 1996. "Hospitals Give Low Marks to State's Report Card." *Wall Street Journal*, March 6, p. F1.

Moe, Terry. 1989. "The Politics of Bureaucratic Structure." In John Chubb and Paul Peterson, eds., *Can the Government Govern?* Washington, DC: The Brookings Institution, pp. 267–329.

Montague, Bill. 1991. "Critics Say Agencies Failed during the Crisis." *USA Today*, August 6, p. B1.

Montague, Jim. 1996. "Report Card Daze." *Hospitals and Health Networks*, 5(January): 33–38.

Moody, John. 1914. *Moody's Analysis of Investments*. Fifth Annual Number. New York: Analyses Publishing Co.

Mooney, Christopher Z. 1992. "Putting It on Paper: The Content of Written Information Used in State Lawmaking." *American Politics Quarterly*, 20(3): 345–65.

Moore, J. Duncan, Jr. 1997. "JCAHO Tries Again." *Modern Healthcare*, February 24, pp. 2–3.

Moore, Mark H. 1995. *Creating Public Value: Strategic Management in Government*. Cambridge, MA: Harvard University Press.

Morone, James and Theodore Marmor. 1981. "Representing Consumer Interests: The Case of American Health Planning." *Ethics*, 91(April): 431–450.

Morrissey, John. 1996. "HEDIS to Expand Performance Guidelines." *Modern Healthcare*, July 22, pp. 2–3.

Morse, Robert. 1995. "The Methodology: How U.S. News Determines the

Rankings in this Guide." *U.S. News & World Report,* September 18, pp. 123–124.

Mukamel, Dana B. 1997. "Risk-Adjusted Outcome Measures and Quality of Care in Nursing Homes." *Medical Care,* 35(4): 367–385.

Mukamel, Dana B. and Alvin I. Mushlin. 1998. "Quality of Care Information Makes a Difference: An Analysis of Market Share and Price Changes Following Publication of the New York State Cardiac Surgery Mortality Reports." *Medical Care,* 36(7): 945–954.

Murnane, Richard J. 1975. *The Impact of School Resources on the Learning of Inner City Children.* Cambridge, MA: Ballinger Publishing Company.

Nash, David. 1996. Thomas Jefferson University, Philadelphia. Telephone interview, December 4.

National Center for Education Statistics. 1993. *NAEP 1992 Mathematics Report Card for the Nation and the States.* Washington, DC: U.S. Department of Education, April.

———— 1997. *NAEP 1996 Mathematics Report Card for the Nation and the States.* Washington, DC: U.S. Department of Education, February.

National Commission for Employment Policy. 1988. "Evaluation of the Effects of JTPA Performance Standards on Clients, Services, and Costs." Washington, DC: National Commission for Employment Policy.

National Committee for Quality Assurance. 1995. *Report Card Pilot Project: Technical Report.* Washington, DC: NCQA.

———— 1996. "Accreditation Status List." Washington, DC: NCQA, September 30.

———— 1997. "HEDIS 3.0: Health Plan Employer Data and Information Set." Washington, DC: NCQA.

Neuman, W. Russell, Marion Just, and Ann Crigler. 1992. *Common Knowledge: News and the Construction of Political Meaning.* Chicago: University of Chicago Press.

Nevo, David. 1994. "Combining Internal and External Evaluation: A Case for School-Based Evaluation." *Studies in Educational Evaluation,* 20(1): 87–98.

Newcomer, Robert, Steven Preston, and Charlene Harrington. 1996. "Health Plan Satisfaction and Risk of Disenrollment among Social / HMO and Fee-for-Service Recipients." *Inquiry,* 33(2): 144–154.

New York State Department of Health. 1995. *Coronary Artery Bypass Surgery in New York Sate, 1991–1993,* June.

New York State Insurance Department. 1995. *Annual Ranking of Automobile Insurance Companies.*

Niskanen, William A. 1971. *Bureaucracy and Representative Government.* Chicago: Aldine-Atherton.

———— 1975. "Bureaucrats and Politicians." *Journal of Law and Economics,* 18(4): 617–643.

Norton, Edward C. 1992. "Incentive Regulation of Nursing Homes." *Journal of Health Economics,* 11(2): 108–128.

O'Connor, Gerald T., et al. 1996. "A Regional Intervention to Improve the Hospital Mortality Associated with Coronary Artery Bypass Graft Surgery." *Journal of the American Medical Association,* 275(11): 841–846.

Odden, Allan. 1990. "Educational Indicators in the United States: The Need for Analysis." *Educational Researcher,* 19(4): 24–33.

OERI State Accountability Study Group. 1988. "Creating Responsible and Responsive Accountability Systems." Office of Educational Research and Improvement, U.S. Department of Education, September.

Olson, Lynn. 1996. Remarks at panel on "Performance Measurement and Data Needs in Health Policy Management" at the annual meeting of Association for Public Policy Analysis and Management, Pittsburgh, October.

Olson, Mancur. 1973. *The Logic of Collective Action.* Cambridge, MA: Harvard University Press.

Orwin, R. G., R. E. Schucker and R. C. Stokes. 1984. "Evaluating the Life Cycle of a Product Warning: Saccharin and Diet Soft Drinks." *Evaluation Review,* 8(6): 801–822.

Osborne, David and Peter Plastrik. 1997. "Grading Governments." *Washington Post Magazine,* April 13, pp. 8–10.

O'Toole, Lawrence J., Jr., Chilik Yu, James Cooley, Gail Cowie, Susan Crow, Terry DeMeo, and Stephanie Herbert. 1997. "Reducing Toxic Chemical Releases and Transfers: Explaining Outcomes for a Voluntary Program." *Policy Studies Journal,* 25(1): 11–26.

Overman, E. Sam and Anthony Cahill. 1994. "Information, Market Growth, and Health Policy: A Study of Health Data Organizations in the States." *Journal of Policy Analysis and Management,* 13(3): 435–453.

Pennsylvania Health Care Cost Containment Council. 1995. *A Consumer Guide to Coronary Artery Bypass Graft Surgery,* June.

Peters, B. Guy. 1996. *American Public Policy: Promise and Performance,* 4th ed. Chatham, NJ: Chatham House.

Peterson, Eric, James G. Jollis, Elizabeth R. DeLong, Lawrence H. Muhlbaier, and Daniel B. Mark. 1997. "The Effects of New York's Bypass Surgery Provider Profiling on Access to Care and Patient Outcomes." Durham, NC: Duke University Medical Center.

Phelps, Charles E. 1992. "Diffusion of Information in Medical Care." *Journal of Economic Perspectives,* 6(3): 23–42.

——— 1995. "Welfare Loss from Variations: Further Considerations." *Journal of Health Economics,* 14(2): 253–260.

Physician Payment Review Commission. 1997. *Annual Report to Congress, 1997.* Washington, DC: Physician Payment Review Commission.

Pierce, Richard, Sidney Shapiro, and Paul Verkuil. 1985. *Administrative Law and Process.* Mineola, NY: The Foundation Press.

Pollard, Joyce. 1989. "Developing Useful Educational Indicator Systems." *Insights on Educational Policy and Practice,* 15(November): 1–4.

Protess, David et al. 1987. "The Impact of Investigative Reporting on Public Opinion and Policymaking." *Public Opinion Quarterly,* 51(2): 166–185.

Putnam, Robert. 1996. "The Strange Disappearance of Civic America." *The American Prospect,* 24(Winter): 34–48.

Rainey, Hal G. 1996. "Building an Effective Organizational Culture." In James L. Perry, ed., *Handbook of Public Administration,* 2nd ed. San Francisco: Jossey-Bass, pp. 151–166.

Raudenbush, Stephen W. 1988. "Educational Applications of Hierarchical Linear Models: A Review." *Journal of Educational Statistics,* 13(2): 85–116.

Raudenbush, Stephen W., and Anthony S. Bryk. 1989. "Quantitative Models for Estimating Teacher and School Effectiveness." In R. Darrell Bock, ed., *Multilevel Analysis of Educational Data.* San Diego, CA: Academic Press, pp. 205–232.

Ravitch, Diane. 1995. *National Standards in American Education: A Citizen's Guide.* Washington, DC: The Brookings Institution.

Reedy, George. 1970. *The Twilight of the Presidency.* New York: World Publishing Co.

Relman, Arnold. 1988. "Assessment and Accountability: The Third Revolution in Medical Care." *New England Journal of Medicine,* 319(18): 1220–1222.

Rich, Richard C., W. David Conn, and William Owens. 1993. "'Indirect Regulation' of Environmental Hazards through the Provision of Information to the Public: The Case of SARA, Title III." *Policy Studies Journal,* 21(1): 16–34.

Richards, Craig E., and Tian Ming Sheu. 1992. "The South Carolina School Incentive Reward Program: A Policy Analysis." *Economics of Education Review,* 11(1): 71–80.

Rivers, Kenneth. 1996. Placentia Linda Hospital, Orange County, California. Telephone interview, September 30.

Roberts, James, Jack Coale, and Robert Redman. 1987. "A History of the Joint Commission on Accreditation of Hospitals." *Journal of the American Medical Association,* 258(7): 936–940.

Robinson, Tim. 1995. "How to Use Health Pages." *Health Pages-Pittsburgh,* 2(2): 3–4.

Roghman, Hugh. 1996. Survey conducted for the authors, May 23.

Rokeach, Milton. 1968. *Beliefs, Attitudes, and Values.* San Francisco, CA: Jossey-Bass.

Rose-Ackerman, Susan. 1992. *Rethinking the Progressive Agenda.* New York: Free Press.

Rosen, Harry and Barbara Green. 1987. "The HCFA Excess Mortality Lists: A Methodological Critique." *Hospital-Health Services Administration,* 32(1): 119–127.

Rosenthal, Alan. 1996. "The Legislature: Unraveling of the Institutional Fabric." In Carl Van Horn, ed., *The State of the States,* 3rd ed. Washington, DC: Congressional Quarterly Press, 108–142.

Ruggie, Mary. 1996. *Realignments in the Welfare State: Health Policy in the United States, Britain, and Canada.* New York: Columbia University Press.

Salamon, Lester, ed. 1989. *Beyond Privatization: The Tools of Government Action.* Washington, DC: The Urban Institute Press.

———— 1992. *America's Nonprofit Sector: A Primer.* New York: The Foundation Center.

Samuelson, Robert. 1997. "Telephone Straddle." *Newsweek,* May 19, p. 63.

Sanders, William L. 1997a. Value-Added Research and Assessment Center, University of Tennessee, Knoxville, TN. Telephone interview, April 17.

———— 1997b. Value-Added Research and Assessment Center, University of Tennessee, Knoxville, TN. Telephone interview, December 5.

Sanders, William L. and Sandra P. Horn. 1994. "The Tennessee Value-Added Assessment System (TVAAS): Mixed-Model Methodology in Educational Assessment." *Journal of Personnel Evaluation in Education,* 8(3): 299–311.

———— 1995. "The Tennessee Value-Added Assessment System (TVAAS): Mixed Model Methodology in Educational Assessment." In Anthony J. Shinkfield and Daniel L. Stufflebeam, eds., *Teacher Evaluation: Guide to Effective Practice.* Boston: Kluwer Academic Press, pp. 337–350.

Sapolsky, Harvey M. 1972. *The Polaris System Development: Bureaucratic and Programmatic Success in Government.* Cambridge, MA: Harvard University Press.

Sappington, David E. M. 1991. "Incentives in Principal-Agent Relationships." *Journal of Economic Perspectives,* 5(2): 45–66.

Sayen, David. 1996. Director, Managed Care Office, Health Care Financing Administration, Philadelphia. Telephone interview, November 22.

Schauffler, Helen Halpin and Tracy Rodriguez. 1996. "Exercising Purchasing Power for Preventive Care." *Health Affairs,* 15(1): 73–85.

Schiavo, Mary. 1997. *Flying Blind, Flying Safe.* New York: Avon Books.

Schlesinger, Mark, Robert Dortward, and Richard Pulice. 1986. "Competitive Bidding and States' Purchase of Services: The Case of Mental Health in Massachusetts." *Journal of Policy Analysis and Management,* 5(2): 245–263.

Schlesinger, Mark, Bradford Gray, and Elizabeth Bradley. 1996. "Charity and Community: The Role of Nonprofit Organization in a Managed Health Care System." *Journal of Health Politics, Policy and Law,* 21(4): 697–751.

Schneider, Anne and Helen Ingram. 1990. "Behavioral Assumptions of Policy Tools." *Journal of Politics,* 52(2): 510–529.

Schneider, Eric C. and Arnold M. Epstein. 1998. "Use of Public Performance Reports: A Survey of Patients Undergoing Cardiac Surgery." *Journal of the American Medical Association,* 279(20): 1638–1642.

Schneider, Mark and Paul Teske with Michael Mintrom. 1995. *Public Entrepreneurs: Agents for Change in American Government.* Princeton, NJ: Princeton University Press.

Scholz, John T. and Wayne Gray. 1997. "Can Government Facilitate Cooperation? An Informational Model of OSHA Enforcement." *American Journal of Political Science*, 41: 693–717.

"School League-Tables: An Antidote to Elitism." 1994. *The Economist*, November 26, pp. 65–66.

"School Report Card Law May Be Dumped." 1996. *Lewiston Morning Tribune*, March 5, p. 11.

Schotter, Andrew. 1990. *The Economic Theory of Social Institutions*. New York: Cambridge University Press.

Schulte, Fred. 1997. Fort Lauderdale Sun-Sentinel. Telephone interview, June 5.

Selcraig, Bruce. 1997. "Toxics Release Inventory." *Sierra*, 82(January / February): 38–43.

Seligman, Joel. 1986. "The SEC and Accounting: A Historical Perspective." In Robert H. Mundheim and Noyes E. Leech, eds., *The SEC and Accounting: The First 50 Years*. Amsterdam: North-Holland, 3–28.

Serrano v. Priest. 1971. *California Reporter*, 96: 601.

Shaughnessy, Peter W. et al. 1994. "Measuring and Assuring the Quality of Home Health Care." *Health Care Financing Review*, 16(1): 35–67.

Shenk, David. 1997. *Data Smog: Surviving the Information Glut*. New York: Harper Collins.

Singh, K. Ajai and Mark L. Power. 1994. "The Effects of Best's Rating Changes on Insurance Company Stock Prices." *Journal of Risk and Insurance*, 59(2): 317–327.

Siu, Albert L. et al. 1992. *Choosing Quality-of-Care Measures Based on the Expected Impact of Improved Quality of Care for the Major Causes of Mortality and Morbidity*. Santa Monica, CA: RAND Corporation.

Skolnick, Jerome H. 1966. *Justice without Trial*. New York: John Wiley.

Smart, Dean. 1996. CalPers (California Public Employees' Retirement System). Telephone interview, December 9.

Smith, David L. 1996. "Analysis of Nevada School Accountability System: School Year 1993–94." Nevada Department of Education, January.

Smith, Elwood. 1995. "Scorecards for Managed Care Plans." *Health Pages-Pittsburgh*, 2(2): 15–23.

Smith, Steven R. and Michael Lipsky. 1993. *Nonprofits for Hire*. Cambridge, MA: Harvard University Press.

Smith, Susan. 1996. Health Standards and Quality Bureau, U.S. Health Care Financing Administration. Telephone interview, May 22.

Smith, Susan J. 1997. "Strong Hospital Heart Surgery Safer." *Rochester Democrat and Chronicle*, September 5, p. A1.

Sommer, David W. 1996. "The Impact of Firm Risk on Property-Liability Insurance Prices." *Journal of Risk and Insurance*, 63(3): 501–514.

Spragins, Ellyn. 1996. "Does Your HMO Stack Up?" *Newsweek*, June 24, pp. 56–63.

Starr, Paul. 1982. *The Social Transformation of American Medicine*. New York: Basic Books.

State of Florida v. PCA Family Health Plan, Inc. 1996. Court of Appeal, First District, State of Florida, Case Nos. 95–1659 and 95–2790, September 11.

Stecklow, Steve. 1995. "Universities Face Trouble for Enhancing Guide Data." *Wall Street Journal,* October 12, p. B1.

———— 1997. "Kentucky's Teachers Get Bonuses, but Some Are Caught Cheating." *Wall Street Journal,* September 2, pp. A1, A5.

Stewart, Debra and Ingrid Martin. 1994. "Intended and Unintended Consequences of Warning Messages." *Journal of Public Policy and Marketing,* 13(1): 1–19.

Stigler, George. 1971. "The Theory of Economic Regulation." *Bell Journal of Economics and Management Science,* 3(1): 3–21.

Stout, Richard R., Martin J. Eisenberg, and James D. Nowlan. 1996. *Performance Rankings of Illinois School Districts.* Springfield, IL: Illinois Tax Foundation.

Stover, Teresa. 1997. Title I Supervisor, McNairy County School District. Telephone interview, December 2.

Strategic Consulting Services. 1994. "Health Plan Report Cards: An Inside Look at Gaming." *Executive Bulletin,* Fall: 3–6.

Straw, Edward F. 1997. Technical Coordinator, Natural Hazards Mitigation, Insurance Services Office. Telephone interview, January 20.

Taylor, Alan, Rick Moses, and Don McDonald. 1996. "Bureau of Service Evaluation Report for 1995." Memorandum, Public Service Commission, Tallahassee, FL, March 13.

Terrill, Stephanie. 1996. National Committee for Quality Assurance, Washington, DC. Telephone interview, October 29.

Thomas, Patricia. 1987. "The Uses of Social Research: Myths and Models." In Martin Bulmer, ed., *Social Science Research and Government: Comparative Essays on Britain and the United States.* New York: Cambridge University Press, pp. 51–60.

Thompson, Fred and L. R. Jones. 1986. "Controllership in the Public Sector." *Journal of Policy Analysis and Management,* 5(3): 547–571.

Toenniessen, Robert. 1997. Office of Assistant Administrator for System Safety, Federal Aviation Administration. Telephone interview, July 2.

Tolchin, Susan, and Martin Tolchin. 1985. *Dismantling America: The Rush to Deregulate.* New York: Oxford University Press.

Tompkins, Philip. 1993. *Organizational Communication Imperatives: Lessons of the Space Program.* Los Angeles: Roxbury Publishing.

Topol, Eric J. and Robert M. Califf. 1994. "Scorecard Cardiovascular Medicine: Its Impact and Future Directions." *Annals of Internal Medicine,* 120(1): 65–70.

Torda, Phyllis. 1997. National Committee for Quality Assurance. Telephone interview, July 9.

Torrence, George W., Michael H. Boyle, and Sargent P. Horwood. 1982. "Application of Multi-Attribute Utility Theory to Measure Social Preferences for Health Status." *Operations Research,* 30(6): 1043–1069.

Tracy, Joseph and Joel Waldfogel. 1997. "The Best Business Schools: A Market-Based Approach." *Journal of Business,* 70(1): 1–31.

Tyack, David. 1974. *The One Best System: A History of American Urban Education.* Cambridge, MA: Harvard University Press.

Tyack, David and Larry Cuban. 1995. *Tinkering toward Utopia: A Century of Public School Reform.* Cambridge, MA: Harvard University Press.

Tyack, David and Elizabeth Hansot. 1982. *Managers of Virtue: Public School Leadership in America, 1820–1980.* New York: Basic Books.

United States Environmental Protection Agency. 1997. "About the Toxics Release Inventory (TRI) Data Collection." Washington, DC: U.S. EPA, Office of Pollution Prevention and Toxics.

United States General Accounting Office. 1990. *Airline Scheduling: Airlines' On-Time Performance.* RCED-90–154. Washington, DC: GAO, June.

———— 1992a. *Utilization Review: Information on External Review Organizations.* Washington, DC: U.S. Government Printing Office.

———— 1992b. *Child Care: States Face Difficulties Enforcing Standards and Promoting Quality.* GAO/HRD-93–13. Washington, DC: GAO, November.

———— 1995. *Health Care: Employers and Individual Consumers Want Additional Information on Quality.* GAO/HEHS-95–201. Washington, DC: GAO, September.

———— 1996a. *Executive Guide: Effectively Implementing the Government Performance and Results Act.* GAO/GGD-96–118. Washington, DC: GAO, June.

———— 1996b. *Medicare: Private-Sector and Federal Efforts to Assess Health Care Quality.* GAO/T-HEHS-96–215. Washington, DC: GAO, September 19.

———— 1996c. *Medicare: HCFA Should Release Data to Aid Consumers, Prompt Better HMO Performance.* GAO/HEHS-97–23. Washington, DC: GAO, October.

———— 1996d. *Regulatory Burden: Measurement Challenges and Concerns Raised by Selected Companies.* GAO/GGD-97–2. Washington, DC: GAO, November.

United States Health Care Financing Administration. 1993. "Medicare Hospital Information Report: 1992 Technical Supplement." Washington, DC: HCFA, June.

United States Interstate Commerce Commission. 1995. *Summary of Service Record, Carriers Transporting More than 1,000 Household Goods Shipments Annually.* Washington, DC: ICC.

USA Today. 1990. "Top Ozone-Depleting Emissions, State by State." 1990. *USA Today,* January 17, p. A2.

Vick, Larry. 1997. Superintendent, Paris Special School System. Telephone interview, December 4.

Vining, Aidan and David Weimer. 1988. "Information Asymmetry Favoring Sellers: A Policy Framework." *Policy Sciences,* 21(4): 281–303.

———— 1990. "Government Supply and Government Production Failure: A Framework Based on Contestability." *Journal of Public Policy,* 10(1): 1–22.

Walker, David. 1995. *The Rebirth of Federalism: Slouching toward Washington.* Chatham, NJ: Chatham House.

Wallin, Bruce. 1997. "The Need for a Privatization Process: Lessons from Development and Implementation." *Public Administration Review,* 5(1): 11–20.

Walsh, Edward. 1997. "Jobs at Stake as Staff Members at 7 Chicago Schools Are Put to the Test." *Washington Post,* June 27, p. A3.

Ware, John and Mary Snyder. 1975. "Dimensions of Patient Attitudes Regarding Doctors and Medical Care Services." *Medical Care,* 13(8): 669–682.

Weimer, David L. 1980a. *Improving Prosecution? The Inducement and Implementation of Innovations for Prosecution Management.* Westport, CT: Greenwood Press.

——— 1980b. "CMIS Implementation: A Demonstration of Predictive Analysis." *Public Administration Review,* 40(3): 231–240.

——— 1983. "Problems of Expedited Implementation." *Journal of Public Policy,* 3(2): 169–190.

——— 1992. "Claiming Races, Broiler Contracts, Heresthetics, and Habits: Ten Concepts for Policy Design." *Policy Sciences,* 25(2): 135–159.

Weimer, David L. and Aidan R. Vining. 1992. *Policy Analysis: Concepts and Practice.* Englewood Cliffs, NJ: Prentice Hall.

Weisbrod, Burton A. 1988. *The Nonprofit Economy.* Cambridge, MA: Harvard University Press.

Weiss, Carol. 1977. "Research for Policy's Sake: The Enlightenment Function of Policy Research." *Policy Analysis,* 3(4): 553–565.

Weiss, Janet A. 1996. "Psychology." In Donald F. Kettl and H. Brinton Milward, eds., *The State of Public Management.* Baltimore, MD: The Johns Hopkins Press, pp. 118–142.

Weiss, Janet A. and Judith E. Gruber. 1984. "Deterring Discrimination with Data." *Policy Sciences,* 17(1): 49–66.

Weiss, Janet A. and Mary Tschirhart. 1994. "Public Information Campaigns as Policy Instruments." *Journal of Policy Analysis and Management,* 13(1): 82–119.

"When a Loved One Needs Care." 1995. *Consumer Reports,* 60(August): 518–527.

Whipple, Christine. 1996. Pittsburgh Business Group on Health. Remarks at panel on Organizational Report Cards, annual meeting of Association of Public Policy and Management, Pittsburgh, November.

White, Halbert. 1980. "A Heteroscedasticity-Consistent Covariance Matrix Estimator and a Direct Test for Heteroscedasticity." *Econometrica,* 48(4): 817–838.

Whiteman, David. 1985. "The Fate of Policy Analysis in Congressional Decision Making: Three Types of Use in Committees." *Western Political Quarterly,* 38(2): 294–311.

——— 1995. *Communication in Congress: Members, Staff, and the Search for Information.* Lawrence, KS: University Press of Kansas.

Wholey, Joseph and Harry Hatry. 1992. "The Case for Performance Monitoring." *Public Administration Review* 52(6): 604–610.

Willms, Douglas J., and Alan C. Kerckhoff. 1995. "The Challenge of Developing New Educational Indicators." *Educational Evaluation and Policy Analysis,* 17(1): 113–131.

Wilson, James Q., ed. 1980. *The Politics of Regulation.* New York: Basic Books.

—— 1989. *Bureaucracy.* New York: Basic Books.

Woodhouse, Geoffrey and Harvey Goldstein. 1988. "Educational Performance Indicators and LEA League Tables." *Oxford Review of Education,* 14(3): 301–320.

Woods, Mary. 1996. Kaiser Permanente, Mid-Atlantic Office, Bethesda, MD. Telephone interview, October 29.

—— 1997. Kaiser Permanente, Mid-Atlantic Office, Bethesda, MD. Telephone interview, March 24.

Young, Alison. 1996. "Good Care is Possible." *Detroit Free Press,* October 11, p. 1.

Zach, Andra. 1996. California Office of Statewide Health Planning and Development, Sacramento, CA. Telephone interviews, October 9 and 28.

Zinman, David. 1991. "Heart Surgeons Rated." *Newsday,* December 18, pp. 3, 35, 37.

Zinn, Jacqueline S. 1994. "Market Competition and the Quality of Nursing Home Care." *Journal of Health Politics, Policy and Law,* 19(3): 555–582.

Index

Accountability, 3, 18, 20, 45, 57, 118, 157, 201; to the public, 21–23; bottom-up, 22, 23, 26–27, 34–35, 37, 197–198; top-down, 23, 27, 34, 35–36, 197, 198; of schools, 43, 76–78, 81, 82, 92–93
Accreditation, 33, 121–122
Accuracy, 11
Aetna Life and Casualty, 147
Agency for Health Care Administration, 54
Airlines, 99, 148–150; report cards on, 65, 214–215; safety, 149, 214
Alexander, Lamar, 81
A.M. Best, 12, 71–73, 108–109, 168–170, 173, 174
American College of Surgeons (ACS), 41
American Express, 120
American Hospital Association, 48
American Medical Association (AMA), 44, 48, 57
American National Standards Institute, 178
American Society of Mechanical Engineers, 178
America's Best Colleges, 166
Art Ensemble of Chicago, 119
Assessment, 3, 36–37, 41–42; problems of, 7–9, 207; of quality, 50. *See also* Outcomes
Associated Press, 160
Association of California School Administrators, 48
Audiences, 26, 37, 94–122, 132–134, 190; parents, 2; corporate purchasers, 5; mass, 5, 17, 100, 109–114, 115, 116, 120, 121; specific organization, 5–7; elite, 17, 99–100, 114–117, 120, 191, 212; government, 26; third-party payers,

27–28, 167–168, 170; external, 60, 124, 222; consumers, 94, 101–103, 105, 191; policymakers, 94, service providers, 94. *See also* Mass media
Auditing, 183–185

Balanced scorecards, 4
Barron's Profiles of American Colleges, 166
Benchmarking, 3–4
Best's Insurance Reports, 72
Bhopal, India, 159
Blaming the messenger (as a dysfunctional response to report cards), 14–15, 139, 147
Boston School Board, 39
Boston University, 138
Brinkley, Joel, 45
Bronx District Attorney's Office, 73
Business school, 65–66, 69, 229–230
Business Week, 69, 229
Butterworth, Bob, 53

California: elementary and secondary schools, 1–2; Teachers Association of, 48; school report cards, 48; hospital report card, 49; Test Bureau of, 81; Office of Statewide Health Planning and Development (OSHPD), 86, 143–144, 208; Sacramento public schools, 106–108; Placentia Linda Hospital, 144; Good Samaritan Hospital, 145; Health Care Association, 179; Medical Association of, 179; acute myocardial infarction study, 207; Cooperative HEDIS Reporting Initiative (CCHRI), 232–233